First Workshop on Commonsense Inference in Natural Language Processing 2019

Hong Kong, China
3 November 2019

ISBN: 978-1-7138-0071-2

EMNLP 2019

Proceedings of the First Workshop on Commonsense Inference in Natural Language Processing

November 3, 2019
Hongkong

Introduction

Welcome to the first Workshop on Commonsense Inference in Natural Language Processing, COIN.

This workshop takes place for the first time and has a focus on research around modeling commonsense knowledge, developing computational models thereof, and applying commonsense inference methods in NLP tasks. This includes any type of commonsense knowledge representation, and explicitly also work that makes use of knowledge bases and approaches developed to mine or learn commonsense from other sources. Evaluation proposals that explore new ways of evaluating methods of commonsense inference, going beyond established natural language processing tasks are also of interest for the workshop.

The workshop included two shared tasks on English reading comprehension using commonsense knowledge. The first task is a multiple choice reading comprehension task on everyday narrations. The second task is a cloze task on news texts.

Several teams participated in the shared tasks, with 4 teams submitting results for task 1, and one team submitting results for both tasks. All models are based on Transformer architectures. The best performing models reach 90.6% accuracy and 83.7% F1-score on task 1 and task 2, respectively.

In total, we received 22 paper submissions (among them 6 shared task papers), out of which 16 were accepted. All workshop papers are presented as talks, while the shared task papers are presented in a poster session. In addition, the workshop includes two invited talks on the topics of commonsense inference and commonsense in question answering.

The program committee consisted of 21 researchers, who we'd like to thank for providing helpful and constructive reviews on the papers. We'd also like to thank all authors for their submissions and interest in our workshop.

Simon, Sheng, Michael and Peter

Organizers:

Simon Ostermann, Saarland University / Nuance Communications

Sheng Zhang, Johns Hopkins University

Michael Roth, Saarland University / University of Stuttgart

Peter Clark, Allen Institute for AI

Program Committee:

Malihe Alikhani, Rutgers University

Ken Barker, IBM Research

Yonatan Bisk, University of Washington

Nathanael Chambers, United States Naval Academy

Hans Chalupsky, USC Information Sciences Institute

Vera Demberg, Saarland University

Andrew S. Gordon, University of Southern California

Jonathan Gordon, Vassar College

William Jarrold, Nuance Communications

Gerard de Melo, Rutgers University

Elizabeth Merkhofer, MITRE Corporation

Todor Mihaylov, Heidelberg University

Ashutosh Modi, Disney Research

Sreyasi Nag Chowdhury, Max-Planck-Institut for Informatics

Juri Opitz, Heidelberg University

Letitia Elena Parcalabescu, Heidelberg University

Debjit Paul, Heidelberg University

Hannah Rashkin, University of Washington

Simon Razniewski, Max Planck Institute for Informatics

Niket Tandon, Allen Institute for AI

Adam Trischler, Microsoft Research

Invited Speaker:

Yejin Choi, University of Washington / Allen Institute for AI

Michael Witbrock, University of Auckland

Table of Contents

Conference Program

Sunday, November 3, 2019

9:00–10:30 **Morning Session**

9:00–9:10 *Introduction*

9:10–10:10 *Invited talk: Commonsense Intelligence—Cracking the Longstanding Challenge in AI*
Yejin Choi

10:10–10:30 *Understanding Commonsense Inference Aptitude of Deep Contextual Representations*
Jeff Da and Jungo Kasai

10:30–11:00 *Coffee break*

11:00–12:20 **Pre-lunch Session**

11:00–11:20 *A Hybrid Neural Network Model for Commonsense Reasoning*
Pengcheng He, Xiaodong Liu, Weizhu Chen and Jianfeng Gao

11:20–11:40 *Towards Generalizable Neuro-Symbolic Systems for Commonsense Question Answering*
Kaixin Ma, Jonathan Francis, Quanyang Lu, Eric Nyberg and Alessandro Oltramari

11:40–12:00 *When Choosing Plausible Alternatives, Clever Hans can be Clever*
Pride Kavumba, Naoya Inoue, Benjamin Heinzerling, Keshav Singh, Paul Reisert and Kentaro Inui

12:00–12:20 *Commonsense about Human Senses: Labeled Data Collection Processes*
Ndapa Nakashole

12:20–14:00 *Lunch break*

14:00–15:20   Post-lunch Session

14:00–15:00   *Invited talk: Learning to Reason: from Question Answering to Problem Solving*
Michael Witbrock

15:00–15:20   *Extracting Common Inference Patterns from Semi-Structured Explanations*
Sebastian Thiem and Peter Jansen

15:20–16:20   Poster session

15:30–16:00   *(including coffee break)*

15:20–16:20   *Commonsense Inference in Natural Language Processing (COIN) - Shared Task Report*
Simon Ostermann, Sheng Zhang, Michael Roth and Peter Clark

15:20–16:20   *KARNA at COIN Shared Task 1: Bidirectional Encoder Representations from Transformers with relational knowledge for machine comprehension with common sense*
Yash Jain and Chinmay Singh

15:20–16:20   *IIT-KGP at COIN 2019: Using pre-trained Language Models for modeling Machine Comprehension*
Prakhar Sharma and Sumegh Roychowdhury

15:20–16:20   *Jeff Da at COIN - Shared Task*
Jeff Da

15:20–16:20   *Pingan Smart Health and SJTU at COIN - Shared Task: utilizing Pre-trained Language Models and Common-sense Knowledge in Machine Reading Tasks*
Xiepeng Li, Zhexi Zhang, Wei Zhu, Zheng Li, Yuan Ni, Peng Gao, Junchi Yan and Guotong Xie

15:20–16:20   *BLCU-NLP at COIN-Shared Task1: Stagewise Fine-tuning BERT for Commonsense Inference in Everyday Narrations*
Chunhua Liu and Dong Yu

16:20–17:30 Afternoon Session

16:20–16:40 *Commonsense inference in human-robot communication*
Aliaksandr Huminski, Yan Bin Ng, Kenneth Kwok and Francis Bond

16:40–16:55 *Diversity-aware Event Prediction based on a Conditional Variational Autoencoder with Reconstruction*
Hirokazu Kiyomaru, Kazumasa Omura, Yugo Murawaki, Daisuke Kawahara and Sadao Kurohashi

16:55–17:15 *Can a Gorilla Ride a Camel? Learning Semantic Plausibility from Text*
Ian Porada, Kaheer Suleman and Jackie Chi Kit Cheung

17:15–17:30 *How Pre-trained Word Representations Capture Commonsense Physical Comparisons*
Pranav Goel, Shi Feng and Jordan Boyd-Graber

Cracking the Contextual Commonsense Code: Understanding Commonsense Reasoning Aptitude of Deep Contextual Representations

Jeff Da   **Jungo Kasai**

Paul G. Allen School of Computer Science & Engineering,
University of Washington, Seattle, WA, USA
`{jzda, jkasai}@cs.washington.edu`

Abstract

Pretrained deep contextual representations have advanced the state-of-the-art on various commonsense NLP tasks, but we lack a concrete understanding of the capability of these models. Thus, we investigate and challenge several aspects of BERT's commonsense representation abilities. First, we probe BERT's ability to classify various object attributes, demonstrating that BERT shows a strong ability in encoding various commonsense features in its embedding space, but is still deficient in many areas. Next, we show that, by augmenting BERT's pretraining data with additional data related to the deficient attributes, we are able to improve performance on a downstream commonsense reasoning task while using a minimal amount of data. Finally, we develop a method of fine-tuning knowledge graphs embeddings alongside BERT and show the continued importance of explicit knowledge graphs.

1 Introduction

Should I put the toaster in the oven? Or does the cake go in the oven? Questions like these are trivial for humans to answer, but machines have a much more difficult time determining right from wrong. Researchers have chased mimicking human intelligence through linguistic commonsense as early as McCarthy (1960):

> ... [machines that] have much in common with what makes us human are described as having common sense. (McCarthy, 1960).

Such commonsense knowledge presents a severe challenge to modern NLP systems that are trained on a large amount of text data. Commonsense knowledge is often implicitly assumed, and a statistical model fails to learn it by this reporting bias

(Gordon and van Durme, 2013). This critical difference of machine learning systems from human intelligence hurts performance when given examples outside the training data distribution (Gordon and van Durme, 2013; Schubert, 2015; Davis and Marcus, 2015; Sakaguchi et al., 2019).

On the other hand, NLP systems have recently improved dramatically with contextualized word representations in a wide range of tasks (Peters et al., 2018; Radford et al., 2018; Devlin et al., 2019). These representations have the benefit of encoding context-specific meanings of words that are learned from large corpora. In this work, we extensively assess the degree to which these representations encode grounded commonsense knowledge, and investigate whether contextual representations can ameliorate NLP systems in commonsense reasoning capability.

We present a method of analyzing commonsense knowledge in word representations through attribute classification on the semantic norm dataset (Devereux et al., 2014), and compare a contextual model to a traditional word type representation. Our analysis shows that while contextual representations significantly outperform word type embeddings, they still fail to encode some types of the commonsense attributes, such as visual and perceptual properties. In addition, we underscore the translation of these deficiencies to downstream commonsense reasoning tasks.

We then propose two methods to address these deficiencies: one implicit and one explicit. Implicitly, we train on additional data chosen via attribute selection. Explicitly, we add knowledge embeddings during the fine-tuning process of contextual representations. This work shows that knowledge graph embeddings improve the ability of contextual embeddings to fit commonsense attributes, as well as the accuracy on downstream reasoning tasks.

1

Proceedings of the First Workshop on Commonsense Inference in Natural Language Processing, pages 1–12
Hongkong, China, November 3, 2019. ©2019 Association for Computational Linguistics

2 Attribute Classification

First, we preform an investigation to see if the output from BERT is able to encode the necessary features to determine if an object has a related attribute. We propose a method to evaluate BERT's representations and compare to previous non-contextual GloVe (Pennington et al., 2014) baselines, using simple logistic classifiers.

2.1 Commonsense Object Attribution

To get labels for attribute features of commonsense features of objects, we utilize CSLB, a semantic norm dataset collected by the Cambridge Centre for Speech, Language, and the Brain (Devereux et al., 2014). Semantic norm datasets are created through reports from human participants asked to label the semantic features of a given object. Thus, a proportion of these features are obvious to humans, but may be difficult to find written in text corpora. This is notably different from the collection methods of prominent commonsense databases, such as ConceptNet (Speer and Havasi, 2013).

CSLB gives 638 different attributes describing a variety of objects provided by 123 participants. To make results consistent between baselines (GloVe) and BERT, we first preprocess the attributes present in CSLB. We removed attributes with two-word names, ambiguous meanings (i.e. homographs), or missing GloVe representations. This gives a 597 attribute vocabulary. Examples of objects described are *zebra*, *wheel*, and *wine*. Example of attributes are *is upright*, *is a toy*, and *is an ingredient*.

2.2 Contextualization

Since BERT is commonly utilized at the sequence embedding level (Devlin et al., 2019), we develop a contextualization module to allow representations of *(object, attribute)* pairs, allowing us to acquire one sequence embedding from BERT for each pair. From a high level, we want to develop a method to transform *(object, attribute)* into simple grammatical sentences.

For each *(object, attribute)* pair, we raise the pair to a sentence structure such that the attribute is describing the object. We would enforce the following representation, in line with the procedure of Devlin et al. (2019):

$$[CLS] \; c_{\text{prefix}} \; \text{noun} \; c_{\text{affix}} \; \text{adj.} \; c_{\text{postfix}} \; [SEP]$$

The goal is to create a simple formula that allows the model to isolate the differences between the object-attribute (noun-adjective) pairs, rather than variation in language. c_{prefix} represents previous context, i.e. context that appears before the word. c_{affix} is context that appears between the noun and the adjective. c_{postfix} is context that closes out the sentence.

We illustrate this algorithm for use with CSLB, but this methodology can be used for any dataset, such as other semantic norm datasets. We use this process for each *(object, attribute)* pair in CSLB. First, we check if any words in the attribute need to be changed. For example, in CSLB, instead of *does deflate*, we use *deflates* as the attribute text, since it simplifies the language. Then, for c_{prefix}, we use either *A* or *An*, and for c_{postfix}, and use a period. For c_{affix}, we use either *is* or nothing, depending on the attribute. Some example sentences would be: *(shirt, made of cotton)* would become "A shirt is made of cotton." and *(balloon, does deflate)* becomes "A balloon deflates." See the appendix for full pseudocode.

We find that this method is a better alternative to simply creating a sequence with the concatenation of the object and the attribute. Some attribute-object pairs translate better to English than others. For example, "wheel does deflate" might be a relatively uncommon and awkward English phrase when compared to more natural phrases such as "shirt made of cotton".

2.3 Determining Attribute Fit

We explore if word embeddings contain the necessary information within their embedding space to classify various semantic attributes. Our procedure involves use of a simple logistic classifier to classify if an *attribute* applies to a candidate *object*. We create a list of *(object, attribute)* pairs as training examples for the logistic classifier (thus, there are $n_{objects} \times n_{attributes}$ training examples in total). We then train logistic classifiers for each attribute, and use leave-one-out accuracy as accuracy – averaging the leave-out-one result across all $n_{objects}$ classifiers, since we leave out a different object each time. For example, to examine the attribute *made of cotton*, we train on all objects except one, using the label 1 if the object is made of cotton, and 0 otherwise. Then, we test to see if the left-out object is classified correctly. We repeat $n_{objects}$ times, removing a different object each

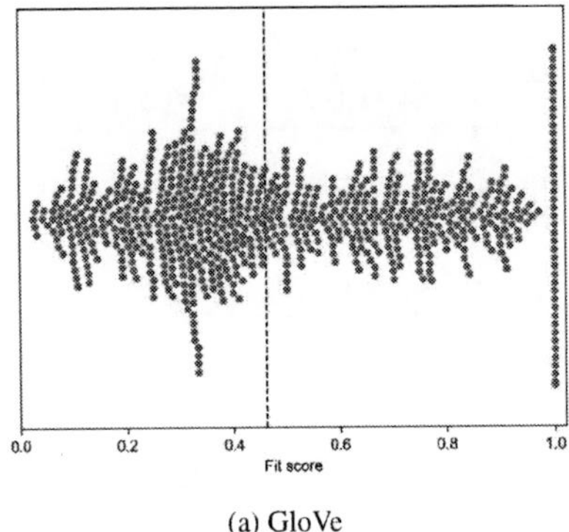
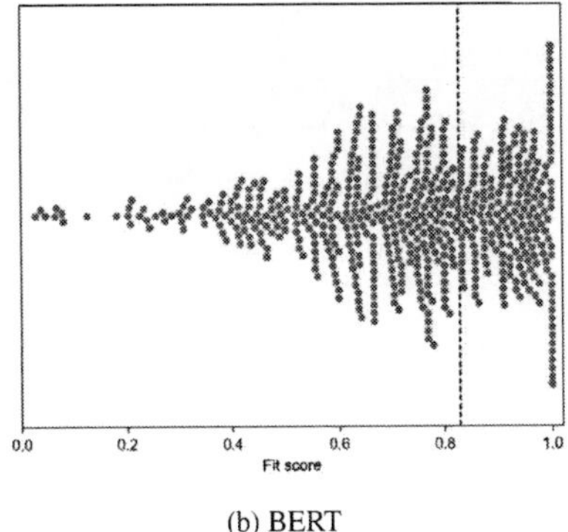

(a) GloVe   (b) BERT

Figure 1: Swarm plots showing attribute fit scores for GloVe (left) and BERT (right). Each dot represents a single attribute, displayed along the x-axis according to the classifier's ability to fit that feature with the given embeddings. The y-axis is not significant, and instead, dots are displaced along the y-axis instead of overlapping to show quantity. The median fit score per embedding type is displayed with a dotted line.

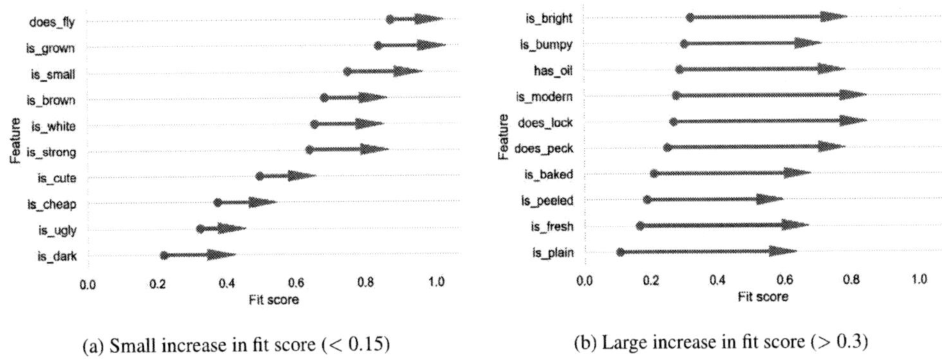

(a) Small increase in fit score (< 0.15)   (b) Large increase in fit score (> 0.3)

Figure 2: Differences between fit scores when using GloVe (start of arrow) or BERT (end of arrows) embeddings.

time. To judge fit, we use F1 score, as F1 score is not affected by dataset imbalance. We consider other classifiers, such as SVD classifiers, but we find that there is no significant empirical difference between the classifiers. For baseline tests, we use the pretrained 300 dimensional GloVe embeddings,[1] as they have shown to perform better than word2vec embeddings (Lucy and Gauthier, 2017). See appendix for specific logistic regression parameters, such as the number of update steps used.

2.4 Attribute Scores

We show our findings for feature fit for each attribute. Figure 1 highlights that BERT is much stronger on this benchmark – the median fit score is nearly double that of the previously reported GloVe baselines. This suggests that BERT en-

codes commonsense traits much better than previous baselines, which is suggestive of its strong scores on several commonsense reasoning tasks. Notably, we can see that much fewer features have a fit score less than 0.5. We observe that many more traits have a perfect fit score of 1.0. However, our results also show that BERT is still unable to fully fit many attributes. This underscores that BERT still lacks much attribution ability, perhaps in areas outside of its training scheme or pre-training data. Seen in Figure 2 is the change in fit scores between GloVe and BERT. We can see that some traits exhibit much larger increases – in particular, physical traits such as *made of wood*, *does lock,* and *has a top*. Traits that are more abstract tend to have a lesser increase. For example, *is creepy* and *is strong* still are not able to be fit by the contextualized BERT module.

---

[1] https://nlp.stanford.edu/projects/glove/

Metric	Visual	Encyclopedic	Functional	Perceptual	Taxonomic	Overall
Median$_{GloVe}$	46.2	38.9	44.4	49.0	89.1	46.1
Median$_{BERT}$	83.3	76.2	78.3	80.0	100	82.7
Δ	**+37.1**	**+37.3**	**+33.9**	**+31.0**	**+10.9**	**+36.6**

Table 1: Comparison of median logistic classifier fit scores (out of 100 percent fit) across categories defined in CSLB.

Category	Lower scoring attributes (fit score $<$ 1.0)	Attributes perfectly fit (fit score = 1.0)
Visual	is triangular, is long and thin, is upright, has two feet, does swing, is rigid	does come in pairs, has a back, has a barrel, has a bushy tail, has a clasp
Encyclopedic	is hardy, has types, is found in bible, is American, does play, is necessary essential	does grow on plants, does grow on trees, does live in rivers, does live in trees, does photosynthesize, has a crew
Functional	does work, does spin, does support, does drink, does breathe, does hang	does DIY, does carry transport goods, does chop, does drive
Perceptual	is chewy, does rattle, is wet, does squeak, is rough, has a strong smell	does bend, has a sting, has pollen, has soft flesh, is citrus, is fermented
Taxonomic	is a home, is a dried fruit, is a garden tool, is a vessel, is a toy, is an ingredient	is a bird of prey, is a boat, is a body part, is a cat, is a citrus fruit, is a crustacean

Table 2: Fine-grained comparison across categories between attributes that lack some level of fit (left) and perfectly fit attributes (right) with classification using BERT representations.

Table 1 shows a comparison of fit scores across different types of attribute categories. These categories are defined per attribute in CSLB (Devereux et al., 2014). Visual attributes define features that can be perceived visually, such as *is curved*. Perceptual defines attributes that can be perceived in other non-visual ways, such as *does smell nice*. Functional describes the ability of an object, such as *is for weddings*. Taxonomic defines a biological or symbolic classification of an object like *is seafood*. Finally, encyclopedic are traits that may be the most difficult to classify, as they are attributes that most pertain to abstract commonsense, such as *is collectible*.

BERT has stronger scores in all categories, and just short of double the overall accuracy. Importantly, however, it struggles to classify many categories of objects. In taxonomic categories, it is able to perfectly fit more than half the objects. We suspect that this is intuitive, as BERT is trained on text corpora that allow for learning relationships between classes of objects and the object itself. GloVe notably also preforms strong in this category, for the same reasons. BERT scores the lowest on encyclopedic traits, which most closely resemble traits that would appear in commonsense tasks. This suggests that BERT maybe be relatively deficient in regards to reasoning about com-monsense attributes.

We also examine specific attributes where BERT is fully fit (with a perfect fit score), and compare those attributes to features where BERT is unable to fit. Table 2 shows examples of both levels of fit. BERT is able to fit many features that would be easily represented in text, such as *does bend*, *does grow on plants*, and *does drive*. It is unable to fit traits that may be less common in text and more susceptible to the reporting bias, such as *is American*, *is chewy*, and *has a strong smell*. Surprisingly, it is also unable to fit several features that would be likely common in text such as *is a toy*, suggesting that BERT's training procedure is lacking coverage of many everyday events perhaps due to the reporting bias.

2.5 Do Knowledge Graphs Help?

We extend our investigation with two inquiries. First, given the large gain in accuracy over GloVe, we wonder if BERT embeddings now encode the same information that external commonsense knowledge graphs (such as ConceptNet (Speer and Havasi, 2013)) provide. Second, we question if it is possible to increase the overall accuracy above the accuracy presented by using BERT embeddings (otherwise, it could mean that the deficit is simply because the logistic classifier does not have

System	Median
GloVe	46.1
BERT$_{LARGE}$	82.7
ConceptNet	23.2
BERT$_{LARGE}$ + ConceptNet	**90.7**

Table 3: Results for attribute classification with ConceptNet as a knowledge graph source.

needed capacity (Liu et al., 2019a)).

We use ConceptNet (Speer and Havasi, 2013) for our experiments. We label each relationship type with an index. (*antonym* as 0, *related_to* as 1, etc.) During classification, we query the knowledge base with the object and the attribute and check if there are any relationships between the two. We embed the indexes of matched relationships to randomly initialized embeddings and concatenate them with the original BERT embeddings. If more than one relationship is found, we randomly choose a relationship to use.

Table 3 shows our results. By itself, the explicit commonsense embeddings do not have enough coverage to learn classifications of each attribute, since the knowledge graph does not contain information about every (*object*, *attribute*) pair. However, by combining the knowledge graph embeddings with the BERT embeddings, we illustrate that knowledge graphs cover information that BERT is unable to generate the proper features for. In addition, the results suggest that BERT is deficient over various attributes, and the traditional knowledge graphs are able to cover this feature space. These results support the hypothesis that BERT simply lacks the features rather than the problem of the logistic classifier.

3 Improving BERT's Representations

We have gained an understanding of the types of commonsense attributes BERT is able to classify and encode in its embeddings, and also have an understanding of the types of attributes that BERT's features are deficient in covering. In Section 2.5, we have shown that commonsense knowledge graphs may also help encode information that extends beyond BERT's embedding features. However, we have yet to know whether this BERT's deficiency will translate to any of BERT's downstream reasoning ability, which is ultimately more important.

We empirically address the gap between at-

Passage: For my anniversary with my husband, I decided to cook him a very fancy and nice breakfast. One thing I had always wanted to do but never got to try was making fresh squeezed orange juice. I got about ten oranges because I wasn't sure how much I was going to need to make enough juice for both me and my husband. I got home and pulled my juicer out from underneath my sink. I began using the juicer to squeeze the juice out of my orange juice. I brought my husband his breakfast with the orange juice, and he said that the juice was his favorite part!
How were the oranges sliced?
a) in half
b) in eighths
When did they plug the juicer in?
a) after squeezing oranges
b) after removing it from the box

Table 4: Example of a prompt from MCScript 2.0 (Ostermann et al., 2018), an everyday commonsense reasoning dataset. Questions often require script knowledge that extends beyond referencing the text.

tribute classification and downstream ability in BERT. First, we demonstrate that there is a correlation between low-scoring attributes and low accuracy on reasoning questions that involve those attributes. Then, we leverage our investigation to build two baseline methods of improving BERT's commonsense reasoning abilities (Figure 4). Since BERT is trained on implicit data, we explore a method of using RACE (Lai et al., 2017) alongside a list of attributes that BERT is deficient in (such as the one in Section 2.4). We also extend our investigation in Section 2.5 on commonsense knowledge graphs by proposing a method to integrate BERT with external knowledge graphs. See appendix for hyperparameters.

3.1 Background: MCScript 2.0

We leverage MCScript 2.0 (Ostermann et al., 2019) for several investigations in this paper. MCScript 2.0 is a downstream commonsense reasoning dataset. Each datum involves one passage, question, and two answers, and the goal is to pick the correct answer out of the two choices. Many questions involve everyday scenarios and objects, which helps us link our semantic norm results to more downstream reasoning capability. Table 4

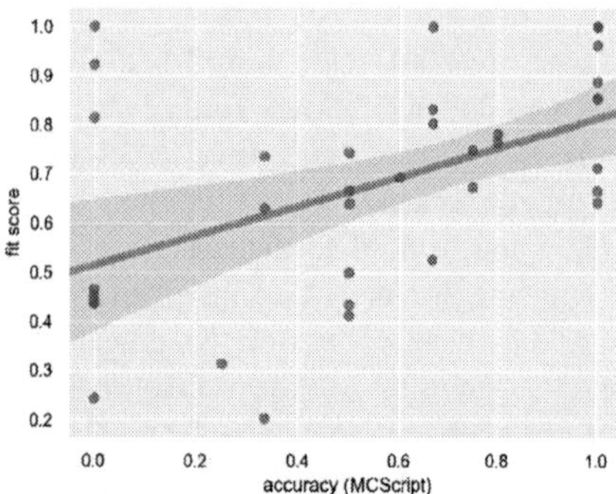

Figure 3: Linear regression fit of accuracy on MCScript 2.0, per attribute, versus fit score, with the inner 90 percent bootstrap confidence intervals highlighted (n = 1000). Each dot represents the accuracy of questions related to one attribute.

shows an example.

3.2 Do Low Classification Scores Result in Low Performance?

We examine if low-scoring attributes result in low downstream performance, and high-scoring attributes also result in high downstream performance. For each question in MCScript, we relate that question to 1 or more of the attributes in the previous experiment. For example, a question might be talking about whether to use a camera flash, and would be thus related to the traits *does have flash*, *is dark*, and *is light*. Here we aim to empirically assess deficiencies in BERT's ability and their downstream implications. For instance, if it is unable to fit *does have flash*, will it have a gap in knowledge in areas regarding camera flash? If a given feature does not have a related question, we do not include it in our experiments. In total, $n_{questions} = 193$, and $n_{attributes} = 92$.

For the MCScript model, we simply classify based on the $[CLS]$ token, as suggested in Devlin et al. (2019). We softmax over the logits between the two answers when producing our final answers, and split the passage-question pair and answer by a $[SEP]$ token. The attribute-related questions here are from the development set only.

Seen in Figure 3 are the results. We do not see a clear pattern, but we can still make several observations. First, we notice that there are simply a lot of items with a high fit score. Next, there are a lot of attributes that BERT simply gets correct. However, notably, BERT is less consistent with getting

items that have a low fit score (< 0.5). We can also notice that all attributes that have high accuracy on MCScript also have a high fit score.

3.3 Implicit Fine-Tune Method

We develop a method of fine-tuning with additional data based on the deficiencies found in the previous section. We fine-tune on additional data, but we select only data related to attributes that BERT is deficient in.

3.3.1 Data Selection

In our experiments, we use RACE (Lai et al., 2017) as our supplementary dataset. While we can fine-tune on the entire dataset, we can also select a subset that directly targets the deficient attributes in semantic norm. To select such a subset, we define a datum as related if any words match between the datum in the supplementary dataset and the deficient feature in semantic norm, stemming all words beforehand. For some attributes, we remove frequent words ("is, "does", and "has") to avoid matching too many sentences within RACE.

Since each datum in RACE involves a question, answer, and passage, we allow matches between either of the three texts, and do not differentiate between matches in the question, answer, and passage. We find that this keeps around a third of the data in RACE (around 44K, out of the 97K data present in RACE). It is also key that this data selection process does not require access to the downstream task dataset. Thus, this procedure has the ability to generalize to other tasks beyond MCScript 2.0.

3.3.2 Fine-Tuning Procedure

We fine-tune BERT's language objectives on RACE. We do not change the properties of either objective, to keep comparability between our analysis and BERT. This mimics Devlin et al. (2019), and thus, we fine-tune the token masking objective and the next sentence prediction objective. Several works have improved on BERT's language objectives (Yang et al., 2019; Liu et al., 2019b), but we keep the language objectives in BERT intact for comparison.

After fine-tuning on RACE, we fine-tune on MCScript with the classification objective only. We do this since we need to build a classification layer for the specific task, as noted in Devlin et al. (2019). We do not freeze the weights in this process, as to keep comparability with the fine-tuning

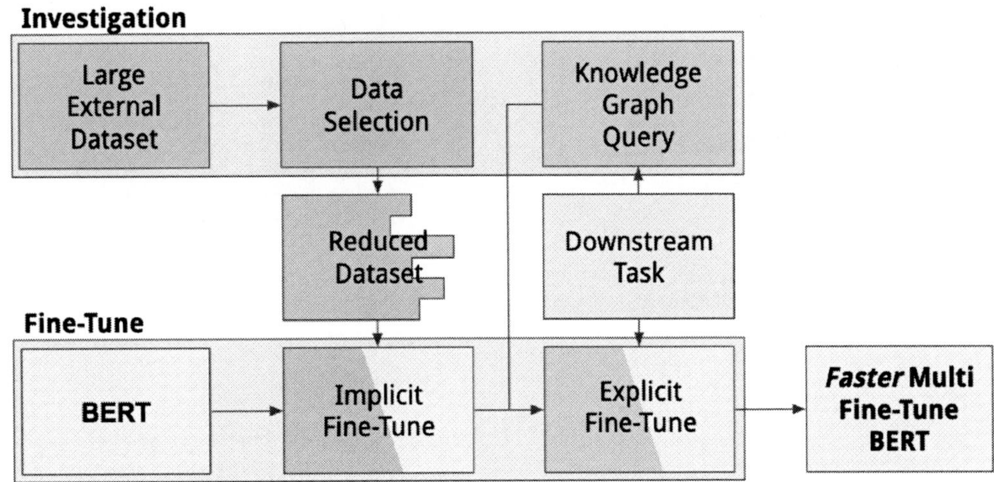

Figure 4: Outline of our baseline method of improving BERT for commonsense reasoning. Our method fine-tunes BERT through multiple facets while optimizing for accuracy and reduced train steps. We use RACE (Lai et al., 2017) as an external dataset, and MCScript 2.0 (Ostermann et al., 2019) as our downstream task.

procedure in Devlin et al. (2019).

3.4 Explicit Fine-Tune Method

Motivated by our results in 2.5, we develop a method of integrating knowledge graph embeddings with the BERT embeddings. First, we query knowledge graphs based on the given text to find relationships between objects in the text. Then, we generate an embedding for each relationship found (similar to Section 2.5). Finally, we fine-tune these embeddings alongside the BERT embeddings.

3.4.1 Knowledge Graph Query

We query a suite of knowledge bases (Concept-Net (Speer and Havasi, 2013), WebChild (Tandon et al., 2017), ATOMIC (Sap et al., 2019)) to create knowledge graph embeddings. First, we examine all relationships, indexing each unique relationship sequentially. Then, during fine-tuning, for each prompt in MCScript 2.0, we query the knowledge bases to find any *(start_node, end_node, edge)* matches between the knowledge base and the current prompt. For example, if *eat* and *dinner* are both present in the text, the relationship *at_location* in ConceptNet would match (Figure 5). We record the index of the matched relationship, keeping a list of matched relationships per word in the prompt. If a *start_node* spans more than one word, we record the match as occurring for the first word in the phrase.

System	Acc.	Data
BERT$_{LARGE}$ + RACE	84.3	98 K
BERT$_{LARGE}$ + RACE (random)	84.0	44 K
BERT$_{LARGE}$ + RACE (selected)	**84.5**	44 K

Table 5: Test set results from the implicit method on MCScript 2.0. "selected" indicates a subset of RACE that consists of misclassified attributes in semantic norm. "random" is a randomly chosen subset.

3.4.2 Fine-Tuning Procedure

We fine-tune our knowledge graph embeddings alongside the BERT fine-tuning procedure. We randomly initialize an embedding for each relationship and each knowledge graph. We choose an embedding for each word in the prompt (randomly, if there is more than one relationship associated), creating a sequence of knowledge graph embeddings. We create a sequence embedding for the 30-dimensional graph embeddings by feeding the sequence through an bidirectional LSTM. Then, during fine-tuning, we classify each datum in MCScript based on the concatenation of the explicit graph sequence representation and the BERT sequence embedding (i.e. $[CLS]$), as per Devlin et al. (2019).

3.5 Results and Analysis

Table 5 shows the results from the implicit method. Accuracy is consistent across the board, with all models giving about a 2% downstream ac-

Figure 5: Visualization of ConceptNet knowledge base queries. The word *eat* is being queried with the other words in the text, with the valid edges discovered displayed against the left.

System	Accuracy
Human (Ostermann et al., 2019)	97.4
Random Baseline	48.9
BERT$_{LARGE}$	82.3
with ConceptNet	83.1
with WebChild	82.7
with ATOMIC	82.5
with all KB	83.3
with all KB + RACE (selected)	**85.5**

Table 6: Test set results for knowledge base embeddings on MCScript 2.0.

curacy boost. However, the model with the less amount of data (RACE, selected from deficiencies only) achieves equivalent accuracy to the entire RACE dataset, while using only half the amount of data. This underscores the importance of the abstract semantic norm task, as the related data selection process was effective in choosing examples that are directly related to deficiencies.

Table 6 shows our results with explicit knowledge embeddings. Each knowledge base improves accuracy, with ConceptNet giving the largest performance boost. ATOMIC gives the smallest boost, likely because the ATOMIC edges involve longer phrases, which means less matches, and the overlap between ATOMIC text and the text present in the task is not as large as either ConceptNet or WebChild.

We can also combine the explicit knowledge base embeddings and the implicit RACE fine-tuning, yielding the highest accuracy (with all KB + RACE (subset) in Table 6). The knowledge embeddings provide a similar +1% absolute improvement (85.5 vs. 84.5), suggesting that the knowledge embeddings cover different aspects and relationships in the text than learned during fine-tuning on RACE.

4   Related Work

Similar to our attribute classification investigation, several other works have used applied semantic norm datasets to computational linguistics (Agirre et al., 2009; Bruni et al., 2012; Kiela et al., 2016). Methodologically, our work is most similar to Lucy and Gauthier (2017), who use a logistic regression classifier to determine fit score of word type embeddings based on leave-one-out verification. Forbes et al. (2019) investigates the commonsense aptitude of contextual representations. However, our work differs in several important ways: 1) we connect our analysis to downstream reasoning aptitude, underscoring the importance of the semantic norm analysis, and 2) we introduce various ways of improving BERT, motivated by our analysis.

In contemporaneous work, various research has been done in improving upon BERT's performance through knowledge augmentation. Implicitly, Sun et al. (2019) explores fine-tuning on in-domain data, similarly to our fine-tuning on the RACE dataset (Lai et al., 2017). They discover an increase in accuracy that is especially prevalent over smaller datasets. Our work differs in that we do not fine-tune on the entire domain data, but rather select a smaller subset of data to fine-tune on. Other work extends BERT to domains where its original training data does not suffice (Beltagy et al., 2019; Lee et al., 2019). RoBERTa (Liu et al., 2019b) also pretrains on RACE, and finds increased results through altering several of BERT's pretraining tasks, claiming that BERT was extensively undertrained. Explicitly, ERNIE, Zhang et al. (2019) introduces information to contextual representations during pretraining. ERNIE uses word-level fusion between the contextual representation and explicit information.

Prior work has developed several benchmark datasets to assess commonsense knowledge of NLP models (Roemmele et al., 2011; Mostafazadeh et al., 2016; Zhang et al., 2017; Zellers et al., 2018, 2019; Ostermann et al., 2018, 2019; Sakaguchi et al., 2019). These benchmarks are typically posed as question answering, but we use semantic norm datasets to specifically assess BERT's ability to represent grounded attributes. Further, we demonstrate that these abstract attributes can be used to enhance BERT's representations and improve the downstream performance.

5 Conclusion

We found that BERT outperforms previous distributional methods on an attribute classification task, highlighting possible reasons why BERT improves the state-of-the-art on various commonsense reasoning tasks. However, we show that BERT still lacks proper attribute representations in many areas. We developed implicit and explicit methods of remedying this deficit on the downstream task. We demonstrated that, individually and combined, both methods can improve scores on the downstream reasoning task. We motivate future work in probing and improving the ability of neural language models to reason about everyday commonsense.

Acknowledgments

The authors thank Maxwell Forbes, Keisuke Sakaguchi, and Noah A. Smith as well as the anonymous reviewers for their helpful feedback. JD and JK are supported by NSF Multimodal and the Funai Overseas Scholarship respectively.

References

Eneko Agirre, Enrique Alfonseca, Keith B. Hall, Jana Kravalova, Marius Pasca, and Aitor Soroa. 2009. A study on similarity and relatedness using distributional and wordnet-based approaches. In *NAACL-HLT*.

Iz Beltagy, Arman Cohan, and Kyle Lo. 2019. Scibert: Pretrained contextualized embeddings for scientific text. *ArXiv*, abs/1903.10676.

Elia Bruni, Gemma Boleda, Marco Baroni, and Nam-Khanh Tran. 2012. Distributional semantics in technicolor. In *Proc. of ACL*.

Ernest Davis and Gary Marcus. 2015. Commonsense reasoning and commonsense knowledge in artificial intelligence. *Commun. ACM*, 58.

Barry J. Devereux, Lorraine K. Tyler, Jeroen Geertzen, and Billi Randall. 2014. The centre for speech, language and the brain (CSLB) concept property norms. *Behavior Research Methods*, 46(4).

Jacob Devlin, Ming-Wei Chang, Kenton Lee, and Kristina Toutanova. 2019. BERT: Pre-training of deep bidirectional transformers for language understanding. In *Proc. of NAACL-HLT*.

Maxwell Forbes, Ari Holtzman, and Yejin Choi. 2019. Do neural language representations learn physical commonsense? *Proc. of the 41st Annual Conference of the Cognitive Science Society*.

Jonathan Gordon and Benjamin van Durme. 2013. Reporting bias and knowledge acquisition. In *Proc. of AKBC*.

Douwe Kiela, Luana Bulat, Anita L. Vero, and Stephen Clark. 2016. Virtual embodiment: A scalable long-term strategy for artificial intelligence research. *ArXiv*, abs/1610.07432.

Guokun Lai, Qizhe Xie, Hanxiao Liu, Yiming Yang, and Eduard H. Hovy. 2017. RACE: Large-scale reading comprehension dataset from examinations. In *Proc. of EMNLP*.

Jinhyuk Lee, Wonjin Yoon, Sungdong Kim, Donghyeon Kim, Sunkyu Kim, Chan Ho So, and Jaewoo Kang. 2019. Biobert: a pre-trained biomedical language representation model for biomedical text mining. *ArXiv*, abs/1901.08746.

Nelson F. Liu, Matthew Ph Gardner, Yonatan Belinkov, Matthew E. Peters, and Noah A. Smith. 2019a. Linguistic knowledge and transferability of contextual representations. In *Proc. of NAACL-HLT*.

Yinhan Liu, Myle Ott, Naman Goyal, Jingfei Du, Mandar S. Joshi, Danqi Chen, Omer Levy, Miranda Paige Linscott Lewis, Luke S. Zettlemoyer, and Veselin Stoyanov. 2019b. Roberta: A robustly optimized bert pretraining approach. *ArXiv*, abs/1907.11692.

Li Lucy and Jon Gauthier. 2017. Are distributional representations ready for the real world? Evaluating word vectors for grounded perceptual meaning. In *Proc. of RoboNLP*.

Jeanette McCarthy. 1960. Programs with common sense.

Nasrin Mostafazadeh, Nathanael Chambers, Xiaodong He, Devi Parikh, Dhruv Batra, Lucy Vanderwende, Pushmeet Kohli, and James F. Allen. 2016. A corpus and cloze evaluation for deeper understanding of commonsense stories. In *Proc. of NAACL-HLT*.

Simon Ostermann, Ashutosh Modi, Michael Roth, Stefan Thater, and Manfred Pinkal. 2018. MCScript: A novel dataset for assessing machine comprehension using script knowledge. In *Proc. of LREC*, Miyazaki, Japan. European Languages Resources Association (ELRA).

Simon Ostermann, Michael Roth, and Manfred Pinkal. 2019. MCScript2.0: A machine comprehension corpus focused on script events and participants. In *Proc. of *SEM*, Minneapolis, Minnesota. Association for Computational Linguistics.

Jeffrey Pennington, Richard Socher, and Christopher Manning. 2014. GloVe: Global vectors for word representation. In *Proc. of EMNLP*, Doha, Qatar. Association for Computational Linguistics.

Matthew Peters, Mark Neumann, Mohit Iyyer, Matt Gardner, Christopher Clark, Kenton Lee, and Luke Zettlemoyer. 2018. Deep contextualized word representations. In *Proc. of NAACL-HLT*.

Alec Radford, Karthik Narasimhan, Tim Salimans, and Ilya Sutskever. 2018. Improving language understanding by generative pre-training.

Melissa Roemmele, Cosmin Adrian Bejan, and Andrew S. Gordon. 2011. Choice of plausible alternatives: An evaluation of commonsense causal reasoning. In *AAAI 2011 Spring Symposium*.

Keisuke Sakaguchi, Ronan Le Bras, Chandra Bhagavatula, and Yejin Choi. 2019. WINOGRANDE: An adversarial winograd schema challenge at scale. *ArXiv*, abs/1907.10641.

Maarten Sap, Ronan Le Bras, Emily Allaway, Chandra Bhagavatula, Nicholas Lourie, Hannah Rashkin, Brendan Roof, Noah A. Smith, and Yejin Choi. 2019. ATOMIC: An atlas of machine commonsense for if-then reasoning. In *Proc. of AAAI*.

Lenhart Schubert. 2015. What kinds of knowledge are needed for genuine understanding? In *Proc of Cognitum*.

R. Speer and Catherine Havasi. 2013. Conceptnet 5: A large semantic network for relational knowledge. In *The People's Web Meets NLP*.

Chi Sun, Xipeng Qiu, Yige Xu, and Xuanjing Huang. 2019. How to fine-tune BERT for text classification? *ArXiv*, abs/1905.05583.

Niket Tandon, Gerard de Melo, and Gerhard Weikum. 2017. WebChild 2.0 : Fine-grained commonsense knowledge distillation. In *Proc. of ACL 2017, System Demonstrations*, Vancouver, Canada. Association for Computational Linguistics.

Zhilin Yang, Zihang Dai, Yiming Yang, Jaime G. Carbonell, Ruslan Salakhutdinov, and Quoc V. Le. 2019. XLNet: Generalized autoregressive pretraining for language understanding. *ArXiv*, abs/1906.08237.

Rowan Zellers, Yonatan Bisk, Roy Schwartz, and Yejin Choi. 2018. SWAG: A large-scale adversarial dataset for grounded commonsense inference. In *Proc. of EMNLP*.

Rowan Zellers, Ari Holtzman, Yonatan Bisk, Ali Farhadi, and Yejin Choi. 2019. HellaSwag: Can a machine really finish your sentence? In *Proc. of ACL*.

Sheng Zhang, Rachel Rudinger, Kevin Duh, and Benjamin Van Durme. 2017. Ordinal common-sense inference. *TACL*, 5.

Zhengyan Zhang, Xu Han, Zhiyuan Liu, Xin Jiang, Maosong Sun, and Qun Liu. 2019. ERNIE: Enhanced language representation with informative entities. In *Proc. of ACL*, Florence, Italy. Association for Computational Linguistics.

A Appendices

A.1 Hyperparameters

Seen in Table 7 is a list of hyperparameters for our experiments. We use the same parameters for both uses of explicit knowledge embeddings.

Regression Classifier	
Penalty	L2
# Penalty Coefficient	1.0
Iteration count	200
Optimizer	lbfgs
Patience	1e-4
Explicit Knowledge Embeddings	
Embedding size	10
Knowledge bases used	3
BERT Fine-Tuning	
Maximum sequence length	450
Train batch size	32
Learning rate	1e-5
Epochs	4
Warmup	20%
LSTM	
Hidden size	32
Dropout	0.0
Bidirectional	Yes

Table 7: Hyperparameters used throughout experiments.

A.2 Contextualization Module Pseudocode

Psuedocode can be found by referencing Algorithm 1.

Algorithm 1: Contextualization Module for CSLB Attributes

contextualize *(object, attribute):*
to_remove = [does]
if *attribute[first word] in to_remove* **then**
    attribute[second word] = make_plural(attribute[second word])
    attribute.remove(attribute[first word])
end if
if *starts_with_vowel(attribute[first word])* **then**
    c_{prefix} = An
else
    c_{prefix} = A
end if
needs_affix = [made]
if *attribute[first word] in needs_affix* **then**
    c_{affix} = is
else
    c_{affix} = None
end if
c_{postfix} = .
return c_{prefix} + object + c_{affix} + attribute + c_{postfix}

A Hybrid Neural Network Model for Commonsense Reasoning

Pengcheng He[1], Xiaodong Liu[2], Weizhu Chen[1], Jianfeng Gao[2]
[1] Microsoft Dynamics 365 AI [2] Microsoft Research
{penhe,xiaodl,wzchen,jfgao}@microsoft.com

Abstract

This paper proposes a hybrid neural network (HNN) model for commonsense reasoning. An HNN consists of two component models, a masked language model and a semantic similarity model, which share a BERT-based contextual encoder but use different model-specific input and output layers. HNN obtains new state-of-the-art results on three classic commonsense reasoning tasks, pushing the WNLI benchmark to 89%, the Winograd Schema Challenge (WSC) benchmark to 75.1%, and the PDP60 benchmark to 90.0%. An ablation study shows that language models and semantic similarity models are complementary approaches to commonsense reasoning, and HNN effectively combines the strengths of both. The code and pre-trained models will be publicly available at https://github.com/namisan/mt-dnn.

1 Introduction

Commonsense reasoning is fundamental to natural language understanding (NLU). As shown in the examples in Table 1, in order to infer what the pronoun "they" refers to in the first two statements, one has to leverage the commonsense knowledge that "demonstrators can cause violence and city councilmen usually fear violence." Similarly, it is obvious to humans what the pronoun "it" refers to in the third and fourth statements due to the commonsense knowledge that "An object cannot fit in a container because either the object (trophy) is too big or the container (suitcase) is too small."

In this paper, we study two classic commonsense reasoning tasks: the Winograd Schema Challenge (WSC) and Pronoun Disambiguation Problem (PDP) (Levesque et al., 2011; Davis and Marcus, 2015). Both tasks are formulated as an anaphora resolution problem, which is a form of co-reference resolution, where a machine (AI

1. *The city councilmen refused the demonstrators a permit because **they** feared violence.* Who feared violence?
   A. **The city councilmen**   B. The demonstrators

2. *The city councilmen refused the demonstrators a permit because **they** advocated violence.* Who advocated violence?
   A. The city councilmen   B. **The demonstrators**

3. *The trophy doesn't fit in the brown suitcase because **it** is too big.* What is too big?
   A. **The trophy**   B. The suitcase

4. *The trophy doesn't fit in the brown suitcase because **it** is too small.* What is too small?
   A. The trophy   B. **The suitcase**

Table 1: Examples from Winograd Schema Challenge (WSC). The task is to identify the reference of the pronoun in bold.

agent) must identify the antecedent of an ambiguous pronoun in a statement. WSC and PDP differ from other co-reference resolution tasks (Soon et al., 2001; Ng and Cardie, 2002; Peng et al., 2016) in that commonsense knowledge, which cannot be explicitly decoded from the given text, is needed to solve the problem, as illustrated in the examples in Table 1.

Comparing with other commonsense reasoning tasks, such as COPA (Roemmele et al., 2011), Story Cloze Test (Mostafazadeh et al., 2016), Event2Mind (Rashkin et al., 2018), SWAG (Zellers et al., 2018), ReCoRD (Zhang et al., 2018), and so on, WSC and PDP better approximate real human reasoning, can be easily solved by native English-speaker (Levesque et al., 2011),

Proceedings of the First Workshop on Commonsense Inference in Natural Language Processing, pages 13–21
Hongkong, China, November 3, 2019. ©2019 Association for Computational Linguistics

and yet are challenging for machines. For example, the WNLI task, which is derived from WSC, is considered the most challenging NLU task in the General Language Understanding Evaluation (GLUE) benchmark (Wang et al., 2018). Most machine learning models can hardly outperform the naive baseline of majority voting (scored at 65.1) [1], including BERT (Devlin et al., 2018a) and Distilled MT-DNN (Liu et al., 2019a).

While traditional methods of commonsense reasoning rely heavily on human-crafted features and knowledge bases (Rahman and Ng, 2012a; Sharma et al., 2015; Schüller, 2014; Bailey et al., 2015; Liu et al., 2017), we explore in this study machine learning approaches using deep neural networks (DNN). Our method is inspired by two categories of DNN models proposed recently.

The first are neural language models trained on large amounts of text data. Trinh and Le (2018) proposed to use a neural language model trained on raw text from books and news to calculate the probabilities of the natural language sentences which are constructed from a statement by replacing the to-be-resolved pronoun in the statement with each of its candidate references (antecedent), and then pick the candidate with the highest probability as the answer. Kocijan et al. (2019) showed that a significant improvement can be achieved by fine-tuning a pre-trained masked language model (BERT in their case) on a small amount of WSC labeled data.

The second category of models are semantic similarity models. Wang et al. (2019); Opitz and Frank (2018) formulated WSC and PDP as a semantic matching problem, and proposed to use two variations of the Deep Structured Similarity Model (DSSM) (Huang et al., 2013) to compute the semantic similarity score between each candidate antecedent and the pronoun by (1) mapping the candidate and the pronoun and their context into two vectors, respectively, in a hidden space using deep neural networks, and (2) computing cosine similarity between the two vectors. The candidate with the highest score is selected as the result.

The two categories of models use different inductive biases when predicting outputs given inputs, and thus capture different views of the data. While language models measure the semantic coherence and wholeness of a statement where the pronoun to be resolved is replaced with its candidate antecedent, DSSMs measure the semantic relatedness of the pronoun and its candidate in their context.

Therefore, inspired by multi-task learning (Caruana, 1997; Liu et al., 2015, 2019b), we propose a hybrid neural network (HNN) model that combines the strengths of both neural language models and a semantic similarity model. As shown in Figure 1, HNN consists of two component models, a masked language model and a deep semantic similarity model. The two component models share the same text encoder (BERT), but use different model-specific input and output layers. The final output score is the combination of the two model scores. The architecture of HNN bears a strong resemblance to that of Multi-Task Deep Neural Network (MT-DNN) (Liu et al., 2019b), which consists of a BERT-based text encoder that is shared across all tasks (models) and a set of task (model) specific output layers. Following (Liu et al., 2019b; Kocijan et al., 2019), the training procedure of HNN consists of two steps: (1) pretraining the text encoder on raw text [2], and (2) multi-task learning of HNN on WSCR which is the most popular WSC dataset, as suggested by Kocijan et al. (2019).

HNN obtains new state-of-the-art results with significant improvements on three classic commonsense reasoning tasks, pushing the WNLI benchmark in GLUE to 89%, the WSC benchmark [3] (Levesque et al., 2011) to 75.1%, and the PDP-60 benchmark [4] to 90.0%. We also conduct an ablation study which shows that language models and semantic similarity models provide complementary approaches to commonsense reasoning, and HNN effectively combines the strengths of both.

2 The Proposed HNN Model

The architecture of the proposed hybrid model is shown in Figure 1. The input includes a sentence S, which contains the pronoun to be resolved, and a candidate antecedent C. The two component models, masked language model (MLM) and se-

---

[1]See the GLUE leaderboard at https://gluebenchmark.com/leaderboard

[2]In this study we use the pre-trained BERT large models released by the authors.

[3]https://cs.nyu.edu/faculty/davise/papers/WinogradSchemas/WS.html

[4]https://cs.nyu.edu/faculty/davise/papers/WinogradSchemas/PDPChallenge2016.xml

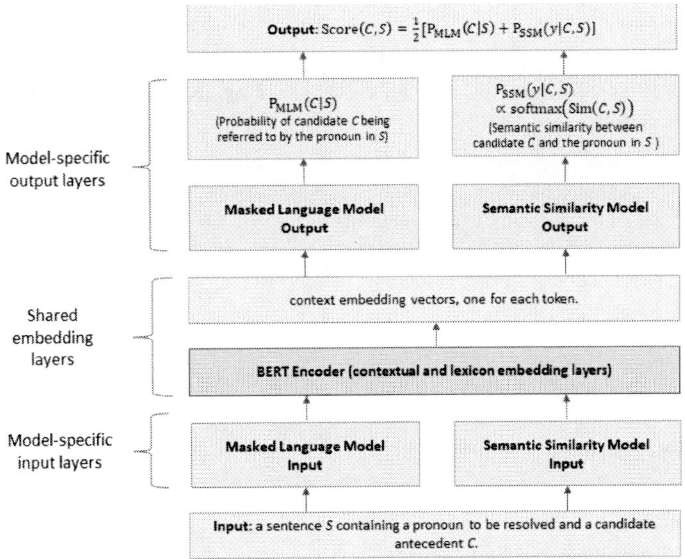

Figure 1: Architecture of the hybrid model for commonsense reasoning. The model consists of two component models, a masked language model (MLM) and a semantic similarity model (SSM). The input includes the sentence S, which contains a pronoun to be resolve, and a candidate antecedent C. The two component models share the BERT-based contextual encoder, but use different model-specific input and output layers. The final output score is the combination of the two component model scores.

mantic similarity model (SSM), share the BERT-based contextual encoder, but use different model-specific input and output layers. The final output score, which indicates whether C is the correct candidate of the pronoun in S, is the combination of the two component model scores.

2.1 Masked Language Model (MLM)

This component model follows Kocijan et al. (2019). In the input layer, a masked sentence is constructed using S by replacing the to-be-resolved pronoun in S with a sequence of N [MASK] tokens, where N is the number of tokens in candidate C.

In the output layer, the likelihood of C being referred to by the pronoun in S is scored using the BERT-based masked language model $P_{mlm}(C|S)$. If $C = \{c_1...c_N\}$ consists of multiple tokens, $\log P_{mlm}(C|S)$ is computed as the average of log-probabilities of each composing token:

$$P_{mlm}(C|S) = \exp\left(\frac{1}{N}\sum_{k=1...N}\log P_{mlm}(c_k|S)\right). \tag{1}$$

2.2 Semantic Similarity Model (SSM)

In the input layer, we treat sentence S and candidate C as a pair (S, C) that is packed together as a word sequence, where we add the [CLS] token as the first token and the [SEP] token between S and C.

After applying the shared embedding layers, we obtain the semantic representations of S and C, denoted as $\mathbf{s} \in \mathbb{R}^d$ and $\mathbf{c} \in \mathbb{R}^d$, respectively. We use the contextual embedding of [CLS] as $\mathbf{s}$. Suppose C consists of N tokens, whose contextual embeddings are $\mathbf{h}_1, ..., \mathbf{h}_N$, respectively. The semantic representation of the candidate C, $\mathbf{c}$, is computed via attention as follows:

$$\alpha_k = \text{softmax}\left(\frac{\mathbf{s}^\top \mathbf{W}_1 \mathbf{h}_k}{\sqrt{d}}\right), \tag{2}$$

$$\mathbf{c} = \sum_{k=1...N} \alpha_k \cdot \mathbf{h}_k. \tag{3}$$

where $\mathbf{W}_1$ is a learnable parameter matrix, and α is the attention score.

We use the contextual embedding of the first token of the pronoun in S as the semantic representation of the pronoun, denoted as $\mathbf{p} \in \mathbb{R}^d$. In the output layer, the semantic similarity between the pronoun and the context is computed using a bilinear model:

$$\text{Sim}(C,S) = \mathbf{p}^\top \mathbf{W}_2 \mathbf{c}, \tag{4}$$

where $\mathbf{W}_2$ is a learnable parameter matrix. Then, SSM predicts whether C is a correct candidate (i.e., (C, S) is a positive pair, labeled as $y = 1$) using the logistic function:

$$P_{ssm}(y = 1|C, S) = \frac{1}{1 + \exp\left(-\text{Sim}(C, S)\right)}. \tag{5}$$

The final output score of pair (S, C) is a linear combination of the MLM score of Eqn. 1 and the SSM score of Eqn. 5:

$$\text{Score}(C, S) = \frac{1}{2}[P_{mlm}(C|S) + P_{ssm}(y = 1|C, S)]. \tag{6}$$

2.3 The Training Procedure

We train our model of Figure 1 on the WSCR dataset, which consists of 1886 sentences, each being paired with a positive candidate antecedent and a negative candidate.

The shared BERT encoder is initialized using the published BERT uncased large model (Devlin et al., 2018a). We then finetune the model on the WSCR dataset by optimizing the combined objectives:

$$\mathcal{L}_{mlm} + \mathcal{L}_{ssm} + \mathcal{L}_{rank}, \tag{7}$$

where $\mathcal{L}_{mlm}$ is the negative log-likelihood based on the masked language model of Eqn. 1, and $\mathcal{L}_{ssm}$ is the cross-entropy loss based on semantic similarity model of Eqn. 5.

$\mathcal{L}_{rank}$ is the pair-wise rank loss. Consider a sentence S which contains a pronoun to be resolved, and two candidates C^+ and C^-, where C^+ is correct and C^- is not. We want to maximize $\Delta = \text{Score}(S, C^+) - \text{Score}(S, C^-)$, where $\text{Score}(.)$ is defined by Eqn. 6. We achieve this via optimizing a smoothed rank loss:

$$\mathcal{L}_{rank} = \log(1 + \exp\left(-\gamma(\Delta + \beta)\right)), \tag{8}$$

where $\gamma \in [1, 10]$ is the smoothing factor and $\beta \in [0, 1]$ the margin hyperparameter. In our experiments, the default setting is $\gamma = 10$, and $\beta = 0.6$.

3 Experiments

We evaluate the proposed HNN on three commonsense benchmarks: WSC (Levesque et al., 2012), PDP60[5] and WNLI. WNLI is derived from WSC, and is considered the most challenging NLU task in the GLUE benchmark (Wang et al., 2018).

3.1 Datasets

Corpus	#Train	#Dev	#Test
WNLI	-	634 + 71	146
PDP60	-	-	60
WSC	-	-	285
WSCR	1322	564	-

Table 2: Summary of the three benchmark datasets: WSC, PDP60 and WNLI, and the additional dataset WSCR. Note that we only use WSCR for training. For WNLI, we merge its official training set containing 634 instances and dev set containing 71 instances as its final dev set.

Table 2 summarizes the datasets which are used in our experiments. Since the WSC and PDP60 datasets do not contain any training instances, following (Kocijan et al., 2019), we adopt the WSCR dataset (Rahman and Ng, 2012b) for model training and selection. WSCR contains 1886 instances (1322 for training and the rest as dev set). Each instance is presented using the same structure as that in WSC.

For the WNLI instances, we convert them to the format of WSC as illustrated in Table 3: we first detect pronouns in the premise using spaCy[6]; then given the detected pronoun, we search its left of the premise in hypothesis to find the longest common substring (LCS) ignoring character case. Similarly, we search its right part of the LCS; by comparing the indexes of the extracted LCSs, we extract the candidates (e.g., the cookstove, the kitchen and the lamplight as shown in Table 3). A detailed example of the conversion process is provided in Table 3.

3.2 Implementation Detail

Our implementation of HNN is based on the PyTorch implementation of BERT[7]. All the models are trained with hyper-parameters depicted as follows unless stated otherwise. The shared layer is initialized by the BERT uncased large model. Adam (Kingma and Ba, 2014) is used as our optimizer with a learning rate of 1e-5 and a batch size of 32 or 16. The learning rate is linearly decayed during training with 100 warm up steps. We select models based on the dev set by greedily searching

---

[5]`https://cs.nyu.edu/faculty/davise/papers/WinogradSchemas/PDPChallenge2016.xml`

[6]`https://spacy.io`

[7]`https://github.com/huggingface/pytorch-pretrained-BERT`

1. **Premise:** The cookstove was warming the kitchen, and *the lamplight made **it** seem even warmer.*
   Hypothesis: *The lamplight made **the cookstove** seem even warmer.*
   Index of LCS in the hypothesis: left[0, 2], right[5, 7]
   Candidate: [3, 4] (the cookstove)

2. **Premise:** The cookstove was warming the kitchen, and *the lamplight made **it** seem even warmer.*
   Hypothesis: *The lamplight made **the kitchen** seem even warmer.*
   Index of LCS in the hypothesis: left[0, 2], right[5, 7]
   Candidate: [3, 4] (the kitchen)

3. **Premise:** The cookstove was warming the kitchen, and *the lamplight made **it** seem even warmer.*
   Hypothesis: *The lamplight made **the lamplight** seem even warmer.*
   Index of LCS in the hypothesis: left[0, 2], right[5, 7]
   Candidate: [3, 4] (the lamplight)

4. **Converted:** The cookstove was warming the kitchen, and *the lamplight made **it** seem even warmer.*
   A. the cookstove B. **the kitchen** C. the lamplight

Table 3: Examples of transforming WNLI to WSC format. Note that the text highlighted by brown is the longest common substring from the left part of pronoun *it*, and the text highlighted by violet is the longest common substring from its right.

epochs between 8 and 10. The trainable parameters, e.g., W_1 and W_2, are initialized by a truncated normal distribution with a mean of 0 and a standard deviation of 0.01. The margin hyperparameter, β in Eqn. 8, is set to 0.6 for MLM and 0.5 for SSM, and γ is set to 10 for all tasks. We also apply SWA (Izmailov et al., 2018) averaging the model weights to reduce the variance during inference. All the texts are tokenized using Word-Pieces, and are chopped to spans containing 512 tokens at most.

3.3 Results

We compare our HNN with a list of state-of-the-art models in the literature, including BERT (Devlin et al., 2018b), GPT-2 (Radford et al., 2019) and DSSM (Wang et al., 2019). The brief description of each baseline is introduced as follows.

1. BERT$_{\text{LARGE-LM}}$ (Devlin et al., 2018b): This is the large BERT model, and we use MLM to predict a score for each candidate following Eq 1.

2. GPT-2 (Radford et al., 2019): During prediction, We first replace the pronoun in a given sentence with its candidates one by one. We use the GPT-2 model to compute a score for each new sentence after the replacement, and select the candidate with the highest score as the final prediction.

3. BERT$_{\text{Wiki-WSCR}}$ and BERT$_{\text{WSCR}}$ (Kocijan et al., 2019): These two models use the same approach as BERT$_{\text{LARGE-LM}}$, but are trained with different additional training data. For example, BERT$_{\text{Wiki-WSCR}}$ is firstly fine-tuned on the constructed Wikipedia data and then on WSCR. BERT$_{\text{WSCR}}$ is directly fine-tuned on WSCR.

4. DSSM (Wang et al., 2019): It is the unsupervised semantic matching model trained on the dataset generated with heuristic rules.

5. HNN: It is the proposed hybrid neural network model.

The main results are reported in Table 4. Compared with all the baselines, HNN obtains much better performance across three benchmarks. This clearly demonstrates the advantage of the HNN over existing models. For example, HNN outperforms the previous state-of-the-art BERT$_{\text{Wiki-WSCR}}$ model with a 11.7% absolute improvement (83.6% vs 71.9%) on WNLI and a 2.8% absolute improvement (75.1% vs 72.2%) on WSC in terms of accuracy. Meanwhile, it achieves a 11.7% absolute improvement over the previous state-of-the-art BERT$_{\text{LARGE-LM}}$ model on PDP60 in accuracy. Note that both BERT$_{\text{Wiki-WSCR}}$ and BERT$_{\text{LARGE-LM}}$ are using language model-based approaches to solve the pronoun resolution problem. On the other hand, We observe that DSSM without pre-training is comparable to BERT$_{\text{LARGE-LM}}$ which is pre-trained on

	WNLI	WSC	PDP60
DSSM (Wang et al., 2019)	-	63.0	75.0
BERT$_{\text{LARGE-LM}}$ (Devlin et al., 2018a)	65.1	62.0	78.3
GPT-2 (Radford et al., 2019)	-	70.7	-
BERT$_{\text{Wiki-WSCR}}$ (Kocijan et al., 2019)	71.9	72.2	-
BERT$_{\text{WSCR}}$ (Kocijan et al., 2019)	70.5	70.3	-
HNN	**83.6**	**75.1**	**90.0**
HNN$_{\text{ensemble}}$	**89.0**	-	-

Table 4: Test results

Premise	Hypothesis	SSM	MLM	Label
In the storm, the tree fell down and crashed through the roof of my house. Now, I have to get it repaired.	Now I have to get the roof repaired.	✗	✓	1
	Now I have to get the tree repaired.	✗	✓	0
The city councilmen refused the demonstrators a permit because they advocated violence.	The demonstrators advocated violence.	✓	✗	1
	The city councilmen advocated violence.	✓	✗	0

Figure 2: Comparison with SSM and MLM on WNLI examples.

	WNLI	WSCR	WSC	PDP60
HNN	**77.1**	**85.6**	**75.1**	**90.0**
-SSM	74.5	82.4	72.6	86.7
-MLM	75.1	83.7	72.3	88.3

Table 5: Ablation study of the two component models in HNN. Note that WNLI and WSCR are reported on dev sets while WSC and PDP60 are reported on test sets.

the large scale text corpus (63.0% vs 62.0% on WSC and 75.0% vs 78.3% on PDP60). Our results show that HNN, combining the strengths of both DSSM and BERT$_{\text{WSCR}}$, has consistently achieved new state-of-the-art results on all three tasks.

To further boost the WNLI accuracy on the GLUE benchmark leaderboard, we record the model prediction at each epoch, and then produce the final prediction based on the majority voting from the last six model predictions. We refer to the ensemble of six models as HNN$_{\text{ensemble}}$ in Table 4. HNN$_{\text{ensemble}}$ brings a 5.4% absolute improvement (89.0% vs 83.6%) on WNLI in terms of accuracy.

3.4 Ablation study

In this section, we study the importance of each component in HNN by answering following questions:

How important are the two component models:

MLM and SSM?

To answer this question, we first remove each component model, either SSM or MLM, and then report the performance impact of these component models. Table 5 summarizes the experimental results. It is expected that the removal of either component model results in a significant performance drop. For example, with the removal of SSM, the performance of HNN is downgraded from 77.1% to 74.5% on WNLI. Similarly, with the removal of MLM, HNN only obtains 75.1%, which amounts to a 2% drop. All these observations clearly demonstrate that SSM and MLM are complementary to each other and the HNN model benefits from the combination of both.

Figure 2 gives several examples showing how SSM and MLM complement each other on WNLI. We see that in the first example, MLM correctly predicts the label while SSM does not. This is due to the fact that "the roof repaired" appears more frequently than "the tree repaired" in the text corpora used for model pre-training. However, in the second pair, since both "the demonstrators" and "the city councilment" could advocate violence and neither occurs significantly more often than the other, SSM is more effective in distinguishing the difference based on their context. The proposed HNN, which combines the strengths of these two models, can obtain the correct results in both cases.

Does the additional ranking loss help?

As shown in Eqn. 7, the training objective of HNN model contains three losses. The first two are based on the two component models, respectively, and the third one, as defined in Eqn. 8, is a ranking loss based on the score function in Eqn. 6. At first glance, the ranking loss seems redundant. Thus, we compare two versions of HNN trained with and without the ranking loss. Experimental results are shown in Table 6. We see that without the ranking loss, the performance of HNN drops on three datasets: WNLI, WSCR and WSC. On the PDP60 dataset, without the ranking loss, the model performs slightly better. However, since the test set of PDP60 includes only 60 samples, the difference is not statistically significant. Thus, we decide to always include the ranking loss in the training objective of HNN.

	WNLI	WSCR	WSC	PDP60
HNN	**77.1**	**85.6**	**75.1**	90.0
HNN-Rank	74.8	85.1	71.9	**91.7**

Table 6: Ablation study of the ranking loss. Note that WNLI and WSCR are reported on dev sets while WSC and PDP60 are reported on test sets.

Is the WNLI task a ranking or classification task?

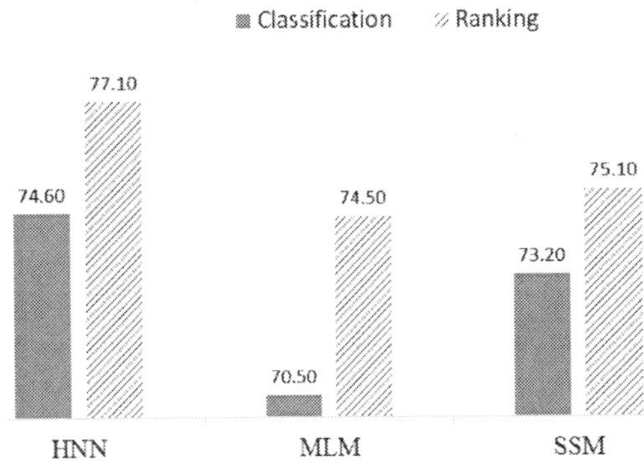

Figure 3: Comparison of different task formulation on WNLI.

The WNLI task can be formulated as either a ranking task or a classification task. To study the difference in problem formulation, we conduct experiments to compare the performance of a model used as a classifier or a ranker. For example, given a trained HNN, when it is used as a classifier we set a threshold to decide label (0/1) for each input. When it is used as a ranker, we simply pick the top-ranked candidate as the correct answer. We run the comparison using all three models HNN, MLM and SSM. As shown in Figure 3, the ranking formulation is consistently better than the classification formulation for this task. For example, the difference in the HNN model is about absolute 2.5% (74.6% vs 77.1%) in terms of accuracy.

4   Conclusion

We propose a hybrid neural network (HNN) model for commonsense reasoning. HNN consists of two component models, a masked language model and a deep semantic similarity model, which share a BERT-based contextual encoder but use different model-specific input and output layers.

HNN obtains new state-of-the-art results on three classic commonsense reasoning tasks, pushing the WNLI benchmark to 89%, the WSC benchmark to 75.1%, and the PDP60 benchmark to 90.0%. We also justify the design of HNN via a series of ablation experiments.

In future work, we plan to extend HNN to other reasoning tasks, especially those where large-scale language models like BERT and GPT do not perform well, as discussed in (Gao et al., 2019; Niven and Kao, 2019).

Acknowledgments

We would like to thank Michael Patterson from Microsoft for his help on the paper.

References

Daniel Bailey, Amelia Harrison, Yuliya Lierler, Vladimir Lifschitz, and Julian Michael. 2015. The winograd schema challenge and reasoning about correlation. In *Knowledge Representation; Coreference Resolution; Reasoning*.

Rich Caruana. 1997. Multitask learning. *Machine learning*, 28(1):41–75.

Ernest Davis and Gary Marcus. 2015. Commonsense reasoning and commonsense knowledge in artificial intelligence. *Communications of the ACM*.

Jacob Devlin, Ming-Wei Chang, Kenton Lee, and Kristina Toutanova. 2018a. Bert: Pre-training of deep bidirectional transformers for language understanding. *arXiv preprint arXiv:1810.04805*.

Jacob Devlin, Ming-Wei Chang, Kenton Lee, and Kristina Toutanova. 2018b. Bert: Pre-training of deep bidirectional transformers for language understanding. *arXiv preprint arXiv:1810.04805*.

Jianfeng Gao, Michel Galley, and Lihong Li. 2019. Neural approaches to conversational ai. *Foundations and Trends® in Information Retrieval*, 13(2-3):127–298.

Po-Sen Huang, Xiaodong He, Jianfeng Gao, Li Deng, Alex Acero, and Larry Heck. 2013. Learning deep structured semantic models for web search using clickthrough data. In *Proceedings of the 22nd ACM international conference on Conference on information & knowledge management*, pages 2333–2338. ACM.

Pavel Izmailov, Dmitrii Podoprikhin, Timur Garipov, Dmitry Vetrov, and Andrew Gordon Wilson. 2018. Averaging weights leads to wider optima and better generalization. *arXiv preprint arXiv:1803.05407*.

Diederik Kingma and Jimmy Ba. 2014. Adam: A method for stochastic optimization. *arXiv preprint arXiv:1412.6980*.

Vid Kocijan, Ana-Maria Cretu, Oana-Maria Camburu, Yordan Yordanov, and Thomas Lukasiewicz. 2019. A surprisingly robust trick for winograd schema challenge. *arXiv preprint arXiv:1905.06290*.

Hector Levesque, Ernest Davis, and Leora Morgenstern. 2012. The winograd schema challenge. In *Thirteenth International Conference on the Principles of Knowledge Representation and Reasoning*.

Hector J Levesque, Ernest Davis, and Leora Morgenstern. 2011. The winograd schema challenge. In *AAAI spring symposium: Logical formalizations of commonsense reasoning*.

Quan Liu, Hui Jiang, Zhen-Hua Ling, Xiaodan Zhu, Si Wei, and Yu Hu. 2017. Combing context and commonsense knowledge through neural networks for solving winograd schema problems. In *AAAI Spring Symposium Series*.

Xiaodong Liu, Jianfeng Gao, Xiaodong He, Li Deng, Kevin Duh, and Ye-Yi Wang. 2015. Representation learning using multi-task deep neural networks for semantic classification and information retrieval. In *Proceedings of the 2015 Conference of the North American Chapter of the Association for Computational Linguistics: Human Language Technologies*, pages 912–921.

Xiaodong Liu, Pengcheng He, Weizhu Chen, and Jianfeng Gao. 2019a. Improving multi-task deep neural networks via knowledge distillation for natural language understanding. *arXiv preprint arXiv:1904.09482*.

Xiaodong Liu, Pengcheng He, Weizhu Chen, and Jianfeng Gao. 2019b. Multi-task deep neural networks for natural language understanding. *arXiv preprint arXiv:1901.11504*.

Nasrin Mostafazadeh, Nathanael Chambers, Xiaodong He, Devi Parikh, Dhruv Batra, Lucy Vanderwende, Pushmeet Kohli, and James Allen. 2016. A corpus and cloze evaluation for deeper understanding of commonsense stories. In *Proceedings of the Conference of the North American Chapter of the Association for Computational Linguistics: Human Language Technologies*.

Vincent Ng and Claire Cardie. 2002. Improving machine learning approaches to coreference resolution. In *Proceedings of the Association for Computational Linguistics*. Association for Computational Linguistics.

Timothy Niven and Hung-Yu Kao. 2019. Probing neural network comprehension of natural language arguments. *arXiv preprint arXiv:1907.07355*.

Juri Opitz and Anette Frank. 2018. Addressing the Winograd schema challenge as a sequence ranking task. In *Proceedings of the First International Workshop on Language Cognition and Computational Models*, pages 41–52, Santa Fe, New Mexico, USA. Association for Computational Linguistics.

Haoruo Peng, Yangqiu Song, and Dan Roth. 2016. Event detection and co-reference with minimal supervision. In *Proceedings of the conference on empirical methods in natural language processing*.

Alec Radford, Jeffrey Wu, Rewon Child, David Luan, Dario Amodei, and Ilya Sutskever. 2019. Language models are unsupervised multitask learners.

Altaf Rahman and Vincent Ng. 2012a. Resolving complex cases of definite pronouns: The winograd schema challenge. In *Proceedings of the Joint Conference on Empirical Methods in Natural Language Processing and Computational Natural Language Learning*.

Altaf Rahman and Vincent Ng. 2012b. Resolving complex cases of definite pronouns: the winograd schema challenge. In *Proceedings of the 2012 Joint Conference on Empirical Methods in Natural Language Processing and Computational Natural Language Learning*, pages 777–789. Association for Computational Linguistics.

Hannah Rashkin, Maarten Sap, Emily Allaway, Noah A. Smith, and Yejin Choi. 2018. Event2mind: Commonsense inference on events, intents, and reactions. In *Proceedings of the Association for Computational Linguistics*.

Melissa Roemmele, Cosmin Adrian Bejan, and Andrew S Gordon. 2011. Choice of plausible alternatives: An evaluation of commonsense causal reasoning. In *AAAI Spring Symposium: Logical Formalizations of Commonsense Reasoning*.

Peter Schüller. 2014. Tackling winograd schemas by formalizing relevance theory in knowledge graphs. In *Knowledge Representation and Reasoning Conference*.

Arpit Sharma, Nguyen H. Vo, Somak Aditya, and Chitta Baral. 2015. Towards addressing the winograd schema challenge: Building and using a semantic parser and a knowledge hunting module. In *Proceedings of the International Conference on Artificial Intelligence*.

Wee Meng Soon, Hwee Tou Ng, and Daniel Chung Yong Lim. 2001. A machine learning approach to coreference resolution of noun phrases. *Computational linguistics*.

Trieu H Trinh and Quoc V Le. 2018. A simple method for commonsense reasoning. *arXiv preprint arXiv:1806.02847*.

Alex Wang, Amapreet Singh, Julian Michael, Felix Hill, Omer Levy, and Samuel R Bowman. 2018. Glue: A multi-task benchmark and analysis platform for natural language understanding. *arXiv preprint arXiv:1804.07461*.

Shuohang Wang, Sheng Zhang, Yelong Shen, Xiaodong Liu, Jingjing Liu, Jianfeng Gao, and Jing Jiang. 2019. Unsupervised deep structured semantic models for commonsense reasoning. In *Proceedings of the 2019 Conference of the North American Chapter of the Association for Computational Linguistics: Human Language Technologies, Volume 1 (Long and Short Papers)*, pages 882–891, Minneapolis, Minnesota. Association for Computational Linguistics.

Rowan Zellers, Yonatan Bisk, Roy Schwartz, and Yejin Choi. 2018. Swag: A large-scale adversarial dataset for grounded commonsense inference. In *Proceedings of the Conference on Empirical Methods in Natural Language Processing*.

Sheng Zhang, Xiaodong Liu, Jingjing Liu, Jianfeng Gao, Kevin Duh, and Benjamin Van Durme. 2018. ReCoRD: Bridging the Gap between Human and Machine Commonsense Reading Comprehension. *arXiv preprint arXiv:1810.12885*.

Towards Generalizable Neuro-Symbolic Systems for Commonsense Question Answering

Kaixin Ma[¶*]   Jonathan Francis[¶§]   Quanyang Lu[†]   Eric Nyberg[¶]   Alessandro Oltramari[§]
[¶]Language Technologies Institute, School of Computer Science, Carnegie Mellon University
[†]Department of Mechanical Engineering, College of Engineering, Carnegie Mellon University
[§]Intelligent IoT, Bosch Research and Technology Center (Pittsburgh, USA)
{kaixinm, jmf1, qlv, ehn}@cs.cmu.edu
alessandro.oltramari@us.bosch.com

Abstract

Non-extractive commonsense QA remains a challenging AI task, as it requires systems to reason about, synthesize, and gather disparate pieces of information, in order to generate responses to queries. Recent approaches on such tasks show increased performance, only when models are either pre-trained with additional information or when domain-specific heuristics are used, without any special consideration regarding the knowledge resource type. In this paper, we perform a survey of recent commonsense QA methods and we provide a systematic analysis of popular knowledge resources and knowledge-integration methods, across benchmarks from multiple commonsense datasets. Our results and analysis show that attention-based injection seems to be a preferable choice for knowledge integration and that the degree of domain overlap, between knowledge bases and datasets, plays a crucial role in determining model success.

1 Introduction

With the recent success of large pre-trained language models (Devlin et al., 2019; Radford et al., 2019; Yang et al., 2019; Liu et al., 2019), model performance has reached or surpassed human-level capability on many previous question-answering (QA) benchmarks (Hermann et al., 2015; Rajpurkar et al., 2016; Lai et al., 2017). However, these benchmarks do not directly challenge model reasoning capability, as they require only marginal use of external knowledge to select the correct answer, i.e., all the evidence required to solve questions in these benchmarks is explicit in the context lexical space. Efforts have been made towards building more challenging datasets that, by design, require models to synthesize external commonsense knowledge and leverage more sophisticated reasoning mechanisms (Zhang et al., 2018; Ostermann et al., 2018), showing that the previous state-of-the-art models often struggle to solve these newer tasks reliably. As a result, commonsense has received a lot of attention in other areas as well, such as natural language inference (Zellers et al., 2018b, 2019) and visual question answering (Zellers et al., 2018a). Despite the importance of commonsense knowledge, however, previous work on QA methods takes a coarse-grained view of commonsense, without considering the subtle differences across the various knowledge types and resources. Such differences have been discussed at length in AI by philosophers, computational linguists, cognitive psychologists (see for instance (Davis, 2014)): at the high level, we can identify *declarative commonsense*, whose scope encompassess factual knowledge, e.g., 'the sky is blue', 'Paris is in France'; *taxonomic knowledge*, e.g., 'football players are athletes', 'cats are mammals'; *relational knowledge*, e.g., 'the nose is part of the skull', 'handwriting requires a hand and a writing instrument'; *procedural commonsense*, which includes prescriptive knowledge, e.g., 'one needs an oven before baking cakes', 'the electricity should be off while the switch is being repaired' (Hobbs et al., 1987); *sentiment knowledge*, e.g., 'rushing to the hospital makes people worried', 'being in vacation makes people relaxed'; and *metaphorical knowledge* (e.g., 'time flies', 'raining cats and dogs'). We believe that it is important to identifiy the most appropriate commonsense knowledge type required for specific tasks, in order to get better downstream performance. Once the knowledge type is identified, we can then select the appropriate knowledge-base(s), and the suitable neural integration mechanisms (e.g., attention-based injection, pre-training, or auxiliary training objectives).

---

[*]Work was done during an internship at Bosch Research.

Proceedings of the First Workshop on Commonsense Inference in Natural Language Processing, pages 22–32
Hongkong, China, November 3, 2019. ©2019 Association for Computational Linguistics

Accordingly, in this work we conduct a comparison study of different knowledge bases and knowledge integration methods, and we evaluate model performance on two multiple-choice QA datasets that explicitly require commonsense reasoning. In particular, we used ConceptNet (Speer et al., 2016) and the recently-introduced ATOMIC (Sap et al., 2019) knowledge resources, integrating them with the *Option Comparison Network* model (OCN; Ran et al. (2019)), a recent state-of-the-art model for multiple choice QA tasks. We evalutate our models on the DREAM (Sun et al., 2019) and CommonsenseQA (Talmor et al., 2019) datasets. An example from DREAM that requires commonsense is shown in Table 1, and an example from CommonsenseQA is shown in Table 2. Our experimental results and analysis suggest that attention-based injection is preferable for knowledge integration and that the degree of domain overlap, between knowledge-base and dataset, is vital to model success.[1]

Dialogue:
M: I hear you drive a long way to work every day.
W: Oh, yes. it's about sixty miles. but it doesn't seem that far, the road is not bad, and there's not much traffic.
Question:
How does the woman feel about driving to work?
Answer choices:
A. She doesn't mind it as the road conditions are good.*
B. She is unhappy to drive such a long way everyday.
C. She is tired of driving in heavy traffic.

Table 1: An example from the DREAM dataset; the asterisk (*) denotes the correct answer.

Question:
A revolving door is convenient for two direction travel, but it also serves as a security measure at a what?
Answer choices:
A. Bank*; B. Library; C. Department Store;
D. Mall; E. New York

Table 2: An example from the CommonsenseQA dataset; the asterisk (*) denotes the correct answer.

2 Related Work

It has been recognized that many recent QA tasks require external knowledge or commonsense to solve, and numerous efforts have been made in injecting commonsense in neural models. Bauer et al. (2018) introduced a pipeline for extracting grounded multi-hop commonsense relation paths from ConceptNet and proposed to inject commonsense knowledge into neural models' intermediate representations, using attention. Similarly, Mihaylov and Frank (2018) also proposed to extract relevant knowledge triples from ConceptNet and use Key-Value Retrieval (Miller et al., 2016) to gather information from knowledge to enhance the neural representation. Zhong et al. (2018) proposed to pre-train a scoring function using knowledge triples from ConceptNet, to model the direct and indirect relation between concepts. This scoring function was then fused with QA models to make the final prediction. Pan et al. (2019a) introduced an entity discovery and linking system to identify the most salient entities in the question and answer-options. Wikipedia abstracts of these entities are then extracted and appended to the reference documents to provide additional information. Weissenborn et al. (2018) proposed a strategy of dynamically refining word embeddings by reading input text as well as external knowledge, such as ConceptNet and Wikipedia abstracts. More recently, Lin et al. (2019) proposed to extract subgraphs from ConceptNet and embed the knowledge using Graph Convolutional Networks (Kipf and Welling, 2016). Then the knowledge representation is integrated with word representation through an LSTM layer and hierarchical attention mechnism. Lv et al. (2019) introduced graph-based reasoning modules that takes both ConceptNet knowledge triples and Wikipedia text as inputs to refine word representations from a pretrained language model and make predictions.

Commonsense knowledge integration has also received a lot of attention on many other tasks. Tandon et al. (2018) proposed to use commonsense knowledge as hard/soft constraints to bias the neural model's prediction on a procedural text comprehension task. Ma et al. (2018) proposed to used embedded affective commonsense knowledge inside LSTM cell to control the information flow in each gate for sentiment analysis task. Li and Srikumar (2019) presented a framework to convert declarative knowlegde into first-order logic that enhance neural networks' training and prediction. Peters et al. (2019) and Levine et al. (2019) both tried to injecting knowlegde into language models by pretraining on knowledge bases.

Previous works only focus on using external

---

[1] From a terminological standpoint, 'domain overlap' here must be interpreted as the overlap between question types in the targeted datasets, and types of commonsense represented in the knowledge bases under consideration.

knowledge sources to improve model performance on certain tasks, disregarding the type of commonsense knowledge and how the domain of the knowledge resource affects results on downstream tasks. In this paper, we examine the roles of knowledge-base domain and specific integration mechanisms on model performance.

3 Approach Overview

In this section, we describe the model architecture used in our experiments. Next, we introduce two popular knowledge resources, we define our knowledge-extraction method, then we illustrate various neural knowledge-integration mechanisms.

3.1 Model architecture

The BERT model (Devlin et al., 2019) has been applied to numerous QA tasks and has achieved very promising performance, particularly on the DREAM and CommonsenseQA datasets. When utilizing BERT on multiple-choice QA tasks, the standard approach is to concatenate the dialogue context and the question with each answer-option, in order to generate a list of tokens which is then fed into BERT encoder; a linear layer is added on top, in order to predict the answer. One aspect of this strategy is that each answer-option is encoded independently: from a cognitive perspective, this aspect contradicts how humans typically solve multiple-choice QA tasks, namely by *weighing* each option to find correlations within them, in addition to correlations with respect to the question. To address this issue, Ran et al. (2019) introduced the *Option Comparison Network* (OCN) that explicitly models pairwise answer-option interactions, making OCN better-suited for multiple-choice QA task structures. We re-implemented OCN while keeping BERT as its upstream encoder.[2] Specifically, given a dialogue D, a question Q, and an answer-option O_k, we concatenate them and encode with BERT to get hidden representation $T_{enc} \in \mathbb{R}^{n \times d}$:

$$T_{enc} = \mathrm{BERT}(D; Q; O_k) \qquad (1)$$

Where d is the size of BERT's hidden representation and n is the total number of words. Next,

---

[2]Because the newly-released XLNet has out-performed BERT on various tasks, we considered using XLNet as the OCN's encoder. However, from our initial experiments, XLNet is very unstable, in that it easily provides degenerate solutions—a problem noted by Devlin et al. (2019) for small datasets. We found BERT to be more stable in our study.

the dialogue encoding $D_{enc} \in \mathbb{R}^{n_d \times d}$, question encoding $Q_{enc} \in \mathbb{R}^{n_q \times d}$, and answer-option encoding $O_{k,enc} \in \mathbb{R}^{n_o \times d}$ are separated from T_{enc}. Here, option-encoding consists both of question and option, i.e. $Q_{enc} \subseteq O_{k,enc}$ and $n_d + n_o = n$, as suggested by Ran et al. (2019). Given a set of options O_k ($k = 1, 2, ...$), these options are compared, pairwise, using standard tri-linear attention (Seo et al., 2016):

$$\mathrm{Att}(u, v) = W_1 \cdot u + W_2 \cdot v + (W_3 \circ v) \cdot u \qquad (2)$$

Where, $W_1, W_2, W_3 \in \mathbb{R}^d$ are trainable weights and $u \in \mathbb{R}^{x \times d}$, $v \in \mathbb{R}^{y \times d}$ are input matrices; x and y here are generic placeholder for input lengths; matrix multiplication and element-wise multiplication are denoted by ($\cdot$) and ($\circ$), respectively. Next, we gather information from all other options, to form a new option representation $O_{k,new} \in \mathbb{R}^{n_o \times d}$. Formally, given option $O_{k,enc}$ and another option $O_{l,enc} \in \mathbb{R}^{n_l \times d}$, $O_{k,new}$ is computed as follows:

$$O_k^l = O_{l,enc} \cdot \mathrm{Att}(O_{l,enc}, O_{k,enc}) \qquad (3)$$

$$\widetilde{O_k^l} = [O_{k,enc} - O_k^l; O_{k,enc} \circ O_k^l] \qquad (4)$$

$$O_{k,new} = \tanh(W_c \cdot [O_{k,enc}; \{\widetilde{O_k^l}\}_{l \neq k}]) \qquad (5)$$

Where, $W_c \in \mathbb{R}^{(d+2d(|O|-1)) \times d}$, $|O|$ denotes total number of options and n_l denotes the number of words in the compared option. Then, a gating mechanism is used to fuse the option-wise correlation information $O_{k,new}$ with the current option-encoding $O_{k,enc}$. Gating values are computed as:

$$G = \mathrm{sigmoid}(W_g[O_{k,enc}; O_{k,new}; \widetilde{Q}]) \qquad (6)$$

$$\widetilde{Q} = Q_{enc} \cdot \mathrm{softmax}(Q_{enc} \cdot V_a)^T \qquad (7)$$

$$O_{fuse} = G \circ O_{k,enc} + (1 - G) \circ O_{k,new} \qquad (8)$$

Here, $W_g \in \mathbb{R}^{3d \times d}$ and $V_a \in \mathbb{R}^{d \times 1}$. Co-attention (Xiong et al., 2016) is applied to re-read the dialogue, given the fused option-correlation features:

$$A_{do} = \mathrm{Att}(D_{enc}, O_{fuse}) \qquad (9)$$

$$A_{od} = \mathrm{Att}(O_{fuse}, D_{enc}) \qquad (10)$$

$$O_d = A_{od} \cdot [D_{enc}; A_{do} \cdot O_{fuse}] \qquad (11)$$

$$\widetilde{O_d} = \mathrm{ReLU}(W_p([O_d; O_{fuse}])) \qquad (12)$$

Here, $W_p \in \mathbb{R}^{3d \times d}$. Finally, self-attention (Wang et al., 2017) is used to compute final option repre-

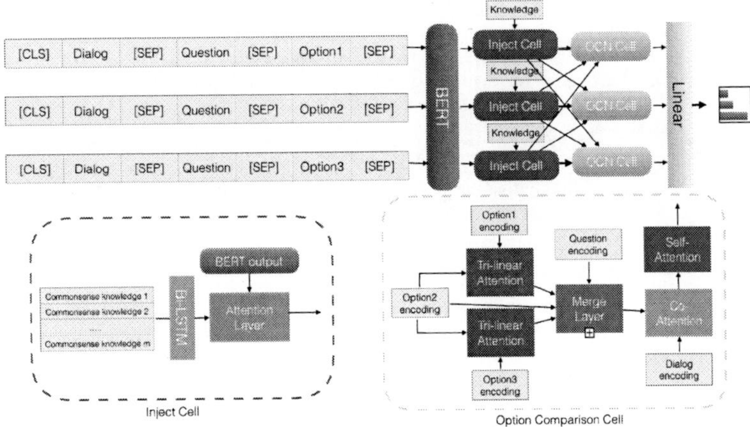

Figure 1: Option Comparison Network with Knowledge Injection

sentation $\widetilde{O_f} \in \mathbb{R}^{n_o \times d}$:

$$O_s = \widetilde{O_d} \cdot \text{Att}(\widetilde{O_d}, \widetilde{O_d}) \quad (13)$$

$$O_f = [\widetilde{O_d}; O_s, \widetilde{O_d} - O_s; \widetilde{O_d} \circ O_s] \quad (14)$$

$$\widetilde{O_f} = \text{ReLU}(W_f \cdot O_f) \quad (15)$$

Unlike the vanilla BERT model, which takes the first token to predict the answer, max-pooling is applied on the sequence dimension of $\widetilde{O_f} \in \mathbb{R}^{n_o \times d}$, in order to generate the final prediction.

3.2 Knowledge bases

The first knowledge-base we consider for our experiments is ConceptNet (Speer et al., 2016). ConceptNet contains over 21 million edges and 8 million nodes (1.5 million nodes in the partition for the English vocabulary), generating triples of the form $(C1, r, C2)$: the natural-language concepts $C1$ and $C2$ are associated by commonsense relation r, e.g., *(dinner, AtLocation, restaurant)*. Thanks to its coverage, ConceptNet is one of the most popular semantic networks for commonsense. ATOMIC (Sap et al., 2019) is a new knowledge-base that focuses on procedural knowledge. Triples are of the form *(Event, r, {Effect|Persona|Mental-state})*, where head and tail are short sentences or verb phrases and r represents an *if-then* relation type. An example would be: *(X compliments Y, xIntent, X wants to be nice)*. Since both DREAM and CommonsenseQA datasets are open-domain and require general commonsense, we think these knowledge-bases are most appropriate for our investigation.

3.3 Knowledge elicitation

ConceptNet. For the DREAM dataset, we find ConceptNet relations that connect dialogues and questions to the answer-options. The intuition is that these relation paths would provide explicit evidence that would help the model find the answer. Formally, given a dialogue D, a question Q, and an answer-option O, we find all ConceptNet relations *(C1, r, C2)*, such that $C1 \in (D + Q)$ and $C2 \in O$, or vice versa. This rule works well for single-word concepts. However, a large number of concepts in ConceptNet are actually phrases, and finding exactly matching phrases in $D/Q/O$ is much harder. To fully utilize phrase-based ConceptNet relations, we relaxed the exact-match constraint to the following:

$$\frac{\text{\# words in C} \cap \text{S}}{\text{\# words in C}} > 0.5 \quad (16)$$

Here, S represents $D/Q/O$, depending on which sequence we try to match the concept C to. Additionally, when the part-of-speech (POS) tag for a concept is available, we make sure it matches the POS tag of the corresponding word in $D/Q/O$. For CommonsenseQA, we use the same procedure to find ConceptNet relations for each answer-option, except that only Q is present and used. Table 3 shows the extracted ConceptNet triples for the CommonsenseQA example in Table 2. It is worth noting that we are able to extract the original ConceptNet sub-graph that was used to create the question, along with some extra triples. Although not perfect, the bold ConceptNet triple does provide some clue that could help the model resolve the correct answer.

Options	Extracted ConceptNet triples
Bank	(revolving door *AtLocation* bank) **(bank RelatedTo security)**
Library	(revolving door *AtLocation* library)
Department Store	(revolving door *AtLocation* store) (security IsA department)
Mall	(revolving door *AtLocation* mall)
New York	(revolving door *AtLocation* New York)

Table 3: Extracted ConceptNet relations for sample shown in Table 2.

Input sentence	Generated ATOMIC relations
Utterance 1	(xAttr dedicated) (xWant to get to work)
Utterance 2	(xAttr far) **(xReact happy)** (xWant to get to their destination)
Option A	**(xAttr calm)** (xWant to avoid the road)
Option B	**(xAttr careless)** (xReact annoyed) (xEffect get tired)
Option C	**(xAttr frustrated)** (xEffect get tired) (xWant to get out of car)

Table 4: Sample generated ATOMIC relations for sample shown in Table 1.

ATOMIC. We observe that many questions in DREAM inquire about agent's opinion and feeling. Superficially, this particular question type seems well-suited for ATOMIC, whose focus is on folk psychology and related general implications; we could frame our goal as evaluating whether ATOMIC can provide relevant knowledge to help answer these questions. However, one challenge to this strategy is that heads and tails of knowledge triples in ATOMIC are short sentences or verb phrases, while rare words and person-references are reduced to blanks and PersonX/PersonY, respectively. This calls for a new matching procedure, different from the ConceptNet extraction strategy, for eliciting ATOMIC-specific relations: we rely on the recently-published COMET model (Bosselut et al., 2019) to generate new ATOMIC relations, with intermediate phrasal resolutions. In particular, we first segmented all dialogues, questions, and answer-options into sentences. We further segment long sentences into sub-sentences, using commas as seperators. Because only verb-phrases satisfy the definition of an "event" in ATOMIC (i.e., relations are only invoked by verbs), we remove all sentences/sub-sentences that do not contain any verb. Next, we use a pre-trained COMET model (Bosselut et al., 2019) to generate all possible ATOMIC relations, for all candidate sentences/sub-sentences and we use greedy-decoding to take the 1-best sequences. Table 4 shows the sample ATOMIC relations, generated using the DREAM example in Table 1. It is interesting to note that the reaction for the woman agent (second utterance) is identified as *happy*, since she said that 'the road is not bad.' If we compare the identified attributes for answer-options,

the one from correct answer seems to be sematically closer than the other two.

3.4 Knowledge injection

Given previously extracted/generated knowledge triples, we need to integrate them with the OCN model. Inspired by Bauer et al. (2018), we propose to use attention-based injection. For ConceptNet knowledge triples, we first convert concept-relation tokens into regular tokens, in order to generate a pseudo-sentence. For example, *"(book, AtLocation, library)"* would be converted to "book at location library." Next, we use the BERT embedding layer to generate an embedding of this pseudo-sentence, with C denoting a ConceptNet relation:

$$H_C = \text{BiLSTM}(C) \qquad (17)$$

If we let $H_C \in \mathbb{R}^{1 \times 2l}$ be the concatenation of the final hidden states and l be the number of hidden units in the LSTM layer, then m ConceptNet relations would yield the commonsense knowledge matrix $H_M \in \mathbb{R}^{m \times 2l}$. We adopt the attention mechanism used in QAnet (Yu et al., 2018) to model the interaction between H_M and the BERT encoding output T_{enc} (from Equation 1):

$$\tilde{H}_M = H_M \cdot W_{proj} \qquad (18)$$
$$S = \text{Att}(H_M, T_{enc}) \qquad (19)$$
$$A_m = \text{softmax}(S) \cdot \tilde{H}_M \qquad (20)$$
$$A_t = \text{softmax}(S) \cdot \text{softmax}(S^T) \cdot T_{enc} \qquad (21)$$
$$T_C = [T_{enc}; A_m; T_{enc} \circ A_m; T_{enc} \circ A_t] \qquad (22)$$
$$T_{out} = \text{ReLU}(T_C \cdot W_a) \qquad (23)$$

Specifically, H_M is first projected into the same dimension as T_{enc}, using $W_{proj} \in \mathbb{R}^{2l \times d}$. Then, the similarty matrix $S \in \mathbb{R}^{n \times m}$ is computed using tri-linear attention, as in Equation 2. We then use S to compute text-to-knowledge attention $A_m \in \mathbb{R}^{n \times d}$ and knowledge-to-text attention $A_t \in \mathbb{R}^{n \times d}$. Finally, the knowledge-aware textual representation $T_{out} \in \mathbb{R}^{n \times d}$ is computed, where $W_a \in \mathbb{R}^{4d \times d}$. T_{out} is fed to subsequent layers (in place of T_{enc}), in order to generate the prediction. The model structure with knowledge-injection is summarized in Figure 1.

For ATOMIC knowledge triples, the injection method is slightly different. Because heads of these knowledge triples are sentences/utterances and the tails contain attributes of the persons (i.e., subject and object of the sentence), it is not possible to directly inject the knowledge triples, as-is. We replace the heads of the ATOMIC knowledge triples with the corresponding speaker for dialogues and leave as blank for the answer-options. Next, we convert the special relation tokens into regular tokens, e.g., "xIntent"⇒"intent" and "oEffect"⇒ "others effect", to make pseudo-sentences. As a result, an ATOMIC relation "*(the road is not bad, xReact, happy)*" would be converted to "*(W, react, happy)*." Moreover, as the ATOMIC knowledge triples are associated with dialogues and answer-options, independently, we inject option relations into $O_{enc} \in \mathbb{R}^{n_o \times d}$ and dialogue relations into D_{enc}, respectively, using the injection method described above.

3.5 Knowledge pre-training

Pre-training large-capacity models (e.g., BERT, GPT (Radford et al., 2019), XLNet (Yang et al., 2019)) on large corpora, then fine-tuning on more domain-specific information, has led to performance improvements on various tasks. Inspired by this, our goal in this section is to observe the effect of pre-training BERT on commonsense knowledge and refining the model on task-specific content from our DREAM and CommonsenseQA corpora. Essentially, we would like to test if pre-training on our external knowledge resources can help the model acquire commonsense. For the ConceptNet pre-training procedure, pre-training BERT on pseudo-sentences formulated from ConceptNet knowledge triples does not provide much gain on performance. Instead, we trained BERT on the *Open Mind Common Sense* (OMCS) corpus (Singh et al., 2002), the original corpus that was used to create ConceptNet. We extracted about 930K English sentences from OMCS and

randomly masked out 15% of the tokens; we then fine-tuned BERT, using a masked language model objective. Then we load this fine-tuned model into OCN and trained on DREAM and CommonsenseQA tasks. As for pre-training on ATOMIC, we again use COMET to convert ATOMIC knowledge triples into sentences; we created special tokens for 9 types of relations as well as blanks. Next, we randomly masked out 15% of the tokens, only masking out tail-tokens. We use the same OMCS pre-training procedure.

Models	Dev Acc	Test Acc
BERT Large(*)	66.0	66.8
XLNet(*)	-	**72.0**
OCN	70.0	69.8
OCN + CN injection	**70.5**	69.6
OCN + AT injection	69.6	**70.1**
OCN + OMCS pre-train	64.0	62.6
OCN + ATOMIC pre-train	60.3	58.8

Table 5: Results on DREAM; the asterisk (*) denotes results taken from leaderboard.

Models	Dev Acc
BERT + OMCS pre-train(*)	68.8
RoBERTa + CSPT(*)	**76.2**
OCN	64.1
OCN + CN injection	67.3
OCN + OMCS pre-train	65.2
OCN + ATOMIC pre-train	61.2
OCN + OMCS pre-train + CN inject	**69.0**

Table 6: Results on CommonsenseQA; the asterisk (*) denotes results taken from leaderboard.

4 Experiments

4.1 Datasets

We choose to evaluate our hypotheses using the DREAM and CommonsenseQA datasets, because some / all questions require commonsense reasoning and because there remains a large gap between state-of-the-art models and human performance.

DREAM is a dialogue-based multiple-choice QA dataset, introduced by Sun et al. (2019). It was collected from English-as-a-foreign-language examinations, designed by human experts. The dataset contains 10,197 questions for 6,444 dialogues in total, and each question is associated with 3 answer-options. The authors point out that 34% of questions require commonsense knowledge to answer, which includes social implication, speaker's intention, or general world knowledge.

CommonsenseQA is a multiple-choice QA dataset that specifically measure commonsense reasoning (Talmor et al., 2019). This dataset is constructed based on ConceptNet (Speer et al.,

2016). Specifically, a source concept is first extracted from ConceptNet, along with 3 target concepts that are connected to the source concept, i.e., a sub-graph. Crowd-workers are then asked to generate questions, using the source concept, such that only one of the target concepts can correctly answer the question. Additionally, 2 more distractor concepts are selected by crowd-workers so that each question is associated with 5 answer-options. In total, the dataset contains 12,247 questions. For CommonsenseQA, we evaluate models on the development-set only, since test-set answers are not publicly available.

4.2 Training details

For ease of comparison, we borrow hyperparameter settings from Pan et al. (2019b); we used the BERT Whole-Word Masking Uncased model (Devlin et al., 2018) for all experiments. For DREAM experiments, we used a max sequence-length of 512, batch-size of 24, learning rate of $1e^{-5}$, and we trained the model for 16 epochs. For CommonsenseQA, we used a max sequence length of 60, batch-size of 32, learning rate of $1e^{-5}$, and trained for 8 epochs. For pre-training on OMCS, we used max sequence length of 35, batch-size of 32, learning rate of $3e^{-5}$, and trained for 3 epochs. For pre-training on ATOMIC, the max sequence length is changed to 45, other hyperparameters remain the same, and we only use the ATOMIC training set. When using OCN on CommonsenseQA, since there is no dialogue, we compute co-attention with Q_{enc}, in place of D_{enc}, in order to keep the model structure consistent.

4.3 Results

DREAM results are shown in Table 5, and CommonsenseQA results are shown in Table 6. For all of our experiments, we run 3 trials with different random seeds and we report average scores in the tables. Evaluated on DREAM, our OCN model got a significant performance boost (+3.0%), compared to BERT-large from previous work. We think the reasons are that OCN is better-suited for the task and that we used BERT Whole-Word Masking Uncased model. OCN with ConceptNet knowledge-injection achieves slightly better results on the development-set, while ATOMIC knowledge-injection helps achieve a small improvement on the test-set. However, we recognize that these improvements are very limited; to our

surprise, OCN pre-trained on OMCS or ATOMIC got significantly lower performance.

As for results on CommonsenseQA, ConceptNet knowledge-injection provides a significant performance boost (+2.8%), compared to the OCN baseline, suggesting that explicit links from question to answer-options help the model find the correct answer. Pre-training on OMCS also provides a small performance boost to the OCN baseline. Since both ConceptNet knowledge-injection and OMCS pre-training are helpful, we combine both approaches with OCN and we are able to achieve further improvement (+4.9%). Finally, similar to the results on DREAM, OCN pre-trained on ATOMIC yields a siginificant performance drop.

5 Error Analysis

To better understand when a model performs better or worse with knowledge-integration, we analyzed model predictions. DREAM dataset provides annotations for about 1000 questions: 500 questions in the development-set and 500 in the test-set. Specifically, questions are manually classified into 5 categories: Matching, Summary, Logic inference, Commonsense inference, and Arithmetic inference; and each question can be classified under multiple categories. We refer readers to Sun et al. (2019) for additional category information. We extracted model predictions for these annotated questions in test-set and grouped them by types. The accuracies for each question-group are shown in Table 7. Note that we omitted 2 categories that have less than 10 questions. For the ConceptNet and the ATOMIC knowledge-injection models, we can see that they did better on questions that involve commonsense (last 3 columns in the table), and the performance on other types are about the same or slightly worse, compared to baseline OCN. As for models pre-trained on OMCS corpus or ATOMIC knowledge-base, we already saw that these model performances drop, compared to the baseline. When we look at the performance difference in each question type, it is clear that some categories account for the performance drop more than others. For example, for both the OMCS pre-trained model and the ATOMIC pre-trained model, performance drops significantly for Matching questions, in particular. On the other hand, for questions that require both commonsense inference and summarization, both models' performances only dropped

Models	M(54)	S(15)	A+L(11)	L(228)	C+L(122)	C(14)	C+S(60)
OCN	88.9	86.7	27.3	75.9	60.7	71.4	70.0
OCN + CN injection	83.3(-5.6)	86.7(+0.0)	18.2(-9.2)	76.8(+0.9)	59.8(-0.9)	64.3(-7.1)	78.3(**+8.3**)
OCN + AT injection	88.9(+0.0)	80.0(-6.7)	27.3(+0.0)	75.9(+0.0)	66.4(**+5.7**)	71.4(+0.0)	75(**+5.0**)
OCN + OMCS pre-train	70.4(-18.5)	73.3(-13.4)	45.4(+18.1)	69.7(-6.2)	48.4(-12.3)	57.1(-14.3)	68.3(**-1.7**)
OCN + ATOMIC pre-train	66.6(-22.3)	86.7(+0.0)	18.2(-9.2)	64.0(-11.9)	51.6(-9.1)	42.9(-28.5)	70.0(**+0.0**)

Table 7: Accuracies for each DREAM question type: **M** means *Matching*, **S** means *Summary*, **L** means *Logic inference*, **C** means *Commonsense inference*, and **A** means *Arithmatic inference*. Numbers beside types denote the number of questions of that type.

Models	AtLoc.(596)	Cau.(194)	Cap.(109)	Ant.(92)	H.Pre.(46)	H.Sub.(39)	C.Des.(28)	Des.(27)
OCN	64.9	66.5	65.1	55.4	69.6	64.1	57.1	66.7
+CN inj.	67.4(+2.5)	70.6(+4.1)	66.1(+1.0)	60.9(+5.5)	73.9(+4.3)	66.7(+2.6)	64.3(+7.2)	77.8(+11.1)
+OMCS	68.8(+3.9)	63.9(-2.6)	62.4(-2.7)	60.9(+5.5)	71.7(+2.1)	59.0(-5.1)	64.3(+7.2)	74.1(+7.4)
+ATOMIC	62.8(-2.1)	66.0(**-0.5**)	60.6(-4.5)	52.2(-3.2)	63.0(-6.6)	56.4(-7.7)	60.7(**+3.6**)	74.1(**+7.4**)
+OMCS+CN	71.6(+6.7)	71.6(+5.1)	64.2(+0.9)	59.8(+4.4)	69.6(+0.0)	69.2(+5.1)	75.0(+17.9)	70.4(+3.7)

Table 8: Accuracies for each CommonsenseQA question type: **AtLoc.** means *AtLocation*, **Cau.** means Causes, **Cap.** means *CapableOf*, **Ant.** means *Antonym*, **H.Pre.** means *HasPrerequiste*, **H.Sub** means *HasSubevent*, **C.Des.** means *CausesDesire*, and **Des.** means *Desires*. Numbers beside types denote the number of questions of that type.

slightly or did not change. Based on these results, we infer that commonsense knowledge-injection with attention is making an impact on models' weight distributions. The model is able to do better on questions that require commonsense but is losing performance on other types, suggesting a direction for future research in developing more robust (e.g., conditional) injection methods. Moreover, pre-training on knowledge-bases seems to have a larger impact on models' weight distributions, resulting in inferior performance. This weight distribution shift also favors of commonsense, as we see that commonsense types are not affected as much as other types. We also conducted similar analysis for CommonsenseQA. Since all questions in CommonsenseQA require commonsense reasoning, we classify questions based on the ConceptNet relation between the question concept and correct answer concept. The intuition is that the model needs to capture this relation in order to answer the question. The accuracies for each question type are shown in Table 8. Note that we have omitted question types that have less than 25 questions. We can see that with ConceptNet relation-injection, all question types got performance boosts, for both OCN model and OCN pre-trained on OMCS, suggesting that knowledge is indeed helpful for the task. In the case of OCN pre-trained on ATOMIC, although the overall performance is much lower than OCN baseline, it is interesting to see that performance for the "Causes" type is not significantly affected. Moreover, performance for "CausesDesire" and "Desires" types actually got much better. As noted by (Sap et al., 2019), "Causes" in ConceptNet is similar to "Effects" and "Reac-

tions" in ATOMIC; and "CausesDesire" in ConceptNet is similar to "Wants" in ATOMIC. This result also correlates with our findings from our analysis on DREAM, wherein we found that models with knowledge pre-training perform better on questions that fit knowledge domain but perform worse on others. In this case, pre-training on ATOMIC helps the model do better on questions that are similar to ATOMIC relations, even though overall performance is inferior. Finally, we noticed that questions of type "Antonym" appear to be the hardest ones. Many questions that fall into this category contain negations, and we hypothesize that the models still lack the ability to reason over negation sentences, suggesting another direction for future improvement.

6 Discussion

Based on our experimental results and error analysis, we see that external knowledge is only helpful when there is alignment between questions and knowledge-base types. Thus, it is crucial to identify the question type and apply the best-suited knowledge. In terms of knowledge-integration methods, attention-based injection seems to be the better choice for pre-trained language models such as BERT. Even when alignment between knowledge-base and dataset is sub-optimal, the performance would not degrade. On the other hand, pre-training on knowledge-bases would shift the language model's weight distribution toward its own domain, greatly. If the task domain does not fit knowledge-base well, model performance is likely to drop. When the domain of the knowledge-base aligns with that of the dataset perfectly, both knowledge-integration methods bring performance boosts and a combination of them could bring further gain.

7 Future Work

We have presented a survey on two popular knowledge bases (ConceptNet and ATOMIC) and recent knowledge-integration methods (attention and pre-training), on commonsense QA tasks. Evaluation on two QA datasets suggests that alignment between knowledge-bases and datasets plays a crucial role in knowledge-integration. We believe it is worth conducting a more comprehensive study of datasets and knowledge-bases and putting more effort towards defining an auxiliary learning objective, in a constrained-optimization (i.e., multi-task learning) framework, that identifies the type of knowledge required, based on data characteristics. In parallel, we are also interested in building a *global commonsense knowledge base* by aggregating ConceptNet, ATOMIC, and potentially other resources like FrameNet (Baker et al., 1998) and MetaNet (Dodge et al., 2015), on the basis of a shared-reference ontology (following the approaches described in (Gangemi et al., 2010) and (Scheffczyk et al., 2010)): the goal would be to assess whether injecting knowledge structures from a semantically-cohesive lexical knowledge base of commonsense guarantees stable model accuracy across datasets.

References

Collin F Baker, Charles J Fillmore, and John B Lowe. 1998. The berkeley framenet project. In *Proceedings of the 17th international conference on Computational linguistics-Volume 1*, pages 86–90. Association for Computational Linguistics.

Lisa Bauer, Yicheng Wang, and Mohit Bansal. 2018. Commonsense for generative multi-hop question answering tasks. In *Proceedings of the 2018 Conference on Empirical Methods in Natural Language Processing*, pages 4220–4230, Brussels, Belgium. Association for Computational Linguistics.

Antoine Bosselut, Hannah Rashkin, Maarten Sap, Chaitanya Malaviya, Asli Celikyilmaz, and Yejin Choi. 2019. COMET: Commonsense transformers for automatic knowledge graph construction. In *Proceedings of the 57th Annual Meeting of the Association for Computational Linguistics*, pages 4762–4779, Florence, Italy. Association for Computational Linguistics.

Ernest Davis. 2014. *Representations of commonsense knowledge*. Morgan Kaufmann.

Jacob Devlin, Ming-Wei Chang, Kenton Lee, and Kristina Toutanova. 2018. Bert: Pre-training of deep bidirectional transformers for language understanding. *arXiv preprint arXiv:1810.04805*.

Jacob Devlin, Ming-Wei Chang, Kenton Lee, and Kristina Toutanova. 2019. BERT: Pre-training of deep bidirectional transformers for language understanding. In *Proceedings of the 2019 Conference of the North American Chapter of the Association for Computational Linguistics: Human Language Technologies, Volume 1 (Long and Short Papers)*, pages 4171–4186, Minneapolis, Minnesota. Association for Computational Linguistics.

Ellen Dodge, Jisup Hong, and Elise Stickles. 2015. Metanet: Deep semantic automatic metaphor analysis. In *Proceedings of the Third Workshop on Metaphor in NLP*, pages 40–49.

Aldo Gangemi, Nicola Guarino, Claudio Masolo, and Alessandro Oltramari. 2010. Interfacing wordnet with dolce: towards ontowordnet. *Ontology and the Lexicon: A Natural Language Processing Perspective*, pages 36–52.

Karl Moritz Hermann, Tomas Kocisky, Edward Grefenstette, Lasse Espeholt, Will Kay, Mustafa Suleyman, and Phil Blunsom. 2015. Teaching machines to read and comprehend. In C. Cortes, N. D. Lawrence, D. D. Lee, M. Sugiyama, and R. Garnett, editors, *Advances in Neural Information Processing Systems 28*, pages 1693–1701. Curran Associates, Inc.

Jerry R Hobbs, William Croft, Todd Davies, Douglas Edwards, and Kenneth Laws. 1987. Commonsense metaphysics and lexical semantics. *Computational linguistics*, 13(3-4):241–250.

Thomas N. Kipf and Max Welling. 2016. Semi-supervised classification with graph convolutional networks. *CoRR*, abs/1609.02907.

Guokun Lai, Qizhe Xie, Hanxiao Liu, Yiming Yang, and Eduard H. Hovy. 2017. RACE: large-scale reading comprehension dataset from examinations. *CoRR*, abs/1704.04683.

Yoav Levine, Barak Lenz, Or Dagan, Dan Padnos, Or Sharir, Shai Shalev-Shwartz, Amnon Shashua, and Yoav Shoham. 2019. Sensebert: Driving some sense into bert. *ArXiv*, abs/1908.05646.

Tao Li and Vivek Srikumar. 2019. Augmenting neural networks with first-order logic. In *Proceedings of the 57th Annual Meeting of the Association for Computational Linguistics*, pages 292–302, Florence, Italy. Association for Computational Linguistics.

Bill Yuchen Lin, Xinyue Chen, Jamin Chen, and Xiang Ren. 2019. Kagnet: Knowledge-aware graph networks for commonsense reasoning. *ArXiv*, abs/1909.02151.

Yinhan Liu, Myle Ott, Naman Goyal, Jingfei Du, Mandar Joshi, Danqi Chen, Omer Levy, Mike Lewis, Luke Zettlemoyer, and Veselin Stoyanov. 2019. Roberta: A robustly optimized BERT pretraining approach. *CoRR*, abs/1907.11692.

Shangwen Lv, Daya Guo, Jingjing Xu, Duyu Tang, Nan Duan, Ming Gong, Linjun Shou, Daxin Jiang, Guihong Cao, and Songlin Hu. 2019. Graph-based reasoning over heterogeneous external knowledge for commonsense question answering. *ArXiv*, abs/1909.05311.

Yukun Ma, Haiyun Peng, and Erik Cambria. 2018. Targeted aspect-based sentiment analysis via embedding commonsense knowledge into an attentive lstm. In *AAAI*.

Todor Mihaylov and Anette Frank. 2018. Knowledgeable reader: Enhancing cloze-style reading comprehension with external commonsense knowledge. In *Proceedings of the 56th Annual Meeting of the Association for Computational Linguistics (Volume 1: Long Papers)*, pages 821–832, Melbourne, Australia. Association for Computational Linguistics.

Alexander Miller, Adam Fisch, Jesse Dodge, Amir-Hossein Karimi, Antoine Bordes, and Jason Weston. 2016. Key-value memory networks for directly reading documents. In *Proceedings of the 2016 Conference on Empirical Methods in Natural Language Processing*, pages 1400–1409, Austin, Texas. Association for Computational Linguistics.

Simon Ostermann, Michael Roth, Ashutosh Modi, Stefan Thater, and Manfred Pinkal. 2018. SemEval-2018 task 11: Machine comprehension using commonsense knowledge. In *Proceedings of The 12th International Workshop on Semantic Evaluation*, pages 747–757, New Orleans, Louisiana. Association for Computational Linguistics.

Xiaoman Pan, Kai Sun, Dian Yu, Heng Ji, and Dong Yu. 2019a. Improving question answering with external knowledge. *CoRR*, abs/1902.00993.

Xiaoman Pan, Kai Sun, Dian Yu, Heng Ji, and Dong Yu. 2019b. Improving question answering with external knowledge. *CoRR*, cs.CL/1902.00993v1.

Matthew E. Peters, Mark Neumann, IV RobertL.Logan, Roy Schwartz, Vidur Joshi, Sameer Singh, and Noah A. Smith. 2019. Knowledge enhanced contextual word representations. *ArXiv*, abs/1909.04164.

Alec Radford, Jeff Wu, Rewon Child, David Luan, Dario Amodei, and Ilya Sutskever. 2019. Language models are unsupervised multitask learners.

Pranav Rajpurkar, Jian Zhang, Konstantin Lopyrev, and Percy Liang. 2016. SQuAD: 100,000+ questions for machine comprehension of text. In *Proceedings of the 2016 Conference on Empirical Methods in Natural Language Processing*, pages 2383–2392, Austin, Texas. Association for Computational Linguistics.

Qiu Ran, Peng Li, Weiwei Hu, and Jie Zhou. 2019. Option comparison network for multiple-choice reading comprehension. *CoRR*, abs/1903.03033.

Maarten Sap, Ronan LeBras, Emily Allaway, Chandra Bhagavatula, Nicholas Lourie, Hannah Rashkin, Brendan Roof, Noah A Smith, and Yejin Choi. 2019. Atomic: An atlas of machine commonsense for if-then reasoning. In *AAAI*.

Jan Scheffczyk, Collin F Baker, and Srini Narayanan. 2010. Reasoning over natural language text by means of framenet and ontologies. *Ontology and the lexicon: A natural language processing perspective*, pages 53–71.

Min Joon Seo, Aniruddha Kembhavi, Ali Farhadi, and Hannaneh Hajishirzi. 2016. Bidirectional attention flow for machine comprehension. *ArXiv*, abs/1611.01603.

Push Singh, Thomas Lin, Erik T. Mueller, Grace Lim, Travell Perkins, and Wan Li Zhu. 2002. Open mind common sense: Knowledge acquisition from the general public. In *On the Move to Meaningful Internet Systems, 2002 - DOA/CoopIS/ODBASE 2002 Confederated International Conferences DOA, CoopIS and ODBASE 2002*, pages 1223–1237, Berlin, Heidelberg. Springer-Verlag.

Robyn Speer, Joshua Chin, and Catherine Havasi. 2016. Conceptnet 5.5: An open multilingual graph of general knowledge. In *AAAI Conference on Artificial Intelligence*.

Kai Sun, Dian Yu, Jianshu Chen, Dong Yu, Yejin Choi, and Claire Cardie. 2019. Dream: A challenge dataset and models for dialogue-based reading comprehension. *Transactions of the Association for Computational Linguistics*, 7:217–231.

Alon Talmor, Jonathan Herzig, Nicholas Lourie, and Jonathan Berant. 2019. CommonsenseQA: A question answering challenge targeting commonsense knowledge. In *Proceedings of the 2019 Conference of the North American Chapter of the Association for Computational Linguistics: Human Language Technologies, Volume 1 (Long and Short Papers)*, pages 4149–4158, Minneapolis, Minnesota. Association for Computational Linguistics.

Niket Tandon, Bhavana Dalvi, Joel Grus, Wen-tau Yih, Antoine Bosselut, and Peter Clark. 2018. Reasoning about actions and state changes by injecting commonsense knowledge. In *Proceedings of the 2018 Conference on Empirical Methods in Natural Language Processing*, pages 57–66, Brussels, Belgium. Association for Computational Linguistics.

Wenhui Wang, Nan Yang, Furu Wei, Baobao Chang, and Ming Zhou. 2017. Gated self-matching networks for reading comprehension and question answering. In *Proceedings of the 55th Annual Meeting of the Association for Computational Linguistics (Volume 1: Long Papers)*, pages 189–198, Vancouver, Canada. Association for Computational Linguistics.

Dirk Weissenborn, Tom'avs Kovcisk'y, and Chris Dyer. 2018. Dynamic integration of background knowledge in neural nlu systems.

Caiming Xiong, Victor Zhong, and Richard Socher. 2016. Dynamic coattention networks for question answering. *ArXiv*, abs/1611.01604.

Zhilin Yang, Zihang Dai, Yiming Yang, Jaime Carbonell, Ruslan Salakhutdinov, and Quoc V. Le. 2019. Xlnet: Generalized autoregressive pretraining for language understanding. Cite arxiv:1906.08237Comment: Pretrained models and code are available at https://github.com/zihangdai/xlnet.

Adams Wei Yu, David Dohan, Thang Luong, Rui Zhao, Kai Chen, and Quoc Le. 2018. Qanet: Combining local convolution with global self-attention for reading comprehension.

Rowan Zellers, Yonatan Bisk, Ali Farhadi, and Yejin Choi. 2018a. From recognition to cognition: Visual commonsense reasoning. *CoRR*, abs/1811.10830.

Rowan Zellers, Yonatan Bisk, Roy Schwartz, and Yejin Choi. 2018b. SWAG: A large-scale adversarial dataset for grounded commonsense inference. In *Proceedings of the 2018 Conference on Empirical Methods in Natural Language Processing*, pages 93–104, Brussels, Belgium. Association for Computational Linguistics.

Rowan Zellers, Ari Holtzman, Yonatan Bisk, Ali Farhadi, and Yejin Choi. 2019. HellaSwag: Can a machine really finish your sentence? In *Proceedings of the 57th Annual Meeting of the Association for Computational Linguistics*, pages 4791–4800, Florence, Italy. Association for Computational Linguistics.

Sheng Zhang, Xiaodong Liu, Jingjing Liu, Jianfeng Gao, Kevin Duh, and Benjamin Van Durme. 2018. Record: Bridging the gap between human and machine commonsense reading comprehension. *CoRR*, abs/1810.12885.

Wanjun Zhong, Duyu Tang, Nan Duan, Ming Zhou, Jiahai Wang, and Jian Yin. 2018. Improving question answering by commonsense-based pre-training. *CoRR*, abs/1809.03568.

When Choosing Plausible Alternatives, Clever Hans can be Clever

Pride Kavumba[1,*] **Naoya Inoue**[1,2,*] **Benjamin Heinzerling**[2,1] **Keshav Singh**[1]
Paul Reisert[2,1] **Kentaro Inui**[1,2]
[1]Tohoku University [2]RIKEN Center for Advanced Intelligence Project (AIP)
{pkavumba, naoya-i, keshav.singh29, inui} @ecei.tohoku.ac.jp
{benjamin.heinzerling, paul.reisert} @riken.jp

Abstract

Pretrained language models, such as BERT and RoBERTa, have shown large improvements in the commonsense reasoning benchmark COPA. However, recent work found that many improvements in benchmarks of natural language understanding are not due to models learning the task, but due to their increasing ability to exploit superficial cues, such as tokens that occur more often in the correct answer than the wrong one. Are BERT's and RoBERTa's good performance on COPA also caused by this? We find superficial cues in COPA, as well as evidence that BERT exploits these cues. To remedy this problem, we introduce Balanced COPA, an extension of COPA that does not suffer from easy-to-exploit single token cues. We analyze BERT's and RoBERTa's performance on original and Balanced COPA, finding that BERT relies on superficial cues when they are present, but still achieves comparable performance once they are made ineffective, suggesting that BERT learns the task to a certain degree when forced to. In contrast, RoBERTa does not appear to rely on superficial cues.

1 Introduction

Pretrained language models such as ELMo (Peters et al., 2018), BERT (Devlin et al., 2019), and RoBERTa (Liu et al., 2019b) have led to improved performance in benchmarks of natural language understanding, in tasks such as natural language inference (NLI, Liu et al., 2019a), argumentation (Niven and Kao, 2019), and commonsense reasoning (Li et al., 2019; Sap et al., 2019). However, recent work has identified superficial cues in benchmark datasets which are predictive of the correct answer, such as token distributions and lexical overlap. Once these cues are neutralized, models perform poorly, suggesting that their good

The woman hummed to herself. What was the *cause* for this?

✓ She was in a good mood.

✗ She was nervous.

(a) Original COPA instance.

The woman trembled. What was the *cause* for this?

✗ She was in a good mood.

✓ She was nervous.

(b) Mirrored COPA instance.

Figure 1: A COPA instance (a) with premise and correct (✓) and wrong (✗) alternatives. Our analysis reveals that the unigram *a* (highlighted orange) is a superficial cue exploited by BERT. We neutralize such superficial cues by creating a mirrored instance (b). After mirroring, the highlighted superficial cue becomes ineffective in predicting the correct answer, since it occurs with equal probability in correct and wrong alternatives.

performance is an instance of the Clever Hans effect[1] (Pfungst, 1911): Models trained on datasets with superficial cues learn heuristics for exploiting these cues, but do not develop any deeper understanding of the task.

While superficial cues have been identified in, among others, datasets for NLI (Gururangan et al., 2018; McCoy et al., 2019), machine reading comprehension (Sugawara et al., 2018), and argumentation (Niven and Kao, 2019), one of the main benchmarks for commonsense reasoning, namely the Choice of Plausible Alternatives (COPA, Roemmele et al., 2011), has not been analyzed so far. Here we present an analysis of superficial cues in COPA.

---

*Equal contribution.

[1]Named after the eponymous horse which appeared to be capable of simple mental tasks but actually relied on cues given involuntarily by its handler.

Proceedings of the First Workshop on Commonsense Inference in Natural Language Processing, pages 33–42
Hongkong, China, November 3, 2019. ©2019 Association for Computational Linguistics

Given a premise, such as *The man broke his toe*, COPA requires choosing the more plausible, causally related alternative, in this case either: because *He got a hole in his sock* (wrong) or because *He dropped a hammer on his foot* (correct). To test whether COPA contains superficial cues, we conduct a dataset ablation in which we provide only partial input to the model. Specifically, we provide only the two alternatives, but not the premise, which makes solving the task impossible and hence should reduce the model to random performance. However, we observe that a model trained only on alternatives performs considerably better than random chance and trace this result to an unbalanced distribution of tokens between correct and wrong alternatives. Further analysis (§4.3) reveals that finetuned BERT (Devlin et al., 2019) perform very well (83.9 percent accuracy) on *easy* instances containing superficial cues, but worse (71.9 percent) on *hard* instances without such simple cues.

To prevent models from exploiting superficial cues in COPA, we introduce *Balanced COPA*. Balanced COPA contains one additional, *mirrored* instance for each original training instance. This mirrored instance uses the same alternatives as the corresponding original instance, but introduces a new premise which matches the *wrong* alternative of the original instance, e.g. *The man hid his feet*, for which the correct alternative is now because *He got a hole in his sock* (See another example in Figure 1). Since each alternative occurs exactly once as correct answer and exactly once as wrong answer in Balanced COPA, the lexical distribution between correct and wrong answers is perfectly balanced, i.e., superficial cues in the original alternatives have become uninformative.

Balanced COPA allows us to study the impact of the presence or absence of superficial cues on model performance.

Since BERT exploits cues in the original COPA, we expected performance to degrade when training on Balanced COPA. However, BERT trained on Balanced COPA performed comparably overall. As we will show, this is due to better performance on the "hard" instances. This suggests that once superficial cues are made uninformative, BERT learns the task to a certain degree.

In summary, our contributions are:

- We identify superficial cues in COPA that allow models to use simple heuristics instead of learning the task (§2);

- We introduce Balanced COPA, which prevents models from exploiting these cues (§3);

- Comparing models on original and Balanced COPA, we find that BERT heavily exploits cues when they are present, but is also able to learn the task when they are not (§4); and

- We show that RoBERTa does not appear to exploit superficial cues.

2   Superficial Cues in COPA

2.1   COPA: Choice of Plausible Alternatives

Causal reasoning is an important prerequisite for natural language understanding. The Choice Of Plausible Alternatives (COPA) (Roemmele et al., 2011) is dataset that aims to benchmark causal reasoning in a simple binary classification setting.[2] COPA requires classifying sentence pairs consisting of the first sentence, the *premise*, and a second sentence that is either cause of, effect of, or unrelated to premise. Given the premise and two *alternatives*, one of which has a causal relation to the premise, while the other does not, models need to choose the more plausible alternative. Figure 1a shows an example of a COPA instance. The overall 1000 instances are split into training set[3] and test set of 500 instances each.

Prior to neural network approaches, the most dominant way of solving COPA was via Pointwise Mutual Information (PMI)-based statistics using a large background corpus between the content words in the premise and the alternatives (Gordon et al., 2011; Luo et al., 2016; Sasaki et al., 2017; Goodwin et al., 2012). Recent studies show that BERT and RoBERTa achieve considerable improvements on COPA (see Table 1).

However, recent work found that the strong performance of BERT and other deep neural models in benchmarks of natural language understanding can be partly or in some cases entirely explained by their capability to exploit superficial cues present in benchmark datasets. For example, Niven and Kao (2019) found that BERT exploits superficial cues, namely the occurrence of certain tokens such as *not*, in the Ar-

---

[2]http://people.ict.usc.edu/~gordon/copa.html

[3]This set is called *development set* by Roemmele et al. (2011), but is used as training set by supervised models.

Model	Accuracy
BigramPMI (Goodwin et al., 2012)	63.4
PMI (Gordon et al., 2011)	65.4
PMI+Connectives (Luo et al., 2016)	70.2
PMI+Con.+Phrase (Sasaki et al., 2017)	71.4
BERT-large (Wang et al., 2019)	70.5
BERT-large (Sap et al., 2019)	75.0
BERT-large (Li et al., 2019)	75.4
RoBERTa-large (finetuned)[4]	90.6
BERT-large (finetuned)*	76.5 ± 2.7
RoBERTa-large (finetuned)*	87.7 ± 0.9

Table 1: Reported results on COPA. With the exception of (Wang et al., 2019), BERT-large and RoBERTa-large yields substantial improvements over prior approaches. See §2 for model details. * indicates our replication experiments.

gument Reasoning Comprehension Task (Habernal et al., 2018). Similarly, Gururangan et al. (2018); Poliak et al. (2018); Dasgupta et al. (2018) showed that a simple text categorization model can perform well on the Stanford Natural Language Inference dataset (Bowman et al., 2015) and MultiNLI (Williams et al., 2018) when given incomplete input, even though the task should not be solvable without the full input. This suggests that the partial input contains unintended superficial cues that allow the models to take shortcuts without learning the actual task. Sugawara et al. (2018) investigated superficial cues that make questions easier across recent machine reading comprehension datasets. Given the fact that superficial cues were found in benchmark datasets for a wide variety of natural language understanding task, does COPA contain such cues, as well?

2.2 Token Distribution

One of the simplest types of superficial cues are unbalanced token distributions, i.e tokens appearing more often or less frequently with one particular instance label than with other labels. For example, Niven and Kao (2019) found that the token *not* occurs more often in one type of instance an argumentation dataset.

Similarly we identify superficial cues — in this case a single token that appears more frequently in correct alternatives or wrong alternatives — in the COPA training set. To find superficial cues in the form of predictive tokens, we use the following measures, defined by Niven and Kao (2019). Let $\mathbb{T}_j^{(i)}$ be the set of tokens in the alternatives for

data point i with label j. The *applicability* α_k of a token k counts how often this token occurs in an alternative with one label, but not the other:

$$\alpha_k = \sum_{i=1}^{n} \mathbb{1} \left[\exists j, k \in \mathbb{T}_j^{(i)} \wedge k \notin \mathbb{T}_{\neg j}^{(i)} \right]$$

The *productivity* π_k of a token is the proportion of applicable instances for which it predicts the correct answer:

$$\pi_k = \frac{\sum_{i=1}^{n} \mathbb{1} \left[\exists j, k \in \mathbb{T}_j^{(i)} \wedge k \notin \mathbb{T}_{\neg j}^{(i)} \wedge y_i = j \right]}{\alpha_k}$$

Finally, the *coverage* ξ_k of a token is the proportion of applicable instances among all instances:

$$\xi_k = \frac{\alpha_k}{n}$$

Table 2 shows the five tokens with highest coverage. For example, *a* is the token with the highest coverage and appears in either a correct alternative or wrong alternative in 21.2% of COPA training instances. Its productivity of 57.5% expresses that it appears in in correct alternatives 7.5% more often than expected by random chance. This suggests that a model could rely on such unbalanced distributions of tokens to predict answers based only on alternatives without understanding the task.

To test this hypothesis, we perform a dataset ablation, providing only the two alternatives as input to RoBERTa, but not the premise, following similar ablations by Gururangan et al. (2018); Niven and Kao (2019). RoBERTa trained[5] in this setting, i.e. on alternatives only, achieves a mean accuracy of 59.6 ($\pm$ 2.3). This is problematic because COPA is designed as a choice between alternatives given the premise. Without a premise given, model performance should not exceed random chance. Consequently, a result better than random chance shows that the dataset allows solving the task in a way that was not intended by its creators. To fix this problem, we create a balanced version of COPA that does not suffer from unbalanced token distributions in correct and wrong alternatives.

3 Balanced COPA (B-COPA)

To allow evaluating models on a benchmark without superficial cues, we need to make them inef-

---

[5]See §4.1 for experimental setup.

Cue	App.	Prod.	Cov.
in	47	55.3	9.40
was	55	61.8	11.0
to	82	40.2	16.4
the	85	38.8	17.0
a	106	57.5	21.2

Table 2: Applicability (App.), Productivity (Prod.) and Coverage (Cov.) of the various words in the *alternatives* of the COPA dev set.

fective. Our approach is to balance the token distributions in correct alternatives and wrong alternatives in the training set. Without unbalanced token distributions, we hope models are able to learn other patterns more closely related to the task, e.g. a pair of causally related events, rather than superficial cues.

3.1 Data Collection

To create the balanced COPA training set, we manually mirror the original training set by modifying the premise. Taking the original training set as a starting point, we duplicate the COPA instances and modify their premises so that incorrect alternatives become correct. Suppose the following original COPA instance:

- **Premise**: The stain came out of the shirt. What was the CAUSE of this?

- **Alternative 1**: I bleached the shirt. (Correct)

- **Alternative 2**: I patched the shirt.

We create the following balanced COPA instance, where the wrong alternative becomes the correct choice now:

- **Premise**: *The shirt did not have a hole anymore.* What was the CAUSE of this?

- **Alternative 1**: I bleached the shirt.

- **Alternative 2**: I patched the shirt. (Correct)

This approach is similar to Niven and Kao (2019), who create a balanced benchmark of the Argument Reasoning Comprehension Task by negating and rotating its ingredients, exploiting the nature of the task. However, due to the nature of COPA, we cannot follow their approach and choose to create new premises.

Dataset	Accuracy	Fleiss' kappa k
Original COPA	100.0	0.973
Balanced COPA	97.0	0.798

Table 3: Results of human performance evaluation of the original COPA and Balanced COPA.

To collect such balanced data, we asked five fluent English speakers who have background knowledge of NLP (see Appendix A for the detailed guideline). Finally, we collected 500 new mirrored instances. Concatenating it with the original training instances, the balanced COPA consists of 1,000 instances in total. The corpus is publicly available at `https://balanced-copa.github.io`.

3.2 Quality Evaluation

To ensure the quality of the mirrored instances, we estimate a human performance using Amazon Mechanical Turk (AMT), a widely-used crowdsourcing platform. We randomly sample 100 instances from the original COPA training set and 100 instances from the balanced COPA, and asked crowdworkers to solve each instance (see Appendix B for an actual screenshot). To avoid noisy workers, we presented our tasks to workers who meet master AMT qualification with at least 10,000 HIT approvals and 99% HIT approval rate. Per HIT, we assign three crowd workers and offer 10 cents reward.

From the collected responses, we calculate the accuracy of workers (by majority voting) and inter-annotator agreement by Fleiss' Kappa (Fleiss, 1981). The human evaluation shows that our mirrored instances are comparable in difficulty to the original ones (see Table 3). However, we found that some mirrored instances are a bit tricky at first glance. But, with a bit more attention, the answer is quite obvious (see Appendix C, for an example).

4 Experiments

4.1 BERT and RoBERTa on COPA

In this section we analyze the performance of two recent pretrained language models on COPA: BERT and RoBERTa, an optimized variant of BERT that achieves better performance on the SuperGLUE benchmark (Wang et al., 2019), which includes COPA.

Model	Method	Training Data	Overall	Easy	Hard	p-value (%)
Goodwin et al. (2012)	PMI	unsupervised	61.8	64.7	60.0	19.8
Gordon et al. (2011)	PMI	unsupervised	65.4	65.8	65.2	83.5
Sasaki et al. (2017)	PMI	unsupervised	71.4	75.3	69.0	4.8*
Word frequency	wordfreq	COPA	53.5	57.4	51.3	9.8
BERT-large-FT	LM, NSP	COPA	76.5 ($\pm$ 2.7)	83.9 ($\pm$ 4.4)	71.9 ($\pm$ 2.5)	0.0*
RoBERTa-large-FT	LM	COPA	87.7 ($\pm$ 0.9)	91.6 ($\pm$ 1.1)	85.3 ($\pm$ 2.0)	0.0*

Table 4: Model performance on the COPA test set (*Overall*), on *Easy* instances with superficial cues, and on *Hard* instances without superficial cues. p-values according to Approximate Randomization Tests (Noreen, 1989), with * indicating a significant difference between performance on *Easy* and *Hard* $p < 5\%$. Methods are pointwise mutual information (PMI), word frequency provided by the wordfreq package (Speer et al., 2018), pretrained language model (LM), and next-sentence prediction (NSP).

We convert COPA instances as follows to make them compatible with the input format required by BERT/RoBERTa. For a COPA instance $\langle p, a_1, a_2, q \rangle$, where p is a premise, a_i is the i-th alternative, and q is a question type (either *effect* or *cause*), we construct BERT's input depending on the question type. We assume that the first sentence and the second sentence in the next sentence prediction task describe a cause and an effect, respectively. Specifically, for each i-th alternative, we define the following input function:

$$\text{input}(p, a_i) = \begin{cases} \text{``[CLS] } p \text{ [SEP] } a_i \text{ [SEP]'' if } q \text{ is effect} \\ \text{``[CLS] } a_i \text{ [SEP] } p \text{ [SEP]'' if } q \text{ is cause} \end{cases}$$

Part of BERT's training objective includes next sentence prediction. Given a pair of sentences, BERT predicts whether one sentence can be plausibly followed by the other. For this, BERT's input format contains two [SEP] tokens to mark the two sentences and the [CLS] token, which is used as the input representation for next sentence prediction. This part of BERT's architecture makes it a natural fit for COPA.

One of the key differences between BERT and RoBERTa is that the next sentence prediction objective is not part of RoBERTa's training objective. Instead, RoBERTa is trained with masked language modeling only, with its input consisting of multiple concatenated sentences. To match this training setting, we encode two sentences in a single segment as follows:

$$\text{input}(p, a_i) = \begin{cases} \text{``<s> } p \; a_i \text{ </s>'' if } q \text{ is effect} \\ \text{``<s> } a_i \; p \text{ </s>'' if } q \text{ is cause} \end{cases}$$

After encoding premise-alternative with BERT or RoBERTa, we take the first hidden representation z_i^0, i.e. the one corresponding to [CLS] or

<s>, in the final model layer and pass it through a linear layer for binary classification:

$$y_i = \boldsymbol{w}^\mathsf{T} \boldsymbol{z}_i^0 + b, \tag{1}$$

where the parameters $\boldsymbol{w} \in \mathbb{R}^h$ and $b \in \mathbb{R}$ are learned on the COPA training set. Finally, we choose the alternative with the higher score, i.e., $a_{\hat{i}}$ with $\hat{i} = \arg\max_{i \in \{1,2\}} y_i$.

For training, we minimize the cross entropy loss with the logits $[y_1; y_2]$ and fine-tune BERT and RoBERTa's parameters. In our experiments, we use pretrained BERT-large (uncased) with 24 layers, 16 self-attention heads (340M parameters) and pretrained RoBERTa-large with 24 layers, 16 self-attention heads (355M parameters).[6]

4.2 Training Details

For training, we consider two configurations: (i) using the original COPA training set (§4.3), and (ii) using B-COPA (§4.4). We randomly split the training data into training data and validation data with the ratio of 9:1. For B-COPA, we make sure that a pair of original instance and its mirrored counterpart always belong to the same split in order to ensure that a model is trained without superficial cues. For testing, we use all 500 instances from the original COPA test set.

We run each experiment three times with different random seeds and average the results. We train for 10 epochs and choose the best model based on the validation score. To reduce GPU RAM usage, we set BERT and RoBERTa's maximum sequence length to 32, which covers all training and test instances. We use Adam (Kingma and Ba, 2015) with warmup, weight decay of 0.01, a batch size

---

[6]`https://huggingface.co/`
`pytorch-transformers/`

Model	Training data	Overall	Easy	Hard
BERT-large-FT	B-COPA	74.5 ($\pm$ 0.7)	74.7 ($\pm$ 0.4)	**74.4** ($\pm$ 0.9)
BERT-large-FT	B-COPA (50%)	74.3 ($\pm$ 2.2)	76.8 ($\pm$ 1.9)	72.8 ($\pm$ 3.1)
BERT-large-FT	COPA	**76.5** ($\pm$ 2.7)	**83.9** ($\pm$ 4.4)	71.9 ($\pm$ 2.5)
RoBERTa-large-FT	B-COPA	**89.0** ($\pm$ 0.3)	88.9 ($\pm$ 2.1)	**89.0** ($\pm$ 0.8)
RoBERTa-large-FT	B-COPA (50%)	86.1 ($\pm$ 2.2)	87.4 ($\pm$ 1.1)	85.4 ($\pm$ 2.9)
RoBERTa-large-FT	COPA	87.7 ($\pm$ 0.9)	**91.6** ($\pm$ 1.1)	85.3 ($\pm$ 2.0)

Table 5: Results of fine-tuned models on Balanced COPA. *Easy*: instances with superficial cues, *Hard*: instances without superficial cues.

of 4, and a gradient accumulation of 8. We optimize hyperparameters for BERT and RoBERTa separately on the validation set. For BERT, we test learning rates of 2e-4, 1e-4, 8e-5, 4e-5, 2e-5, and 1e-5, and use warm up proportion of 0.1, with gradient norm clipping of 1.0. For RoBERTa, we test learning rates of 1e-5, 8e-6, 6e-6, 4e-6, 2e-6, and 1e-6, and use warm up proportion of 0.06, with no gradient norm clipping.

4.3 Evaluation on Easy and Hard subsets

To investigate the behaviour of BERT and RoBERTa trained on the original COPA, which contains superficial cues, we split the test set into an *Easy* subset and a *Hard* subset. The *Easy subset* consists of instances that are correctly solved by the premise-oblivious model described in §2. To account for variation between the three runs with different random seeds, we deem an instance correctly classified only if the premise-oblivous model's prediction is correct for all three runs. This results in the *Easy* subset with 190 instances and the *Hard* subset comprising the remaining 310 instances. Such an easy/hard split follows similar splits in NLI datasets (Gururangan et al., 2018).

We then compare BERT and RoBERTa with previous models on the *Easy* and *Hard* subsets.[7] As Table 4 shows, previous models perform similarly on both subsets, with the exception of Sasaki et al. (2017).[8] Overall both BERT (76.5%) and RoBERTa (87.7%) considerably outperform the

best previous model (71.4%). However, BERT's improvements over previous work can be almost entirely attributed to high accuracy on the *Easy* subset: on this subset, finetuned BERT-large improves 8.6 percent over the model by (Sasaki et al., 2017) (83.9% vs. 75.3%), but on the *Hard* subset, the improvement is only 2.9 percent (71.9% vs. 69.0%). This indicates that BERT relies on superficial cues. The difference between accuracy on *Easy* and *Hard* is less pronounced for RoBERTa, but still suggests some reliance on superficial cues. We speculate that superficial cues in the COPA training set prevented BERT and RoBERTa from focusing on task-related non-superficial cues such as causally related event pairs.

4.4 Evaluation on Balanced COPA (B-COPA)

How will BERT and RoBERTa behave when there are no superficial cues in the training set? To answer this question, we now train BERT and RoBERTa on B-COPA and evaluate on the *Easy* and *Hard* subsets. The results are shown in Table 5. The smaller performance gap between *Easy* and *Hard* subsets indicates that training on B-COPA encourages BERT and RoBERTa to rely less on superficial cues. Moreover, training on B-COPA improves performance on the Hard subset, both when training with all 1000 instances in B-COPA, and when matching the training size of the original COPA (500 instances, *B-COPA 50%*). Note that training on *B-COPA 50%* exposes the model to lexically less diverse training instances than the original COPA due to the high overlap between mirrored alternatives (see §3).

These results show that once superficial cues are removed, the models are able to learn the task to a high degree. This contrasts with Niven and Kao (2019), who found that BERT's performance

---

[7]For previous models, we use the prediction keys available on `http://people.ict.usc.edu/~gordon/copa.html`

[8]We conjecture that word frequency is another superficial cue exploited by models. To verify this we train a classifier based on word frequencies only (Speer et al., 2018) and find that this classifier is able to identify the correct alternative better than random chance, but this result is not significant ($p = 9.8\%$).

Model	Training data	Overall	Easy	Hard
BERT-large	B-COPA	70.5 ($\pm$ 2.5)	72.6 ($\pm$ 2.3)	**69.1** ($\pm$ 2.7)
BERT-large	B-COPA (50%)	69.9 ($\pm$ 1.9)	71.2 ($\pm$ 1.3)	69.0 ($\pm$ 3.5)
BERT-large	COPA	**71.7** ($\pm$ 0.5)	**80.5** ($\pm$ 0.4)	66.3 ($\pm$ 0.8)
RoBERTa-large	B-COPA	**76.7** ($\pm$ 0.8)	73.3 ($\pm$ 1.5)	**78.8** ($\pm$ 2.0)
RoBERTa-large	B-COPA (50%)	72.4 ($\pm$ 2.0)	72.1 ($\pm$ 1.7)	72.6 ($\pm$ 2.1)
RoBERTa-large	COPA	76.4 ($\pm$ 0.7)	**79.6** ($\pm$ 1.0)	74.4 ($\pm$ 1.1)
BERT-base-NSP	None	**66.4**	66.2	**66.7**
BERT-large-NSP	None	65.0	**66.9**	62.1

Table 6: Results of non-fine-tuned models on Balanced COPA. *Easy*: instances with superficial cues, *Hard*: instances without superficial cues.

on the Argument Reasoning Comprehension Task (Habernal et al., 2018) does not exceed random chance level after superficial cues are made uninformative. A likely explanation for this contrast is the difference in the inherent task difficulties. Argument reasoning comprehension is a high level natural language understanding task requiring world knowledge and complex reasoning skills, while COPA can be largely solved with associative reasoning, as the performance of the PMI-based baselines shows (Table 4). A second possible explanations is BERT's insensitivity to negations (Ettinger, 2019). Since Niven and Kao (2019) made superficial cues uninformative by adding negated instances to the dataset, BERT's insensitivity to negations makes distinguishing between instances and negated instances difficult (see §3).

4.5 Analysis of sentence pair embeddings

The findings presented in the previous sections, namely BERT's and RoBERTa's good performance on COPA in spite of the rather small amount of training data, leads us to the following hypothesis that pretraining enables these models to create an embedding space in which embeddings of plausible sentence pairs are distinguishable from embeddings of less plausible pairs.

To investigate how well the respective embedding spaces of BERT and RoBERTa separate plausible and less-plausible pairs, we train BERT-large and RoBERTa-large *without fine-tuning*. Specifically, we freeze model weights and train a classifier by parameterizing w and b in Equation 1 as a soft-margin Support Vector Machine (SVM,

Cortes and Vapnik, 1995).[9] We also report results for a simple model that only uses BERT's pretrained next sentence predictor (BERT-base-NSP, BERT-large-NSP), i.e., we choose the alternative with the higher next sentence prediction score. The results are shown in Table 6. The relatively high accuracies of BERT-large, RoBERTa-large and BERT-*-NSP show that these pretrained models are already well-equipped to perform this task "out-of-the-box".

4.6 Analysis of sensitivity to cues

To analyze the sensitivity of BERT and RoBERTa to superficial cues and to content words, we employ a gradient-based approach, following (Brunner et al., 2019). Specifically, we define the sensitivity $s_{i,t}$ of the classification score in i-th COPA test instance to input token t, as follows:

$$s_{i,t} = \frac{||\boldsymbol{g_t}||}{\sum_{t' \in T_i} ||\boldsymbol{g_{t'}}||}, \boldsymbol{g_t} = \frac{\partial y}{\partial \boldsymbol{x_t}}, \qquad (2)$$

where T_i is a sequence of all input tokens in the i-th COPA test instance, y is a score function defined by Equation (1), and $\boldsymbol{x_t} \in \mathbb{R}^{1024}$ is a position-augmented token embedding of t. We then define the sensitivity $S(k)$ to cue k over all COPA test instances as the average over all m COPA test instances: $S(k) = \frac{1}{m} \sum_i^m s_{i,k}$.

We are interested in the change of sensitivity towards cue t of a model trained on original COPA compared to a model trained on Balanced COPA. We plot this difference as a function of the cue's productivity (Figure 2). We observe that BERT trained on Balanced COPA is less sensitive to a

---

[9]We tune the SVM hyperparameter $C \in \{0.0001, 0.001, 0.01, 0.1, 1\}$ on the validation set.

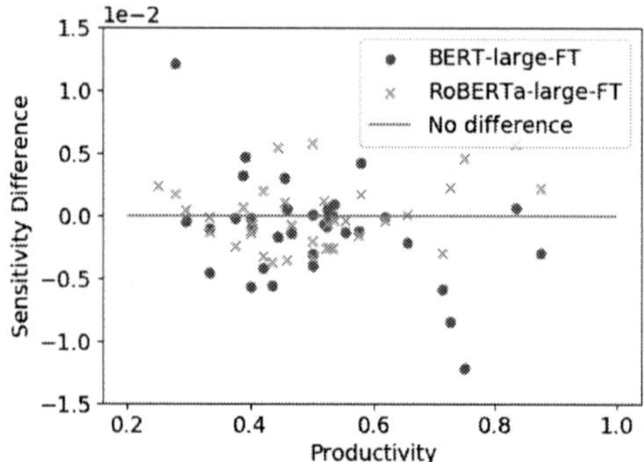

Figure 2: Change of sensitivity to superficial cues (in §2) from COPA-trained models to B-COPA-trained models as a function of their productivity.

Cue	S^{COPA}	$S^{\text{B-COPA}}$	Diff.	Prod.
woman	7.98	4.84	-3.14	0.25
mother	5.16	3.95	-1.21	0.75
went	6.00	5.15	-0.85	0.73
down	5.52	4.93	-0.58	0.71
into	4.07	3.51	-0.56	0.40

Table 7: Sensitivity of BERT-large to superficial cues identified in §2 (unit: 10^{-2}). Cues with top-5 reduction are shown. S^{COPA}, $S^{\text{B-COPA}}$ indicate the mean contributions of BERT-large trained on COPA, and BERT-large trained on B-COPA, respectively.

few highly productive superficial cues than BERT trained on original COPA. Note the decrease in the sensitivity for cues of productivity from 0.7 to 0.9. These cues are shown in Table 7. However, for cues with lower productivity, the picture is less clear, in case of RoBERTa, there are no noticeable trends in the change of sensitivity.

5 Conclusions

We established that COPA, an important benchmark of commonsense reasoning, contains superficial cues, specifically single tokens predictive of the correct answer, that allow models to solve the task without actually understanding it. Our experiments suggest that BERT's good performance on COPA can be explained by its ability to exploit these superficial cues. BERT performs well on *Easy* instances with such superficial cues, and comparable to previous methods on *Hard* instances without such cues. RoBERTa, in contrast, represents a real improvement considerably outperforms both BERT and previous methods on *Hard* instances as well.

To allow evaluating models on a benchmark without predictive single tokens, we created the Balanced COPA dataset. Balanced COPA neutralizes this kind of superficial cue by mirroring instances from the original COPA dataset, thereby removing any differences in token distributions between correct and wrong alternatives. Surprisingly, we found that both BERT and RoBERTa finetuned on Balanced COPA perform comparably overall to the models finetuned on the original COPA. However, a more detailed analysis revealed quite different behaviour. Whereas BERT finetuned on original COPA heavily exploited superficial cues, we now find evidence that BERT finetuned on balanced COPA appears to learn some aspects of the task with similar accuracies on both *Easy* and *Hard* instances. Even more surprisingly, RoBERTa benefits from training on Balanced COPA instances and achieves higher accuracy than on the original COPA with superficial cues.

Two important questions remain unanswered at present, which we plan to explore in future work: Even in the presence of superficial cues, RoBERTa does not seem to rely on them. First, why does RoBERTa not appear to rely on superficial cues, even when they are available? And second, are the results of our experiments on Balanced COPA specific to BERT and RoBERTa or are all pretrained language models able to exploit superficial cues in COPA and able to solve the task by other means if no such cues are present?

Acknowledgements

This work was partially supported by JSPS KAKENHI Grant Number 19K20332 and JST CREST Grant Number JPMJCR1513, including AIP challenge.

References

Samuel R. Bowman, Gabor Angeli, Christopher Potts, and Christopher D. Manning. 2015. A large annotated corpus for learning natural language inference. In *Proceedings of the 2015 Conference on Empirical Methods in Natural Language Processing (EMNLP)*. Association for Computational Linguistics.

Gino Brunner, Yang Liu, Dami'an Pascual, Oliver Richter, and Roger Wattenhofer. 2019. On the validity of self-attention as explanation in transformer models. *ArXiv*, abs/1908.04211.

Corinna Cortes and Vladimir Vapnik. 1995. Support-vector networks. *Mach. Learn.*, 20(3):273–297.

Ishita Dasgupta, Demi Guo, Andreas Stuhlmüller, Samuel J Gershman, and Noah D. Goodman. 2018. Evaluating compositionality in sentence embeddings. *ArXiv*, abs/1802.04302.

Jacob Devlin, Ming-Wei Chang, Kenton Lee, and Kristina Toutanova. 2019. BERT: Pre-training of deep bidirectional transformers for language understanding. In *Proceedings of the 2019 Conference of the North American Chapter of the Association for Computational Linguistics: Human Language Technologies, Volume 1 (Long and Short Papers)*, pages 4171–4186, Minneapolis, Minnesota. Association for Computational Linguistics.

Allyson Ettinger. 2019. What bert is not: Lessons from a new suite of psycholinguistic diagnostics for language models.

Joseph L. Fleiss. 1981. *Statistical methods for rates and proportions*, 2nd edition. Wiley, New York.

Travis Goodwin, Bryan Rink, Kirk Roberts, and Sanda Harabagiu. 2012. UTDHLT: COPACETIC system for choosing plausible alternatives. In **SEM 2012: The First Joint Conference on Lexical and Computational Semantics – Volume 1: Proceedings of the main conference and the shared task, and Volume 2: Proceedings of the Sixth International Workshop on Semantic Evaluation (SemEval 2012)*, pages 461–466, Montréal, Canada. Association for Computational Linguistics.

Andrew S. Gordon, Cosmin Adrian Bejan, and Kenji Sagae. 2011. Commonsense Causal Reasoning Using Millions of Personal Stories. In *25th Conference on Artificial Intelligence (AAAI-11)*, San Francisco, CA.

Suchin Gururangan, Swabha Swayamdipta, Omer Levy, Roy Schwartz, Samuel Bowman, and Noah A. Smith. 2018. Annotation artifacts in natural language inference data. In *Proceedings of the 2018 Conference of the North American Chapter of the Association for Computational Linguistics: Human Language Technologies, Volume 2 (Short Papers)*, pages 107–112, New Orleans, Louisiana. Association for Computational Linguistics.

Ivan Habernal, Henning Wachsmuth, Iryna Gurevych, and Benno Stein. 2018. The argument reasoning comprehension task: Identification and reconstruction of implicit warrants. In *Proceedings of the 2018 Conference of the North American Chapter of the Association for Computational Linguistics: Human Language Technologies, Volume 1 (Long Papers)*, pages 1930–1940, New Orleans, Louisiana. Association for Computational Linguistics.

Diederik P. Kingma and Jimmy Ba. 2015. Adam: A method for stochastic optimization. In *3rd International Conference on Learning Representations, ICLR 2015, San Diego, CA, USA, May 7-9, 2015, Conference Track Proceedings*.

Zhongyang Li, Tongfei Chen, and Benjamin Van Durme. 2019. Learning to rank for plausible plausibility. In *Proceedings of the 57th Annual Meeting of the Association for Computational Linguistics*, pages 4818–4823, Florence, Italy. Association for Computational Linguistics.

Xiaodong Liu, Pengcheng He, Weizhu Chen, and Jianfeng Gao. 2019a. Multi-task deep neural networks for natural language understanding. *arXiv preprint arXiv:1901.11504*.

Yinhan Liu, Myle Ott, Naman Goyal, Jingfei Du, Mandar Joshi, Danqi Chen, Omer Levy, Mike Lewis, Luke Zettlemoyer, and Veselin Stoyanov. 2019b. Roberta: A robustly optimized BERT pretraining approach. *CoRR*, abs/1907.11692.

Zhiyi Luo, Yuchen Sha, Kenny Q. Zhu, Seung-won Hwang, and Zhongyuan Wang. 2016. Commonsense causal reasoning between short texts. In *Proceedings of the Fifteenth International Conference on Principles of Knowledge Representation and Reasoning, KR'16*, pages 421–430. AAAI Press.

Tom McCoy, Ellie Pavlick, and Tal Linzen. 2019. Right for the wrong reasons: Diagnosing syntactic heuristics in natural language inference. In *Proceedings of the 57th Annual Meeting of the Association for Computational Linguistics*, pages 3428–3448, Florence, Italy. Association for Computational Linguistics.

Timothy Niven and Hung-Yu Kao. 2019. Probing neural network comprehension of natural language arguments. In *Proceedings of the 57th Annual Meeting of the Association for Computational Linguistics*, pages 4658–4664, Florence, Italy. Association for Computational Linguistics.

Eric W Noreen. 1989. *Computer-intensive methods for testing hypotheses*. Wiley New York.

Matthew Peters, Mark Neumann, Mohit Iyyer, Matt Gardner, Christopher Clark, Kenton Lee, and Luke Zettlemoyer. 2018. Deep contextualized word representations. In *Proceedings of the 2018 Conference of the North American Chapter of the Association for Computational Linguistics: Human Language Technologies, Volume 1 (Long Papers)*, pages 2227–2237, New Orleans, Louisiana. Association for Computational Linguistics.

Oskar Pfungst. 1911. *Clever Hans:(the horse of Mr. Von Osten.) a contribution to experimental animal and human psychology*. Holt, Rinehart and Winston.

Adam Poliak, Jason Naradowsky, Aparajita Haldar, Rachel Rudinger, and Benjamin Van Durme. 2018. Hypothesis only baselines in natural language inference. In *Proceedings of the Seventh Joint Conference on Lexical and Computational Semantics*, pages 180–191, New Orleans, Louisiana. Association for Computational Linguistics.

Melissa Roemmele, Cosmin Adrian Bejan, and Andrew S Gordon. 2011. Choice of plausible alternatives: An evaluation of commonsense causal reasoning. In *AAAI Spring Symposium on Logical Formalizations of Commonsense Reasoning*, Stanford University.

Maarten Sap, Hannah Rashkin, Derek Chen, Ronan Le Bras, and Yejin Choi. 2019. Socialiqa: Commonsense reasoning about social interactions. *ArXiv*, abs/1904.09728.

Shota Sasaki, Sho Takase, Naoya Inoue, Naoaki Okazaki, and Kentaro Inui. 2017. Handling multiword expressions in causality estimation. In *IWCS 2017 — 12th International Conference on Computational Semantics — Short papers*.

Robyn Speer, Joshua Chin, Andrew Lin, Sara Jewett, and Lance Nathan. 2018. Luminosoinsight/wordfreq: v2.2.

Saku Sugawara, Kentaro Inui, Satoshi Sekine, and Akiko Aizawa. 2018. What makes reading comprehension questions easier? In *Proceedings of the 2018 Conference on Empirical Methods in Natural Language Processing*, pages 4208–4219, Brussels, Belgium. Association for Computational Linguistics.

Alex Wang, Yada Pruksachatkun, Nikita Nangia, Amanpreet Singh, Julian Michael, Felix Hill, Omer Levy, and Samuel R. Bowman. 2019. SuperGLUE: A stickier benchmark for general-purpose language understanding systems. *arXiv preprint 1905.00537*.

Adina Williams, Nikita Nangia, and Samuel Bowman. 2018. A broad-coverage challenge corpus for sentence understanding through inference. In *Proceedings of the 2018 Conference of the North American Chapter of the Association for Computational Linguistics: Human Language Technologies, Volume 1 (Long Papers)*, pages 1112–1122, New Orleans, Louisiana. Association for Computational Linguistics.

A Balanced COPA New Premise Guidelines

We instructed dataset creators with the following guidelines:

1. Ensure as much lexical overlap in new premise as the original premise.

2. Ensure little lexical overlap between premise and alternative, but if a word occurs both in premise and alternatives, it is acceptable to include it in the premise.

3. Maintain, as much as possible, the length and style between the new premise and the original premise.

4. Ensure that there is no direct association between the correct alternative and premise.

5. Avoid slang.

B Amazon Mechanical Turk Form

Task

1. Read the following situation description:

The customer filed a complaint with the store manager.

2. Tell us which of the following is the most likely CAUSE of this situation:

(a) *The sales associate undercharged the customer.*

(b) *The sales associate acted rude to the customer.*

Figure 3: Amazon Mechanical Turk task form

C Example of an instance with low inter-annotator agreement

I received a package in the mail. What happened as a result? (effect)

✓ The package triggered my curiosity.

✗ I took the package to the post office.

(a) Original COPA instance.

I received someone's package in the mail. What happened as a result? (effect)

✗ The package triggered my curiosity.

✓ I took the package to the post office.

(b) Mirrored COPA instance.

Figure 4: An example of one of mirrored COPA instances with low inter-annotator agreement. Paying attention to the highlighted word is key to picking the correct alternative.

Commonsense about Human Senses: Labeled Data Collection Processes

Ndapa Nakashole
Computer Science and Engineering
University of California, San Diego
La Jolla, CA 92093
nnakashole@eng.ucsd.edu

Abstract

We consider the problem of extracting from text commonsense knowledge pertaining to human senses such as sound and smell. First, we consider the problem of recognizing mentions of human senses in text. Our contribution is a method for acquiring labeled data. Experiments show the effectiveness of our proposed data labeling approach when used with standard machine learning models on the task of sense recognition in text. Second, we propose to extract novel, common sense relationships pertaining to sense perception concepts. Our contribution is a process for generating labeled data by leveraging large corpora and crowd-sourcing questionnaires.

1   Introduction

Information extraction methods produce structured data in the form of knowledge bases of factual assertions. Such knowledge bases are useful for porting inference, question answering, and reasoning (Bollacker et al., 2008; Hoffart et al., 2012; Mitchell et al., 2015). However, progress on the common sense front, as opposed to named entities such as locations, and people, is still limited (Havasi et al., 2007; Tandon et al., 2011).

One of the factors impeding progress in common sense knowledge acquisition is the lack of labeled data. Prior work has shown that it can be straightforward to obtain training data for identifying relationships between named entities such as companies and their headquarters, or people and their birth places (Havasi et al., 2007; Tandon et al., 2011; Bollacker et al., 2008; Hoffart et al., 2012; Mitchell et al., 2015). Examples of such relationships can be found in semi-structured formats on the Web(Wu and Weld, 2008; Wang and Cohen, 2008). This is not the case for common sense relationships.

We therefore consider the problem of extracting from text commonsense knowledge pertaining to human senses such as sound and smell. We split the problem into two parts, for each part we propose approaches for obtaining labeled data, and train standard machine learning models.

1. In the first part of this work, the goal is to detect mentions of concepts that are discernible by sense. For example, recognize that "chirping birds" is a mention of an audible concept (sound), and "burning rubber" is a mention of an olfactible concept (smell). We aim to detect *mentions* of concepts without performing co-reference resolution or clustering mentions. Therefore, our setting resembles the established task of entity recognition (Finkel et al., 2005; Ratinov and Roth, 2009), with the difference being that we focus on un-named entities.

We propose a data labeling method, that leverages crowd-sourcing and large corpora. This approach provides the flexibility to control the size and accuracy of the available labeled data for model training. Additionally, we train several standard machine learning models including to recognize mentions of sound and smell concepts in text. In our experiments, we show that the combination of our data labeling approach, and a suitable learning model are an effective solution to sense recognition in text.

2. In the second part of this work, we seek to extract novel common sense relationships about concepts that are discernible by sense.

Our contributions in this part of the work are as follows: first, we propose to extract novel relationships that are sparse in existing knowledge bases. Second, we propose a pro-

43

Proceedings of the First Workshop on Commonsense Inference in Natural Language Processing, pages 43–52
Hongkong, China, November 3, 2019. ©2019 Association for Computational Linguistics

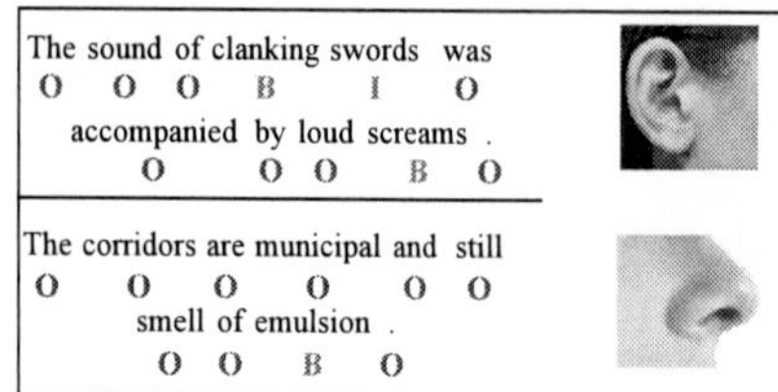

Figure 1: Example beginning-inside-outside (BIO) labeled sentences with mentions of sound (top) and smell (bottom) concepts.

cess for generating labeled data by leveraging large corpora and crowd-sourcing questionnaires. Third, using the resulting labeled data, we train standard machine learning methods (both linear model and memory neural network models), obtaining high accuracy on the task of extracting these previously under-explored relationships.

In summary, we propose minimal-effort approaches for obtaining labeled data on two key tasks: mention recognition, and relationship extraction for concepts pertaining to human senses. In the first, task we make use of Hearst patterns, and crowd sourcing, and for the second task, we make use of part-of-speech tag sequences and crowd-sourcing. Although these processes are not new, we have applied them to a novel setting of common sense about human senses, and showed their effectiveness. We trained standard machine learning methods, and showed that the labeled data generated by our processes lead to high quality models.

2 Recognizing Mentions of Human Senses

In this part of the work, we would like to detect mentions of concepts discernible by sense, we focus on mentions of *audible (sound)* and *olfactible (smell)* concepts. We treat sense recognition in text as a sequence labeling task where each sentence is a sequence of tokens labeled using the BIO tagging scheme (Ratinov and Roth, 2009). The BIO labels denote tokens at the *beginning, inside, and outside* of a relevant mention, respectively. Example BIO tagged sentences are shown in Figure 1.

2.1 Data Labeling Methodologies

There is a lack of easy to identify labeled data on the Web for common sense information extraction,

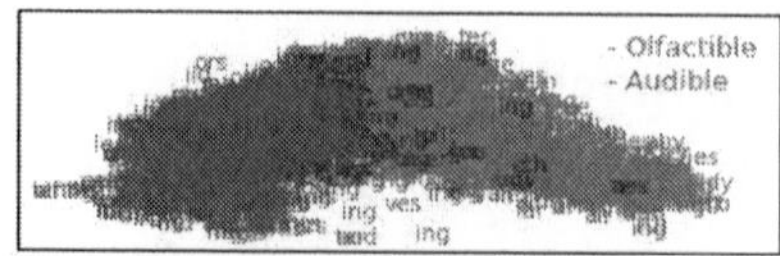

Figure 2: A PCA projection of the embeddings of audible and olfactible phrases labeled by the pattern approach.

an issue which affects named-entity centric information extraction to a lesser degree (Wang and Cohen, 2008; Wu and Weld, 2008). We consider three data labeling approaches: *i)* Automatically generate training data using judiciously specified patterns. *ii)* Solicit input on crowd-sourcing platforms. *iii)* Leverage both i) and ii) in order to overcome their respective limitations.

2.1.1 Pattern-based Corpus Labeling

To label data with patterns, we begin by specifying patterns that we apply to a large corpus. For our concepts of interest, sound, and smell, we specify the following two patterns. " sound of <y>", and " smell of <y>", We then apply these patterns to a large corpus. In our experiments, we used the English part of ClueWeb09. [1]. The result is a large collection of occurrences such as: " sound of *breaking glass*", "smell of *perfume*", etc. The collections contains 134,473 sound phrases, and 18,183 smell phrases.

Figure 2, shows a 2D projection of the 300-dimensional word vectors[2] of the discovered audible and olfactible phrases. We see a strong hint of two clusters. We later provide a quantitative analysis of this data.

2.1.2 Crowd-Sourced Supervision

The second way of obtaining labeled data that we consider is crowd-sourcing. We used the Amazon Mechanical Turk crowd-sourcing platform.

Crowd Task Definition. To obtain labeled examples, we could do a "cold call" and ask crowd workers to list examples of phrases that refer to senses. However, such an approach requires crowd workers to think of examples without clues or memory triggers. This is time consuming and error prone. We propose to exploit a large corpus to obtain preliminary labeled data, making it possible to only need crowd workers to filter the data through a series of *"yes/no/notsure"* questions. These types of questions require little effort

---

[1] http://lemurproject.org/clueweb09/
[2] https://code.google.com/archive/p/word2vec/

	% Majority Yes	*Fleiss* κ
Audible	73.4%	0.51
Olfactible	89.6%	0.33

Table 1: Crowd-sourced labeling of phrases generated by the pattern approach of section 2.1.1.

from crowd workers while mitigating the amount of noisy input that one could get from open-ended questions. We randomly selected 1000 phrases labeled by the pattern approach as described in Section 2.1.1 to be sound/smell phrases, 500 for each sense type. Each phrase was given to 3 different workers to annotate *"yes/no/notsure"*. We consider a phrase to be a true mention of the labeled sense if the majority of the participants chose "yes". This annotation task serves two purposes: 1) to provide us with human labeled examples of sound and smell concepts ii) to provide a quantitative evaluation of pattern generated labels. **Crowd Annotation Results.** Table 1 is a summary of the annotation results. First, we can see that the accuracy of the patterns is quite high, which was hinted at in Figure 2. Second, The inter-annotator agreement rates are moderate, but lower for olfactible phrases. This is also reflected by the fact that there were around 3 times as many "not sure" responses in the smell annotations as there were in the sound annotation task (27 vs 10). Nonetheless, the output of these tasks provide us with another option for labeled data that we can use to train our models.

2.1.3 Joint Pattern & Crowd-Sourced Labeling

A third way of obtaining labeled data is to leverage both pattern-based and crowd-sourced labeling approaches. One central question pertains to how we can combine the two sources in a way that exploits the advantages of each approach while mitigating their limitations. We seek to start with the crowd-sourced labeled, which is small but more accurate, and expand it with the pattern-generated labeled data, which is large but less accurate. We define a function that determines how to expand the data. Let $x_i^c \in D^c$ be a crowd labeled phrase, and $x_i^p \in D^p$ be a pattern labeled phrase. Then x_i^p is added to our training labeled data D^{pc} if $sim(x_i^c, x_i^p) >= \alpha$ where sim is the cosine similarity between the vector representations of the phrases. For vector representations of phrases, we

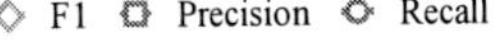
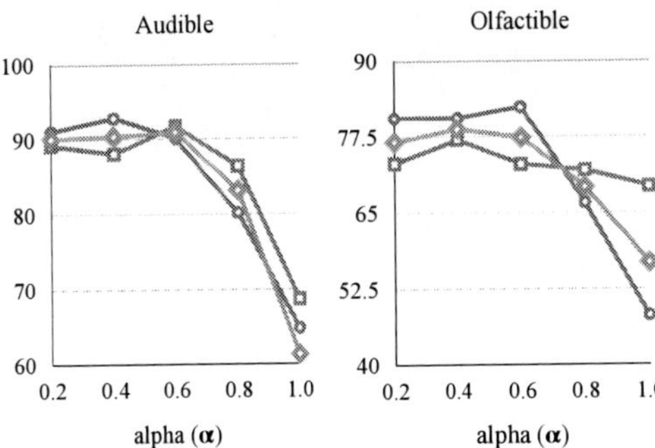

Figure 3: Performance as α is varied to control size and accuracy of labeled data.

use the same pre-trained Google word embeddings as those used to plot Figure 2. For phrases longer than one word, we use vector averaging. The effect of varying α, for a fixed prediction model, can be seen in Figure 3. When $\alpha = 1$, that is we are only using the crowd-sourced labeled data, performance is at its worst. This is because even though the human labeled data is more accurate, it is much smaller, leading to potential model overfitting problems. A more subtle finding is that with low α values (i.e., <0.4 for audible concepts), we have the highest recall, but not the best precision, this can be explained by the fact that, with low α values, we are allowing more of the automatically labeled data to be part of the training data, thereby potentially adding noise to the model. However, the advantage of the mixture approach comes from the fact that, there comes a point where precision goes up, recall slightly degrades but we obtain the best F1 score. In Figure 3, we see these points at $\alpha = 0.6$ and $\alpha = 0.4$ for the audible and olfactible concepts respectively. We use these values to generate the labeled data used to train models described in the rest of the paper.

2.2 Learning Models

We treat sense recognition in text as sequence prediction problem, we would like to estimate: $P(y_i | x_{i-k}, ..., x_{i+k}; y_{i-l}, ..., y_{i-1})$. where x refers to words, and y refers to BIO labels.

Conditional Random Fields (CRFs) (Lafferty et al., 2001) have been widely used named entity recognition (Ratinov and Roth, 2009; Finkel et al., 2005), a task similar to our own. While the CRF models performed reasonably well on our task, we sought to obtain improvements by training variations of Long Short Memory (LSTM) re-

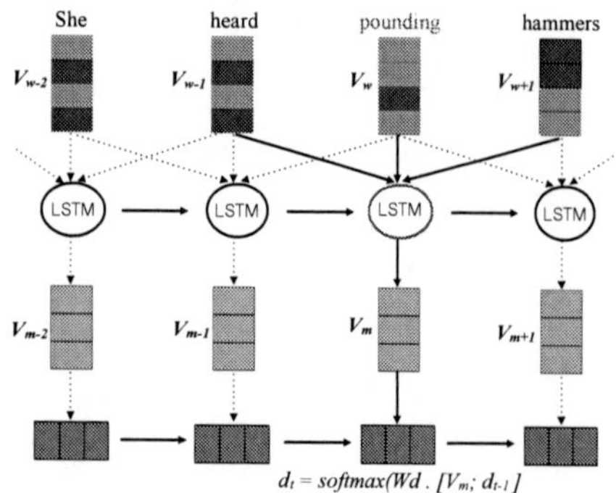

Figure 4: Our neural network architecture for the task of recognizing concepts that are discernible by sens-esss.

Sound	Smell
honking cars	burning rubber
snoring	chlorine
gunshots	citrus blossoms
live music	fresh paint

Table 2: Examples of sound and smell concepts recognized by our method.

current neural networks (Hochreiter and Schmidhuber, 1997). We found variations of LSTM sequence classifiers to do better than the CRF model, and also better than standard LSTMs. In particular, the well-studied combination of CRF and LSTMs works better.

Word and Character Features. As input, the LSTM neural network model takes a sentence and, as output, produces a probability distribution over the BIO tags for each word in the sentence. To BIO tag each word in the sentence, we use word features. We chose the word features to be their word embeddings. As additional features, we model the character composition of words in order to capture morphology. Neural encodings of character-level features have been shown to yield performance gains in natural language tasks (Ling et al., 2015; Chiu and Nichols, 2016). In all our experiments, we initialize the word embeddings with the Google news pre-trained word embeddings [3]. The character embeddings are learned from scratch.

Prediction and Output Layer Recurrence. We represent each word as a mention within a short context window of length m. We use the LSTM to encode these windows contexts in order to make a prediction for each word. The LSTM window encoding is then used to make predictions over the BIO labels. The output for each word is decoded by a linear layer and a *softmax* layer into probabilities over the BIO tag labels. Crucially, we modify the standard LSTM by modeling temporal dependencies by introducing a recurrence in the output layer. Therefore, the prediction d_t

at time step t takes into account the prediction d_{t-1} at the previous time t-1. Formally, we have: $d_t = \text{softmax}(W_d \cdot [v_m; v_{c_a}; v_s; d_{t-1}])$, where $\text{softmax}(z_i) = e^{z_i} / \sum_j e^{z_j}$. We illustrate the model in Figure 4. We found this model to consistently perform well on the senses of sound and smell.

Model Evaluation. To evaluate the models, we set aside 200 of the 1000 crowd-annotated phrases as test data, meaning we have 100 test instances for each sense type (sound/smell). The rest of the data, 400 per sense type was used for generating training data using the combined crowd and pattern approach described in Section 2.1.3. We set $\alpha = 0.6$ and $\alpha = 0.4$, based on Figure 3, for audible and olfactible concepts respectively. With these α values, the combination approach produced *1,962* and *1,702* training instances for audible and olfactible concepts respectively

Performance of the various models is shown in Table 3. The abbreviations denote the following: **LSTM** refers to a vanilla LSTM model, using only word embeddings as features, **+ OR** refers to the LSTM plus the output recurrence, **+ CHAR** refers to the LSTM plus the character embeddings as features. **+ OR + CHAR** refers to the LSTM plus the output recurrence and character embeddings as features. For the **CRF**, we use the commonly used features for named entity recognition: words, prefix/suffices, and part-of-speech tag (Ratinov and Roth, 2009). We can see that for both senses, the model that uses both character embedding features, and an output recurrence layer yields the best F1 score. Examples of sounds and smells our method can recognize are shown in Table 2.

2.3 Sense Mention Recognition Related Work

Our task is related to entity recognition however in this paper we focused on novel types of entities, which can be used to improve extraction of common sense knowledge. Entity recognition systems are traditionally based on a sequen-

---

[3] https://code.google.com/p/word2vec/

Method	F1	P	R
	Audible		
CRF	89.38	87.83	90.99
LSTM	89.64	88.87	90.42
+ OR	89.780	88.60	90.99
+CHAR	87.78	88.18	87.39
+ OR + CHAR	**90.91**	91.740	90.09
	Olfactible		
CRF	75.73	79.59	72.22
LSTM	69.96	62.96	78.70
+ OR	78.380	76.320	80.56
+ CHAR	69.57	60.69	81.48
+ OR + CHAR	**78.73**	76.990	80.56

Table 3: Performance of the various models on the task of sense recognition.

tial model, for example a CRF, and involve feature engineering (Lafferty et al., 2001; Ratinov and Roth, 2009). Like other neural approaches, our approach does not require feature engineering (Hammerton, 2003; Collobert et al., 2011; dos Santos and Guimarães, 2015; Chiu and Nichols, 2016; Shimaoka et al., 2016), the only features we use are word and character embeddings. The work of (Lample et al., 2016) introduced a CRF on top of LSTM for the task of named entity recognition.

2.4 Summary on Sense Mention Recognition

We have presented a method for recognizing concepts that are discernible by sense by proposing a process for collecting data, and then training standard machine learning methods. The concepts our method recognizes present opportunities for discovering additional types of common sense knowledge, for example, learning relationships that encode information such as which objects produce which sounds, in which environments can certain sounds be found, what is the sentiment of various types of smell, etc. These type of relations can significantly improve coverage of common sense in knowledge bases, thereby improving their utility. We explore this direction in the next section.

3 Relationships for Concepts Discernible By Sense

Now that we have a way of recognizing mentions of sense concepts in text, we can move on to relationships between such concepts.

To focus our task, we consider three rela-

tions pertaining to sense perception of sound and smell. Namely: 1) *soundSourceRelation*, 2) *soundSceneRelation*, and 3) *smellSentimentRelation*.

3.1 Sound-Source Relationship

The sound-source relationship represents information pertaining to which objects produce which sounds. For example, that planes and birds are capable of *flying*, the wind *blows*, and geckos *bark*. Obtaining sufficient labeled data to learn an extractor for this relationship is non-trivial, we propose one approach in the next section.

Labeled Data Generation. One option for obtaining labeled data is to directly request for it on crowd-sourcing platform by asking crowd workers to list examples of sounds and their sources. However, such an approach requires crowd workers to think of examples without clues or memory triggers. This is time consuming and error prone. Therefore, as we did in the recognition task, we again propose to exploit a large corpus to obtain preliminary labeled data. This way, we again only need crowd workers to filter the data through a series of *"yes/no/notsure"* questions. These type of questions require little effort from crowd workers while mitigating the amount of noisy input that one could get from open-ended questions.

To pose *"yes/no/notsure"* questions, we need a list of plausible sound-source pairs. To this end, we propose a lightly supervised corpus-based technique. First, we identify which phrases refer to sounds using the approach described in the first Section 2

One important observation we made was that about 20,000 (15%) of the 134,471 phrases are bigrams of the form: "verb noun" or "noun verb" where in both cases, the verb is in the gerund or present participle V-*ing* form. For example, *birds chirping, cars honking, squealing brakes*, etc. From phrases of this kind, we create verb-noun pairs, that we treat as plausible sound-source pairs where the verb is the *sound* and the noun is the *source*. We then asked crowd-workers to decide if the source (noun) produces the sound (verb). Thus from "birds chirping" we generate the question, "Is *chirping* a sound produced by *birds*?"; Negative examples include: "surrounding nature", and "Standing ovation", i.e., standing is not a sound made by ovation. We generated 634 such questions, from which we obtained a moderate inter-

	$Fleiss\ \kappa$
soundSource	0.57
soundEnvironment	0.35
smellSentiment	0.43

Table 4: Fleiss κ. inter-annotator agreement rates for the three relations on yes/no type crowd-sourcing tasks.

Learning Model	Accuracy
LM: LSTM encoder	**0.90**
LM: (Source - Target)	0.88
LM: (Target - Source)	0.87
LM: Vector Concatenation	0.83
MM: 1 hop	0.87
MM: 3 hops	0.85

Table 5: Accuracy of the linear models (LM) and memory networks models (MM) on the sound-source relation.

annotator agreement rate of Fleiss $\kappa = 0.57$, see Table 4. We use the resulting labeled data to train two types of learning methods.

Linear Learning Model. The learning problem for the sound-source relationship is as follows: given a bi-gram phrase n of the form "verb noun" or "noun verb", we wish to classify yes or no if a given noun, denoted by w_{src}, produces the verb, denoted by word w_{snd}, as a sound. As a simple linear solution to this problem, we train a logistic regression classifier. The features we use are the vectors representing the word embeddings of w_{src} and w_{snd}, denoted by v_{src}, and v_{snd}. In our experiments, we use the 300-dimensional Google News pre-trained embeddings [4]. There are several ways in which we combine v_{src}, and v_{snd} into a single feature vector:

Vector Concatenation: $v = concat(v_{src}, v_{snd})$
Size of v, $|v| = |v_{src}| + |v_{snd}|$
LSTM encoder : $v = lstm(v_{src}, v_{snd})$
An LSTM (Hochreiter and Schmidhuber, 1997) recurrent neural network is used to encode the phrase containing v_{src} and v_{snd}. $|v| = h$, where h is the hidden layer size of the neural network.
Source minus sound: $v = v_{src} - v_{snd}$
$|v| = |v_{src}| = |v_{snd}|$
Sound minus source: $v = v_{snd} - v_{src}$
$|v| = |v_{src}| = |v_{snd}|$

Memory Networks Learning Model. In addition to the variations of the linear model, we also trained a non-linear model in the form of memory networks (Sukhbaatar et al., 2015). Memory networks combine their inference component with a memory component. The memory component serves as a knowledge base or history vault to recall words or facts from the past. For the task of relation extraction, the memory network model learns a scoring function to rank relevant memories (words) with respect to how much they express a given relationship. This is done for a given argument pair as a query, i.e., a sound-source

pair. At prediction time, the model finds k relevant memories (words) according to the scoring function and conditions its output on these memories. In our experiments, we explore different values of k, effectively changing how many memories (words), the model conditions on. We report results for up to $k = 3$ as we did not see improvements for larger values of k.

Sound-Source Evaluation. Both the linear model and the memory networks models were implemented using Tensorflow. For the memory networks, we implemented the end-to-end version as described in (Weston et al., 2014; Sukhbaatar et al., 2015). Of the 634 crowd-sourced labeled examples described, we used 100 as test data, the rest as training data. Model parameters such as hidden layer size of the memory networks were tuned using cross-validation on the training data. As shown in Table 2, we obtain high accuracy across all models. The best performing model is a linear model with an LSTM encoding of the sound phrases, achieving accuracy of 90%. Surprisingly, we could not obtain better results with the memory networks model. Increasing the memory size or the number of hops (how often we iterate over the memories) did not help. One possible reason is the size of our training data, in previous work (Weston et al., 2014; Sukhbaatar et al., 2015), the memory networks were trained on 1,000 or more examples per problem type whereas our training data is half the size. Nevertheless, the memory networks module still produces good accuracy, with best performance of 87%.

3.2 Sound-Scene Relationship

The sound-scene relationship represents information about which sounds are found in which scenes. For example, birds chirping can be found in a forest. Therefore, this kind of information can

---

[4] https://code.google.com/archive/p/word2vec/

also be used in context recognition systems (Eronen et al., 2006), in addition to providing common sense knowledge that could be useful in language understanding tasks.

Labeled Data Generation. We would like to obtain labeled data in the form of scenes and their sounds. For example, (beach, waves crashing), (construction, hammering), (street, sirens), (street, honking cars). To obtain this type of labeled data, we again would like to only use *"yes/no/notsure"* crowd-sourcing questions. To generate plausible sound-scene pairs, first we find all sentences that mention at least one scene and one sound concept. To detect sound concepts, we use the approach described in Section 2. To detect mentions of scenes, we specified a list of 36 example scenes, which includes scenes such as beach, park, airport most of our scenes are part of the list of acoustic scenes from a scene classification challenge [5]. For every sentence that mentions both an acoustic scene and a sound concept, we apply a dependency parser[6]. This step produces dependencies that form a directed graph, with words being nodes and dependencies being edges.

Dependency graph shortest paths between entities have been found to be a good indicator of relationships between entities (Xu et al., 2015; Nakashole et al., 2013b). We use shortest paths as features in order classify sound-scene pairs. To obtain training data, we sort the paths by frequency, that is, how often we have seen the path occur with different sound-scene pairs. We then consider pairs that occur with frequent shortest paths to be plausible sound-scene pairs which we can present to crowd-workers in *"yes/no/notsure"* questions. We randomly selected 584 sound-scene pairs, and the corresponding sentences that mention them, which were then presented to crowd workers in questions. The inter-annotator agreement rate on this task is Fleiss $\kappa = 0.35$, see Table 4.

Learning Models and Evaluation. For the linear model, we consider three options for features. *Shortest Paths (SP)*: LSTM encoding of the dependency shortest path. *Sentence (S)*: an LSTM encoding of the sentence. *SP + S*: encoding of both the shortest path and the sentence are used as features. For the memory network models, we considered using the contents of both the shortest

[5]http://www.cs.tut.fi/sgn/arg/dcase2016/
[6]https://pypi.python.org/pypi/practnlptools/1.0

Learning Model	Accuracy
LM: shortest path	**0.81**
LM: shortest path +sentence:	0.80
LM: sentence	0.75
MM: 1 hop	0.75
MM: 3 hops	0.80

Table 6: Accuracy on the sound-scene relation.

Learning Model	Accuracy
LM: LSTM encoder	**0.84**
LM: vector addition	0.81
MM: 1 hop	0.82
MM: 3 hops	0.82

Table 7: Accuracy on the sound-sentiment relation.

paths and the sentences to produce memories. We use 100 of the 584 labeled data for testing, the rest for training. The shortest paths performed better, for space reasons we omit the results of using sentences as memories. As shown in Table 6, the linear model with the shortest path achieves the best accuracy of 81%. However, the best performing memory networks model with 3 memory hops is not significantly worse at 80% accuracy.

3.3 Smell-Sentiment Relationship

For the smell-sentiment relationship, the goal is to extract information about which smells are considered pleasant, unpleasant or neutral. In general, sentiment is both subjective and context dependent. However, as we show through crowd-sourced annotations, there is substantial consensus even on sentiment of smells.

Labeled Data Generation. First we generate a list of plausible smells phrases, following a similar approach to Section 2. We then used these phrases to evaluate sentiment of smells in a Mechanical Turk task. We present a phrase within a sentence context. We then asked crowd workers to choose if the phrase refers to a smell that is *"pleasant/unpleasant/neutral/notsure/notasmell"*. We generated 600 such questions on which we obtained a moderate inter-annotator agreement rate of Fleiss $\kappa = 0.43$, see Table 4. While this is not a yes/no task, it is still a simple multiple choice task with the same advantages of the yes/no tasks as we described earlier.

Learning Models and Evaluation. We again use the same earning models. For the linear model, we consider two options for features. **LSTM encoder**: LSTM encoding of the smell phrase **Vector addition**: vector addition encoding of the smell phrase. For the memory network models, the contents of the sentence that mentions the phrases are stored as memories. We use 100 of the 600 labeled data for testing, the rest for training. As can be seen in Table 7, the linear model with LSTM encoded phrases achieved the highest accuracy of 84%.

3.4 Summary on Relationships

In this work, we extracted novel common sense relations, using standard machine learning methods. To obtain labeled data, we proposed a combination of large corpora, and multiple choice crowdsourced questions. These type of questions require little effort from crowd workers while mitigating the amount of noise one might get from open-ended questions. We have also proposed and trained models on this data, achieving high accuracy for all relations. Scaling up our approach to more relations is an exciting future direction for our work. Scale is not expected to be prohibitive, given the minimally-supervised nature of our approach.

4 Conclusion

Cyc (Lenat, 1995), and ConceptNet (Havasi et al., 2007) are well-known examples of knowledge bases of everyday common sense knowledge. These projects are decades long efforts involving either experts or crowd-sourcing. Other knowledge bases focus on facts about named entities such as people, locations, and companies (Bollacker et al., 2008; Hoffart et al., 2012; Mitchell et al., 2015). Common sense contained in these knowledge bases is still limited . We considered the problem of extracting from text commonsense knowledge pertaining to human senses such as sound and smell. We proposed minimal-effort approaches for obtaining labeled data on two key tasks: mention recognition, and relationship extraction. In the first task we make use of Hearst patterns, and crowd sourcing, and for the second task, we make use of part-of-speech tag sequences and crowd-sourcing. Although these processes are not new, we have applied them to a novel setting of common sense about human senses, and showed their effectiveness. We trained standard machine learning methods, and showed that the labeled data generated by our processes lead to high quality models.

In the future, we would like to apply our methods to a broader class of common sense assertion, and to go develop novel machine learning methods that improve accuracy on both of these tasks.

References

Yoshua Bengio, P. Simard, and Paolo Frasconi. 1994. Learning long-term dependencies with gradient descent is difficult. *IEEE Transactions on Neural Networks. Special Issue on Recur.*

Kurt Bollacker, Colin Evans, Praveen Paritosh, Tim Sturge, and Jamie Taylor. 2008. Freebase: A collaboratively created graph database for structuring human knowledge. In *SIGMOD*, SIGMOD '08, pages 1247–1250.

Sergey Brin. 1998. Extracting patterns and relations from the world wide web. In *WebDB*, pages 172–183.

Jason P. C. Chiu and Eric Nichols. 2016. Named entity recognition with bidirectional lstm-cnns. *TACL*, 4:357–370.

Ronan Collobert, Jason Weston, Léon Bottou, Michael Karlen, Koray Kavukcuoglu, and Pavel P. Kuksa. 2011. Natural language processing (almost) from scratch. *Journal of Machine Learning Research*, 12:2493–2537.

Antti J Eronen, Vesa T Peltonen, Juha T Tuomi, Anssi P Klapuri, Seppo Fagerlund, Timo Sorsa, Gaëtan Lorho, and Jyri Huopaniemi. 2006. Audio-based context recognition. *Audio, Speech, and Language Processing, IEEE Transactions on*, 14:321–329.

Christaine Fellbaum. 1998. A semantic network of English verbs. In *WordNet: An Electronic Lexical Database*, pages 69–104. The MIT Press.

Jenny Rose Finkel, Trond Grenager, and Christopher D. Manning. 2005. Incorporating non-local information into information extraction systems by gibbs sampling. In *ACL*.

James Hammerton. 2003. Named entity recognition with long short-term memory. In *HLT-NAACL*, pages 172–175.

Catherine Havasi, Robert Speer, and Jason Alonso. 2007. Conceptnet 3: a flexible, multilingual semantic network for common sense knowledge. In *RANLP*, pages 27–29.

Marti A. Hearst. 1992. Automatic acquisition of hyponyms from large text corpora. In *COLING*, pages 539–545.

Sepp Hochreiter and Jürgen Schmidhuber. 1997. Long short-term memory. *Neural Computation*, 9(1):1–42.

Johannes Hoffart, Fabian M. Suchanek, Klaus Berberich, and Gerhard Weikum. 2012. YAGO2: A spatially and temporally enhanced knowledge base from Wikipedia. *Artificial Intelligence*, 194:28–61.

Johannes Hoffart, Mohamed Amir Yosef, Ilaria Bordino, Hagen Fürstenau, Manfred Pinkal, Marc Spaniol, Bilyana Taneva, Stefan Thater, and Gerhard Weikum. 2011. Robust disambiguation of named entities in text. In *Proceedings of the 2011 Conference on Empirical Methods in Natural Language Processing, EMNLP 2011, 27-31 July 2011, John McIntyre Conference Centre, Edinburgh, UK, A meeting of SIGDAT, a Special Interest Group of the ACL*, pages 782–792.

Anurag Kumar, Bhiksha Raj, and Ndapandula Nakashole. 2017. Discovering sound concepts and acoustic relations in text. In *2017 IEEE International Conference on Acoustics, Speech and Signal Processing (ICASSP)*, pages 631–635. IEEE.

Matthieu Labeau, Kevin Löser, and Alexandre Allauzen. 2015. Non-lexical architecture for fine-grained POS tagging. In *EMNLP, 2015*, pages 232–237.

John D. Lafferty, Andrew McCallum, and Fernando C. N. Pereira. 2001. Conditional random fields: Probabilistic models for segmenting and labeling sequence data. In *ICML*, pages 282–289.

Guillaume Lample, Miguel Ballesteros, Sandeep Subramanian, Kazuya Kawakami, and Chris Dyer. 2016. Neural architectures for named entity recognition. In *NAACL HLT 2016, The 2016 Conference of the North American Chapter of the Association for Computational Linguistics: Human Language Technologies, San Diego California, USA, June 12-17, 2016*, pages 260–270.

Douglas B. Lenat. 1995. Cyc: A large-scale investment in knowledge infrastructure. *Commun. ACM*, 38(11).

Wang Ling, Chris Dyer, Alan W. Black, Isabel Trancoso, Ramon Fermandez, Silvio Amir, Luís Marujo, and Tiago Luís. 2015. Finding function in form: Compositional character models for open vocabulary word representation. In *EMNLP*, pages 1520–1530.

Tom M. Mitchell, William W. Cohen, Estevam R. Hruschka Jr., Partha Pratim Talukdar, Justin Betteridge, Andrew Carlson, Bhavana Dalvi Mishra, Matthew Gardner, Bryan Kisiel, Jayant Krishnamurthy, Ni Lao, Kathryn Mazaitis, Thahir Mohamed, Ndapandula Nakashole, Emmanouil Antonios Platanios, Alan Ritter, Mehdi Samadi, Burr Settles, Richard C. Wang, Derry Tanti Wijaya, Abhinav Gupta, Xinlei Chen, Abulhair Saparov, Malcolm Greaves, and Joel Welling. 2015. Never-ending learning. In *AAAI*, pages 2302–2310.

Ndapandula Nakashole, Tomasz Tylenda, and Gerhard Weikum. 2013a. Fine-grained semantic typing of emerging entities. In *Proceedings of the 51st Annual Meeting of the Association for Computational Linguistics, ACL*, pages 1488–1497.

Ndapandula Nakashole, Gerhard Weikum, and Fabian M. Suchanek. 2013b. Discovering semantic relations from the web and organizing them with PATTY. *SIGMOD Record*, 42(2):29–34.

Ndapandula T Nakashole. 2012. Automatic extraction of facts, relations, and entities for web-scale knowledge base population.

Lev-Arie Ratinov and Dan Roth. 2009. Design challenges and misconceptions in named entity recognition. In *CoNLL*, pages 147–155.

Cícero Nogueira dos Santos and Victor Guimarães. 2015. Boosting named entity recognition with neural character embeddings. *CoRR*, abs/1505.05008.

Sonse Shimaoka, Pontus Stenetorp, Kentaro Inui, and Sebastian Riedel. 2016. An attentive neural architecture for fine-grained entity type classification. *arXiv preprint arXiv:1604.05525*.

Sainbayar Sukhbaatar, Arthur Szlam, Jason Weston, and Rob Fergus. 2015. End-to-end memory networks. In *Advances in Neural Information Processing Systems 28: Annual Conference on Neural Information Processing Systems 2015, December 7-12, 2015, Montreal, Quebec, Canada*, pages 2440–2448.

Niket Tandon, Bhavana Dalvi, Joel Grus, Wen-tau Yih, Antoine Bosselut, and Peter Clark. 2018. Reasoning about actions and state changes by injecting commonsense knowledge. In *Proceedings of the 2018 Conference on Empirical Methods in Natural Language Processing,*, pages 57–66.

Niket Tandon, Gerard de Melo, and Gerhard Weikum. 2011. Deriving a web-scale common sense fact database. In *AAAI*.

Niket Tandon, Gerard de Melo, and Gerhard Weikum. 2014. Acquiring comparative commonsense knowledge from the web. In *AAAI*, pages 166–172.

Richard C. Wang and William W. Cohen. 2008. Iterative set expansion of named entities using the web. In *Proceedings of the 8th IEEE International Conference on Data Mining (ICDM 2008), December 15-19, 2008, Pisa, Italy*, pages 1091–1096.

Jason Weston, Sumit Chopra, and Antoine Bordes. 2014. Memory networks. *arXiv preprint https://arxiv.org/abs/1410.3916*.

Derry Tanti Wijaya, Ndapandula Nakashole, and Tom Mitchell. 2015. "a spousal relation begins with a deletion of engage and ends with an addition of divorce": Learning state changing verbs from wikipedia revision history. In *Proceedings of the 2015 conference on empirical methods in natural language processing*, pages 518–523.

Fei Wu and Daniel S. Weld. 2008. Automatically refining the wikipedia infobox ontology. In *Proceedings of the 17th International Conference on World Wide Web, WWW 2008, Beijing, China, April 21-25, 2008*, pages 635–644.

Yan Xu, Lili Mou, Ge Li, Yunchuan Chen, Hao Peng, and Zhi Jin. 2015. Classifying relations via long short term memory networks along shortest dependency paths. In *Proceedings of the 2015 Conference on Empirical Methods in Natural Language Processing, EMNLP 2015, Lisbon, Portugal, September 17-21, 2015*, pages 1785–1794.

Extracting Common Inference Patterns from Semi-Structured Explanations

Sebastian Thiem and **Peter Jansen**
School of Information, University of Arizona
{sthiem,pajansen}@email.arizona.edu

Abstract

Complex questions often require combining multiple facts to correctly answer, particularly when generating detailed explanations for why those answers are correct. Combining multiple facts to answer questions is often modeled as a "multi-hop" graph traversal problem, where a given solver must find a series of interconnected facts in a knowledge graph that, taken together, answer the question and explain the reasoning behind that answer. Multi-hop inference currently suffers from semantic drift, or the tendency for chains of reasoning to "drift" to unrelated topics, and this semantic drift greatly limits the number of facts that can be combined in both free text or knowledge base inference. In this work we present our effort to mitigate semantic drift by extracting large high-confidence multi-hop inference patterns, generated by abstracting large-scale explanatory structure from a corpus of detailed explanations. We represent these inference patterns as sets of generalized constraints over sentences represented as rows in a knowledge base of semi-structured tables. We present a prototype tool for identifying common inference patterns from corpora of semi-structured explanations, and use it to successfully extract 67 inference patterns from a "matter" subset of standardized elementary science exam questions that span scientific and world knowledge.

1 Introduction

Combining separate pieces of knowledge to answer complex natural language questions is a central contemporary challenge in natural language inference. For complex questions, a single passage in a corpus or single fact in a knowledge base is often insufficient to arrive at an answer, and multiple sentences or facts must be combined through some inference process. A benefit and goal of this "multi-hop" inference process is for the set of combined facts to form a human-readable explanation detailing why the inference and answer are correct.

Most recent approaches to combining knowledge to answer questions (e.g. Das et al., 2017; Jansen et al., 2017; Ding et al., 2019) model inference as a progressive construction, iteratively adding nodes (facts) one at a time to a graph that represents the inference (and explanation) required to answer a question. This approach suffers from the phenomenon of semantic drift (Fried et al., 2015), which is the observation that determining whether two facts can be meaningfully combined to answer a question is an extremely noisy process, and most often results in adding erroneous facts unrelated to answering a question that causes the inference to fail. A common signal to determine whether two facts might be combined is whether those facts have shared words or entities. For example, for a question asking about the possible *effects of sunlight on an ice cube*, a given solver might choose to meaningfully connect the facts *"melting means changing from a [solid] to a liquid by adding heat energy"* and *"water is a kind of [solid], called ice, at temperatures below 0°C"* on the shared word *solid*. Unfortunately, using shared words alone, either of these facts could also be connected to the fact *"sound travels fastest through a [solid]"*, which is irrelevant to answering this problem, and allows further traversals to unrelated facts about sound that can produce incorrect answers.

Jansen (2018) empirically demonstrated that combining facts based on lexical overlap has very low chance of success, which was measured at between 0.1% and 5% for elementary science questions, depending on the source corpus of the facts being retrieved. This is a significant limitation, as even elementary science questions require combining an average of 4 to 6 facts (and as many as 16 facts) that span scientific and common-sense or world knowledge in order to answer and provide

Proceedings of the First Workshop on Commonsense Inference in Natural Language Processing, pages 53–65
Hongkong, China, November 3, 2019. ©2019 Association for Computational Linguistics

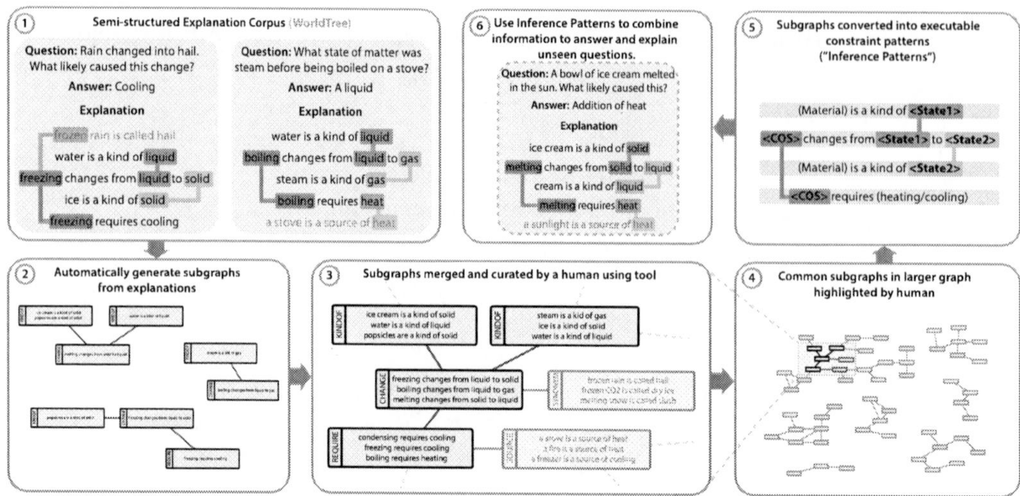

Figure 1: An overview of our inference pattern extraction approach. A corpus of semi-structured explanations (2) is preprocessed through a set of heuristics that generate a large number of small (often disconnected) subgraphs in a large graph (2). Those subgraphs are merged and curated (3). Inference patterns, or subgraphs of nodes can then be extracted from the curated graph, by the user (4). These patterns for executable constraint satisfaction patterns that can be executed over the knowledge base (5). In this work we address steps 2 through 5, whereas using these inference patterns to answer and explain unseen questions (6) is part of ongoing efforts.

a detailed explanation for their reasoning (Jansen et al., 2018, 2016), and such a low probability of successfully traversing the knowledge graph places strong limits on the length of inferences that can be made (Khashabi et al., 2019). In response to this challenge, a number of datasets such as Hot-potQA (Yang et al., 2018) and WorldTree (Jansen et al., 2018) have emerged to provide explicit gold explanations that serve as training and evaluation instruments for multi-hop inference models.

Jansen (2017) proposed combining "common explanatory patterns", or groups of frequently interconnected facts observed in explanations, as a possible means of mitigating the semantic drift associated with combining facts one at a time. Human-authored explanations contain meaningful connections between their component facts. Each edge in an explanatory pattern extracted from a human-authored explanation is a high-confidence edge that does not require a solver to use other more noisy signals (such as lexical overlap) to populate, reducing the opportunity for semantic drift. An empirical evaluation using the WorldTree explanation corpus demonstrated that this approach could in principle regenerate the majority of unseen gold explanation graphs by using only 2 or 3 hops between these "explanatory pattern" subgraphs, which is substantially fewer hops than the up to 16 hops required if aggregating single facts. The disadvan-

tages of this technique are that (a) it requires the (currently manual) construction of a large corpus of detailed explanations to learn these common explanatory patterns from, which is an expensive process, and (b) it requires developing automatic or semi-automatic methods to abstract the structure of training explanations to mitigate sparsity and allow known explanations to generalize to unseen scenarios.

In this work, we explore a hybrid human-in-the-loop method and tool for abstracting the structure of common explanatory patterns found in the WorldTree corpus of structured explanations. We use this tool to extract 67 inference patterns, specified as constraint satisfaction patterns over a knowledge base of tables, from detailed explanations to standardized elementary science exam questions. Our long-term interests are in generating a corpus of common inference patterns at scale, and constructing an inference system that combines and uses those patterns to answer questions and produce detailed explanations for its answers. Conceptually, this is similar to Explanation-Based Learning (De-Jong and Mooney, 1986; Baillargeon and DeJong, 2017), but using semi-structured text and constraint patterns instead of first-order logic. This approach is also similar to efforts at using scripts or semantic frames for inference (e.g. Wang et al., 2015; Ostermann et al., 2017), or automatically extracted proxies (e.g. Khashabi et al., 2018), though confined to the subdomain of elementary science, and semi-automatically extracted from semi-structured explanation graphs.

2 Approach and Workflow

The workflow describing our process of taking a corpus of semi-structured explanations through the inference pattern discovery process is described in Figure 1, with further details below.

2.1 Semi-Structured Explanation Corpus

Our technique for discovering inference patterns requires extracting these patterns from a pre-existing corpus of semi-structured explanations. We make use of the WorldTree explanation corpus[1] (Jansen et al., 2018), a set of 1,680 detailed explanation graphs for standardized elementary science questions. These questions represent the elementary (3rd through 5th grade) subset of the Aristo Reasoning Challenge (ARC) corpus[2] (Clark, 2015), a set of 4-choice multiple choice elementary and middle-school science questions drawn from 12 US states.

Each question in Worldtree is paired with an explanation graph composed of a set of facts that, taken together, provide a detailed explanation for why the answer to a given question is correct. Each "fact" is a natural language sentence that takes the form of a row in a knowledge base of 62 semi-structured tables containing a total of 4,950 unique rows. Each table centers around encoding a particular type of knowledge, such as taxonomic relations (e.g. *a bird is a kind of animal*), part-of relations (*a wing is a part of a bird*), property knowledge (*metals are electrical conductors*), or other more complex relations, such as changes (*boiling means changing from a liquid to a gas by adding heat energy*), coupled relationships (*as altitude increases, air pressure deceases*), causality (*bacteria can cause diseases by infecting organisms*), and if-then relationships (*if an animal relies on plants for food, then it must store enough food for winter*).

Each semi-structured table contains between 2 and 16 content columns, which form an $n - ary$ relation between the columns in a given row, and are often used by inference frameworks (e.g. Pasupat and Liang, 2015; Sun et al., 2016; Khashabi et al.,

2016) as they afford more fine-grained decomposition than triple representations (e.g. Etzioni et al., 2011; Schmitz et al., 2012) common in other inference methods (e.g. Das et al., 2017; Khot et al., 2017; Kwon et al., 2018). The knowledge base construction was data-driven, where each fact exists because it was authored to be used in at least one real explanation. As such, the knowledge base contains a mix of scientific and world knowledge, some of which is commonly found in other knowledge bases (e.g., taxonomic, part-of, used-for, Speer and Havasi, 2012; Tandon et al., 2017), while other kinds of knowledge (e.g. coupled relationships, how processes change actors, if-then relationships centered around elementary science concepts) are less common. When authoring explanations, the annotation protocol required annotators to attempt to reference existing rows (facts) first rather than create duplicate knowledge. The most highly reused row (*an animal is a kind of organism*) occurs in 89 different explanations, and 31% of rows in the knowledge base occur in more than one explanation. This suggests that a subset of core facts are frequently reused, but that some form of abstraction or generalization of explanations would be required for those core facts to connect to the 69% of facts used in only a single explanation, or to knowledge imported from other knowledge bases that is not currently used in any explanation.

2.2 Automatic Generation of Subgraphs

In this work we frame the process of discovering inference patterns as a process of clustering similar groups of facts together, and discovering meaningful connections between different groups of facts in the forms of constraints (see Figure 1, steps 2 to 5). These constraints take the form of edges between two tables, that can be satisfied by one row from each table having the same words in specific columns (see Figure 1, step 5, for an example).

Clustering Facts: Clustering similar facts requires recognizing that certain groups of facts tend to describe specific instances of a high-level process, even when those facts may have little or no lexical overlap with each other (as in grouping *"freezing means changing from a liquid to a solid"* and *"boiling means changing from a liquid to a gas"*, in the context of a *change of state of matter* process).

Discovering Connections: Discovering connections (i.e. edges) between two or more groups of facts that tend to occur together in gold explanation

---

[1] http://www.cognitiveai.org/explanationbank/
[2] http://www.allenai.org/data.html

Error Class
Sparsity in Explanation Annotation

Fact 1	**Friction** occurs when two **object's surfaces** move against each other
Fact 2	As an **object's** smoothness increases, it's **friction** will decrease when it's **surface** moves against another **surface**.
Issue	These facts are not observed together in a single question's explanation, so they are not connected.

Sparsity in Knowledge Base

Fact 1	If food is **cooked** then **heat** energy is added to that food.
Fact 2	A stove generates **heat** for **cooking**.
Missing	A campfire generates **heat** for **cooking**.
Issue	Missing facts in the knowledge base limit the generalization of patterns to new scenarios (e.g. campfire).

Permissiveness in automatically populated edges

Fact 1	Melting means changing from a solid to a liquid by adding heat **energy**
Fact 2	Wax is an electrical **energy** insulator
Issue	Creating edges based on shared words (here, **"energy"**) does not always generate meaningful connections.

Permissiveness in automatically populated column links

Fact 2	A tape **measure*** is used to **measure distance**.
Fact 2	centimeters (cm) are a unit used for **measuring** is **distance**.
Issue	Ideally this edge should generalize to all kinds of measuring tools and units (e.g. **X** is used to measure **Y**, **Z** is a unit for measuring **Y**). The connection between **tape measure*** in Fact 1 and **measure** in Fact 2 makes generalization unlikely, and should be removed.

Table 1: Example classes of errors when automatically generating inference pattern graphs. Fact 1 and Fact 2 represent facts (rows) drawn from the knowledge base of semi-structured tables. Boldface words represent lexical connections between those facts (edges between tables, on the specific columns those words occupy).

graphs. For example, facts about *change of state* processes *(freezing, boiling, melting, condensing)* may tend to connect to other groups of facts that discuss specific solids, liquids, or gasses that are undergoing the change of state (as in *"water is a kind of liquid"*, or *"ice is a kind of solid"*).

Our initial hypothesis was that it would be possible to extract a large corpus of inference patterns automatically from a sufficiently large and structured corpus of explanations. Instead, we discovered that both the clustering and connection processes are susceptible to a number of common opportunities for error (described in Table 1) that limit this process in practice. In addition to these error classes, we discovered challenges due to inference patterns existing at different levels of abstraction, with patterns at different levels of abstraction frequently overlapping. For example, a high-level domain-specific pattern might describe the process of *changing from one state of matter to another through the addition or subtraction of heat energy,* while describing *specific substances* and *sources of heat or cooling.* A substantially more low-level, domain-general, and common pattern in the corpus is taxonomic inheritance – the idea that if X is a kind of Y, and Y is a kind of Z, then X is a kind of Z (e.g. *a bird is a kind of animal, an animal is a kind of living thing, therefore a bird is a kind of living thing*). Similar low-level science-domain patterns are common (e.g. X is a kind of Y, Y is made of Z, as in *"an ice cube is a kind of object,*

and objects are made of matter"). High-level and low-level patterns frequently overlap – that is, a high-level pattern may contain one or more low-level patterns. This caused challenges for the pilot experiments in entirely automatic extraction, either "over-grouping" facts into a single pattern that a human annotator would likely consider different patterns, or vice-versa.

Because of the high-precision requirements of multi-hop inference, our pragmatic solution to the above technical challenge is to build a hybrid system that combines automatic and manual methods. First, a preprocessing system assembles and connects groups of facts using a set of minimal high-precision low-recall heuristics. We then provide the user with a graphical tool to streamline the workflow for manually editing groupings, adding or removing edges between groups of facts, and speeding the inspection and repair of any errors made by the automated heuristics. Summary statistics on the proportion of these changes and errors on our analysis are included in Table 2.

2.3 Merging and Curating Subgraphs

To facilitate the assembly of subgraphs into large high-quality inference patterns, we developed and iterated the graphical authoring tool shown in Figure 2. The tool includes four main components:

Graph View: The graph view allows the annotator to inspect the entire graph in its current state, and to merge nodes (that represent groups of facts/table

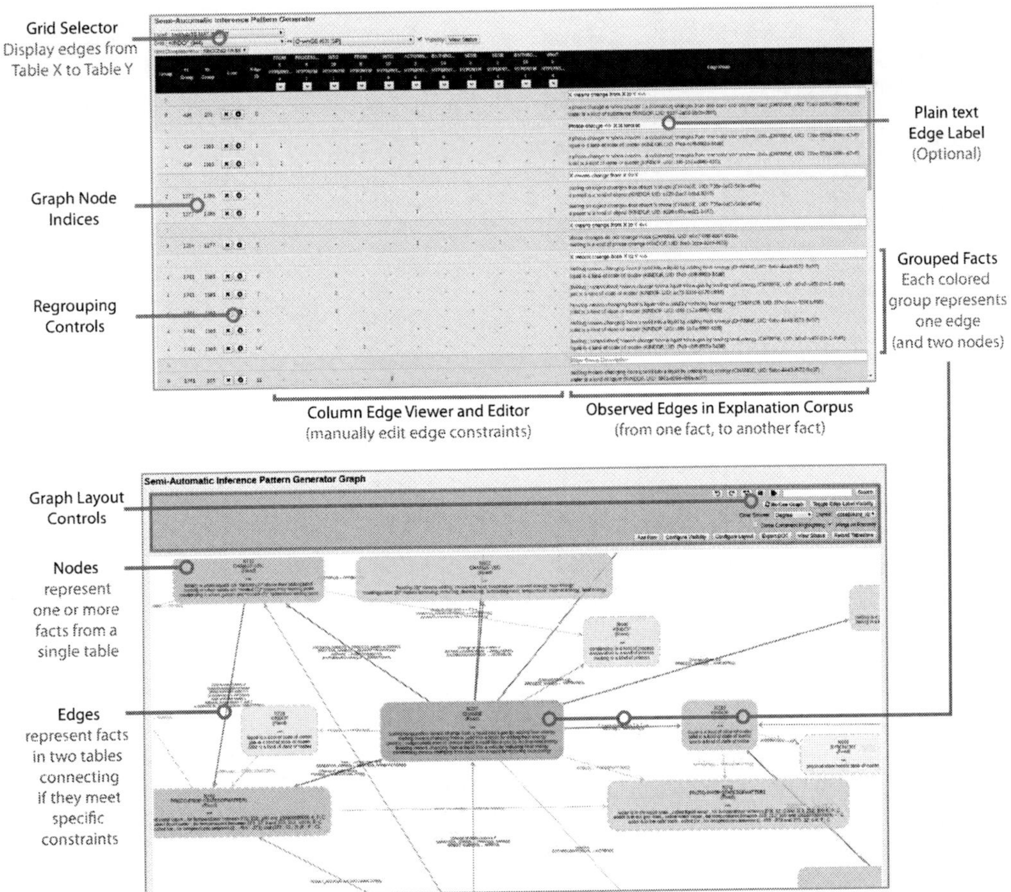

Figure 2: A screenshot of the grid view (top) and graph view (bottom) of our inference pattern extraction tool. The constraint view and the tablestore spreadsheet integration are not shown for space.

rows) together to perform the fact clustering procedure. The graph view also allows the annotator to highlight specific subgraphs to mark as inference patterns, which enables further functionality in the constraint view.

Grid View: The grid view enables the curation of the edges between nodes by visually displaying them in an interface that allows the user to (a) remove automatically populated edges that are not meaningful, (b) remove only part of edges (i.e. specific links between columns between two tables), and (c) manually edit the automatic clustering by dragging and dropping specific rows in one edge group either into another existing group, or into a new group.

Constraint View: Once a user has identified and marked a subgraph to extract as an inference pattern, the constraint view allows "running" that inference pattern to generate all possible sets of rows in the tablestore that satisfy that pattern's constraints. As subgraphs extracted directly from the large curated graph built from the explanation corpus tend to require edits to their nodes and constraints before they are generic and runnable inference patterns, the constraint view also includes a number of debugging tools to facilitate diagnosing constraints that are unable to be satisfied.[3]

Table View: The tool also includes an interface to a Google Sheet[4] storing a live copy of the Tablestore that the annotator can edit to refine existing knowledge, or incorporate additional knowledge, while curating and debugging inference patterns.

The tool runs in a Chrome browser window, and is implemented as a Javascript application with a node.js backend server. We make use of Cy-

---

[3] We include exports from the constraint view tool for all extracted patterns in our supplementary material.

[4] http://sheets.google.com

Measure	Count
Graph Nodes:	
Nodes before merging	700
Nodes after merging	540 (77%)
Graph Edges:	
Edges before curation	637
Edges after curation	771 (21%)
Grid Row-to-Row Connections:	
Row-to-row connections before curation	1384
Row-to-row connections modified	631 (46%)
Row-to-row connections removed	224 (16%)
Grid Edge Constraints:	
Edge constraints before curation	2101
Edge constraints removed	133 (6%)
Edge constraints marked optional	27 (1%)

Table 2: Manual edits done to the automatically generated graph and grid during the merging and curation steps. Values in parentheses represent percent change.

Inference Pattern	Nodes	Edges
Alloys	5	4
*Altitude**	8	10
Building requires measuring	11	13
Burning-Preventing Harm	12	15
Change of State	68	128
Chemical Changes	11	12
Containers contain things	6	6
Cooking Food	9	11
Electrical Conductivity	27	52
Friction	15	24
*General Motion**	3	3
*Ice Wedging**	4	4
*Long lasting vs replacing**	5	4
Magnetism	14	20
Manufacturers use mats. for products	5	5
Measurements	22	34
Navigation lost at sea	6	7
Physical Changes	13	14
Seeing	19	29
*Soil erosion**	6	6
*Solutions - Dissolving substances**	4	5
*Sources of Heat**	3	2
*Sunlight as a source of energy**	14	30
*Sunlight location and shadow size**	7	7
*Taste**	9	11
Taxonomic Inheritance	2	1
*Texture**	4	3
Thermal Conductivity	27	34
*Touch-Hardness**	4	3

Table 3: A list of high-level inference patterns discovered in the corpus of explanations for *Matter* science exam questions using this tool. A full list of patterns is provided in Table 5 (see `Appendix`). An asterisk (*) signifies patterns that are partial or otherwise limited in size because they overlap with other topics (e.g. from Earth or Life Science) not examined in this preliminary study.

toscape.js (Franz et al., 2015) as a graph visualization plugin, while primarily using the CoSE-Bilkent graph layout algorithm (Dogrusoz et al., 2009) modified to allow variable edge lengths based on the maximum degree of connected nodes to make the graph easier to visualize when assembling densely-connected patterns. The tool was iterated for usability to maximize throughput for the merging and curation steps, and includes functionality for quickly finding knowledge in the graph while seamlessly moving between graph (graphical) and grid (tabular) views, filtering subsets of nodes and edges by various metrics (completeness, table connection, user-selected utility rating), and keeping track of where the annotator is in the curation workflow. A Scala preprocessing tool reads in gold explanations (which can be filtered to include only subsets of questions by a question classification label, such as only *matter*, *energy*, or *life science* questions), applies the initial clustering heuristics, and outputs tab delimited files that are then read in by the tool. Edges between rows in WorldTree are determined by rows have overlapping content lemmas (defined as nouns, verbs, adjectives, or adverbs), with Stanford CoreNLP (Manning et al., 2014) used for lemmatization and POS tagging.

3 Preliminary Evaluation

To evaluate the utility of our approach, we made use of the tool to extract inference patterns present in all questions in the training subset of the WorldTree corpus categorized as belonging to the *Matter* topic, one of the 9 broad science curriculum categories of question topics, using the ARC question classification labels of Xu et al. (2019). This represents 43 of 902 (5%) of questions and explanations in the training corpus, covering topics such as Changes of State of Matter *(e.g. melting, boiling)*, Measuring Properties of Matter *(e.g. temperature, mass)*, Physical vs Chemical Changes *(e.g. length vs composition)*, Properties of Materials *(e.g. electrical or thermal conductivity, taste)*, Properties of Objects *(e.g. shape or volume)*, and Mixtures *(e.g. alloys)*.

3.1 Initial merging and curation

The preprocessing procedure generated 273 grids for this subset of the explanation corpus, representing the specific pairs of tables (e.g. KINDOF ↔ CHANGE) that have direct connections in the explanations for these questions. A total of 1,384 unique row-row connections populated these grids, and required manual verification. Summary statistics for the edits to these grids is shown in Table 2.

State of Matter (changing between states of known substances)

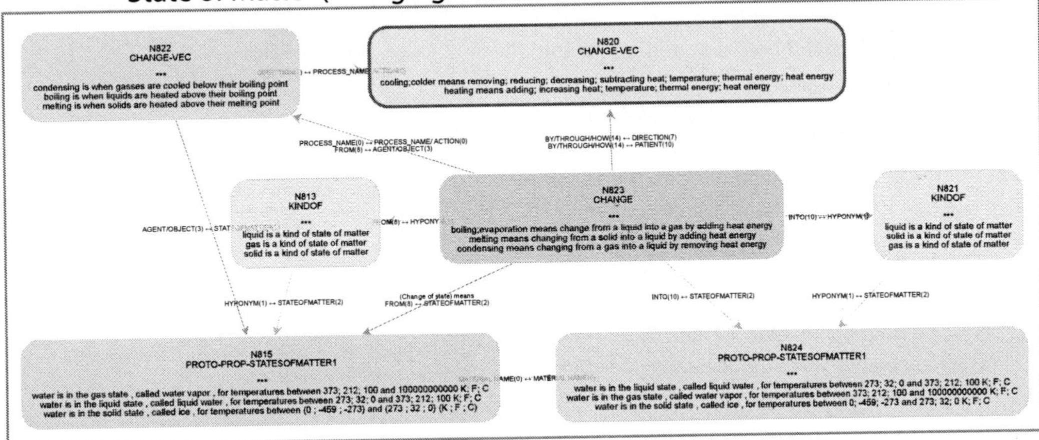

Phase Changes

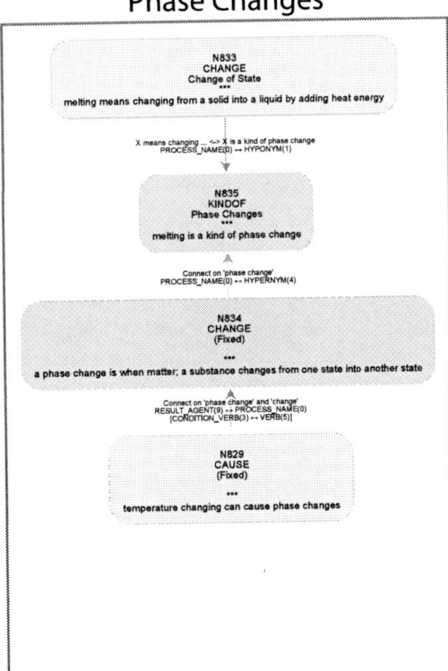

Alloys (composition)

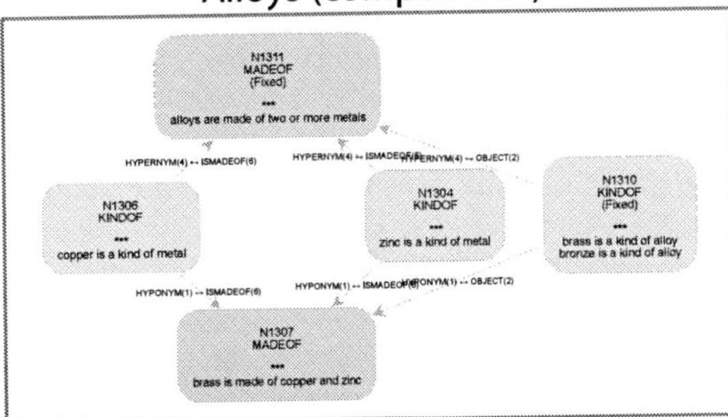

Containers contain objects/materials

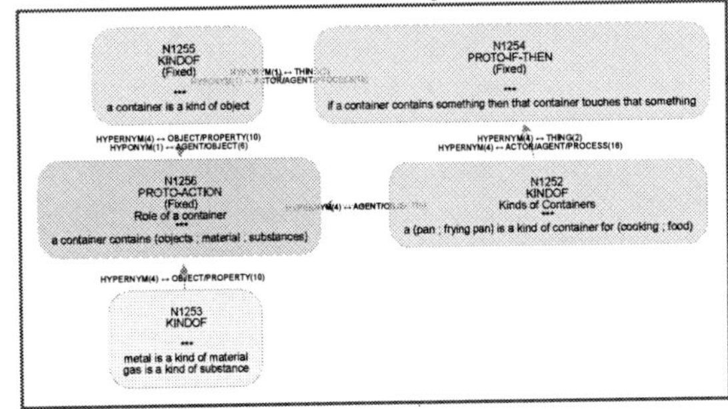

Animals see objects with eyes

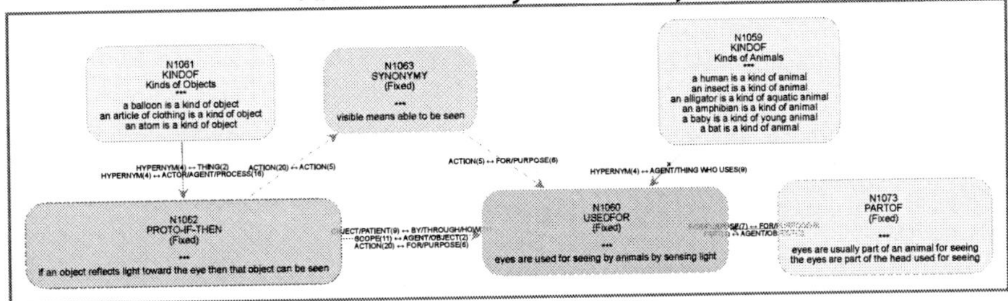

Figure 3: Example inference patterns extracted from the WorldTree explanation corpus using this tool. Nodes represent one or more example facts (table rows) from a specific table (e.g. CHANGE), and edges represent constraints between table rows that must be satisfied. Facts shown in nodes are examples, and not an exhaustive list of all rows that meet the constraints for a given inference pattern.

On average, each grid generally required minimal to moderate editing. Figure 4 (see `Appendix`) shows the full graph before and after the initial merging and curation process.

3.2 Extracting Inference Patterns

Due to it's size, the graph after merging and curation is included in the supplementary material. Manual inspection of the curated graph using the Graph View revealed 29 high-level inference patterns shown in Table 3, each containing between 3 and 66 nodes, and up to 107 edges.[5] These represent the high-level inferences being described in the *Matter* subset of the explanation corpus, and include scientific reasoning processes for topics such as *Measuring Properties with Instruments* and *Thermal Conductivity*, while also describing common world knowledge such as *Seeing*, *Tasting*, and *Cooking Food*. These world-knowledge-centered explanation patterns tend to be either directly required to answer questions (for example, about observing *material properties*), or to process the examples the questions are grounded in (such as *temperature* or *state changes* caused by cooking food). While high-level patterns can be classified as belonging more to scientific or world knowledge, the individual knowledge present in each pattern is generally a mix of both, including nodes that match either scientific knowledge (e.g. *"Matter in the gas phase has variable volume"*) or world knowledge at either a high-level (e.g., *"a balloon is a flexible container"*) or low-level (e.g., *"if a container contains something, then that container touches that something"*).

Examining the 29 high-level inference patterns, we further subdivided them into 38 smaller, more reusable component inference patterns that describe narrower inferences for a given problem domain. For example, the high-level *Change of State* inference pattern was subdivided into 3 smaller and more specialized patterns such as *Changing between states of known substances, Phase Changes,* and *Evaporating Liquids*, each containing between 4 and 9 nodes. Examples of these inference patterns are shown in Figure 3, while the full corpus of

---

[5]These large inference patterns (up to 66 nodes and 107 edges) represent large topical patterns generated from analyzing many questions on similar topics, and were not derived from any one question. In these cases, it is likely that only a small subset of these larger inference patterns would be used to answer a given question. We describe further subdividing these larger patterns into smaller reusable pieces further in Section 3.2.

Change of State

Freezing means changing from a liquid to a solid by reducing heat energy
A liquid is a kind of state of matter
Water is in the liquid state, called liquid water, for temperatures between 0 C and 100 C
A solid is a kind of state of matter
Water is in the solid state, called liquid water, for temperatures between -273 C and 0 C
Cooling means reducing heat energy
Freezing is when liquids are cooled below freezing point

Phase Changes

Boiling means changing from a liquid to a gas by adding heat energy
Boiling is a kind of phase change
A phase change is when a substance changes from one state to another state
Temperature changes can cause phase changes

Alloys

Alloys are made of two or more metals
Bronze is a kind of alloy
Bronze is made of copper and tin
Tin is a kind of metal
Copper is a kind of metal

Containers contain objects

A container is a kind of object
If a container contains something, then that container touches that something
A bowl is a kind of container
A container contains objects
A rock is a kind of object

Table 4: A small subset of example combinations of knowledge base facts that satisfy the constraints of inference patterns extracted from the explanation corpus. Each example was generated from the inference pattern, and is not found in the training corpus.

patterns generated is included in the supplementary material.

3.3 Executing constraint patterns

Our long-term goal is to use the extracted inference patterns to answer unseen questions, and enable generating detailed coherent multi-fact explanations for the reasoning behind those answers. We are currently building a scripting language and development environment for easily authoring and evaluating constraint-based inference patterns.

In the near-term, to evaluate the executability of each pattern, we incorporate a constraint satisfaction framework into the extraction tool allowing the user to test each extracted pattern by querying the tablestore knowledge base and enumerating valid combinations of table rows that satisfy the constraints of a given inference pattern. Our Javascript table constraint solver is able to process approximately 2 million constraint evaluations per second, which generally satisfies exhaustively testing small patterns in under one minute.[6] The graphical interface allows disabling subsections of larger inference patterns for speed to exhaustively test larger inference patterns piece-wise, or limiting specific nodes to only a small subset of possible facts to speed evaluation.

Examples of valid combinations of facts satisfying the extracted inference patterns in Figure 3 are shown in Table 4. Each of these short explanations was not observed in the training corpus, but rather was generated by satisfying the constraints of an inference pattern by querying the knowledge base, and could form explanations for unseen questions – either in whole, or as part of a combination of several patterns together (such as combining *Changes of State* and *Phase Changes*). At our current state of development, each inference pattern generally matches between one and several thousand unique patterns in the knowledge base, but precise counts are limited by the speed of our current constraint satisfaction solver.

4   Conclusion and Future Work

We present a method and tool for extracting inference patterns from corpora of explanations, where these inference patterns provide a mechanism to combine large amounts of knowledge with high-confidence. While this ability to combine facts into meaningful multi-fact patterns exceeds what is currently possible using contemporary algorithms for multi-hop reasoning, several challenges remain.

First, while significantly faster and more data-driven than our manual attempts at constructing inference patterns, the end-to-end process of constructing an explanation for a question, authoring knowledge base facts, merging and curating a central graph, extracting patterns from that graph, and debugging generic patterns currently comes at a significant labour cost – an average of approximately 2 hours per question[7] – that we are working to further reduce to allow the technique to scale. We hypothesize that a number of the time costs associated with this process scale sublinearly, and are currently working on demonstrating this by

refining the protocol and evaluating on an order-of-magnitude more explanations.

Second, while these inference patterns have utility for answering and explaining science exam questions, this needs to be empirically demonstrated by incorporating the patterns into a question answering system to measure the overall recall of this technique. We are actively pursuing both the construction of a corpus of science-domain explanation patterns, at scale, while concurrently developing methods of using these inference patterns to answer questions and provide compelling multi-fact explanations for their answers.

5   Supplementary Material

This work contains supplementary material, including additional tables and figures in the `Appendix` below, and a corpus of 67 extracted inference patterns available at `http://www.cognitiveai.org/explanationbank/`.

6   Acknowledgements

We thank Elizabeth Wainwright, Steven Marmorstein, Zhengnan Xie, and Jaycie Martin for contributions to the WorldTree explanation corpus, who were funded by the Allen Institute for Artificial Intelligence (AI2). This work is supported by the National Science Foundation (NSF Award #1815948, "Explainable Natural Language Inference", to PJ).

References

Renée Baillargeon and Gerald F DeJong. 2017. Explanation-based learning in infancy. *Psychonomic bulletin & review*, 24(5):1511–1526.

Peter Clark. 2015. Elementary school science and math tests as a driver for AI: take the aristo challenge! In *Proceedings of the Twenty-Ninth AAAI Conference on Artificial Intelligence, January 25-30, 2015, Austin, Texas, USA.*, pages 4019–4021. AAAI Press.

Rajarshi Das, Shehzaad Dhuliawala, Manzil Zaheer, Luke Vilnis, Ishan Durugkar, Akshay Krishnamurthy, Alex Smola, and Andrew McCallum. 2017. Go for a walk and arrive at the answer: Reasoning over paths in knowledge bases using reinforcement learning. *AKBC*.

Gerald DeJong and Raymond Mooney. 1986. Explanation-based learning: An alternative view. *Machine learning*, 1(2):145–176.

Ming Ding, Chang Zhou, Qibin Chen, Hongxia Yang, and Jie Tang. 2019. Cognitive graph for multi-hop reading comprehension at scale. *ACL*.

---

[6] We are currently developing a high-performance stand-alone constraint satisfaction solver for these types of lexicalized table-based constraint satisfaction problems.

[7] Approximate durations of the most time consuming steps (average per question): explanation construction: 15 minutes; merging/graph curation/high-level pattern identification: 45 minutes; subpattern identification/debugging: 45 minutes.

Ugur Dogrusoz, Erhan Giral, Ahmet Cetintas, Ali Civril, and Emek Demir. 2009. A layout algorithm for undirected compound graphs. *Information Sciences*, 179(7):980–994.

Oren Etzioni, Anthony Fader, Janara Christensen, Stephen Soderland, and Mausam Mausam. 2011. Open information extraction: The second generation. In *Proceedings of the 20th International Joint Conference on Artificial Intelligence (ICJAI)*, pages 3–10.

Max Franz, Christian T Lopes, Gerardo Huck, Yue Dong, Onur Sumer, and Gary D Bader. 2015. Cytoscape. js: a graph theory library for visualisation and analysis. *Bioinformatics*, 32(2):309–311.

Daniel Fried, Peter Jansen, Gustave Hahn-Powell, Mihai Surdeanu, and Peter Clark. 2015. Higher-order lexical semantic models for non-factoid answer reranking. *Transactions of the Association for Computational Linguistics*, 3:197–210.

Peter Jansen. 2018. Multi-hop inference for sentence-level textgraphs: How challenging is meaningfully combining information for science question answering? *TextGraphs*.

Peter Jansen, Niranjan Balasubramanian, Mihai Surdeanu, and Peter Clark. 2016. What's in an explanation? characterizing knowledge and inference requirements for elementary science exams. In *Proceedings of COLING 2016, the 26th International Conference on Computational Linguistics: Technical Papers*, pages 2956–2965, Osaka, Japan.

Peter Jansen, Rebecca Sharp, Mihai Surdeanu, and Peter Clark. 2017. Framing qa as building and ranking intersentence answer justifications. *Computational Linguistics*.

Peter Jansen, Elizabeth Wainwright, Steven Marmorstein, and Clayton Morrison. 2018. Worldtree: A corpus of explanation graphs for elementary science questions supporting multi-hop inference. In *Proceedings of the Eleventh International Conference on Language Resources and Evaluation (LREC-2018)*.

Peter A Jansen. 2017. A study of automatically acquiring explanatory inference patterns from corpora of explanations: Lessons from elementary science exams. In *6th Workshop on Automated Knowledge Base Construction (AKBC 2017)*.

Daniel Khashabi, Erfan Sadeqi Azer, Tushar Khot, Ashish Sabharwal, and Dan Roth. 2019. On the capabilities and limitations of reasoning for natural language understanding. *arXiv preprint arXiv:1901.02522*.

Daniel Khashabi, Tushar Khot, Ashish Sabharwal, Peter Clark, Oren Etzioni, and Dan Roth. 2016. Question answering via integer programming over semi-structured knowledge. In *Proceedings of the International Joint Conference on Artificial Intelligence*, IJCAI'16, pages 1145–1152.

Daniel Khashabi, Tushar Khot, Ashish Sabharwal, and Dan Roth. 2018. Question answering as global reasoning over semantic abstractions. In *Thirty-Second AAAI Conference on Artificial Intelligence*.

Tushar Khot, Ashish Sabharwal, and Peter Clark. 2017. Answering complex questions using open information extraction. In *Proceedings of the 55th Annual Meeting of the Association for Computational Linguistics, ACL 2017, Vancouver, Canada, July 30 - August 4, Volume 2: Short Papers*, pages 311–316.

Heeyoung Kwon, Harsh Trivedi, Peter Jansen, Mihai Surdeanu, and Niranjan Balasubramanian. 2018. Controlling information aggregation for complex question answering. In *European Conference on Information Retrieval*, pages 750–757. Springer.

Christopher D Manning, Mihai Surdeanu, John Bauer, Jenny Finkel, Steven J Bethard, and David McClosky. 2014. The stanford corenlp natural language processing toolkit. In *Proceedings of 52nd Annual Meeting of the Association for Computational Linguistics: System Demonstrations*, pages 55–60.

Simon Ostermann, Michael Roth, Stefan Thater, and Manfred Pinkal. 2017. Aligning script events with narrative texts. In *Proceedings of the 6th Joint Conference on Lexical and Computational Semantics (*SEM 2017)*, pages 128–134, Vancouver, Canada. Association for Computational Linguistics.

Panupong Pasupat and Percy Liang. 2015. Compositional semantic parsing on semi-structured tables. In *Proceedings of the 53rd Annual Meeting of the Association for Computational Linguistics (ACL)*.

Michael Schmitz, Robert Bart, Stephen Soderland, Oren Etzioni, et al. 2012. Open language learning for information extraction. In *Proceedings of the 2012 Joint Conference on Empirical Methods in Natural Language Processing and Computational Natural Language Learning*, pages 523–534. Association for Computational Linguistics.

Robert Speer and Catherine Havasi. 2012. Representing general relational knowledge in conceptnet 5. In *LREC*, pages 3679–3686.

Huan Sun, Hao Ma, Xiaodong He, Wen-tau Yih, Yu Su, and Xifeng Yan. 2016. Table cell search for question answering. In *Proceedings of the 25th International Conference on World Wide Web (WWW)*, pages 771–782.

Niket Tandon, Gerard De Melo, and Gerhard Weikum. 2017. Webchild 2.0: Fine-grained commonsense knowledge distillation. In *Proceedings of ACL 2017, System Demonstrations*, pages 115–120.

Hai Wang, Mohit Bansal, Kevin Gimpel, and David McAllester. 2015. Machine comprehension with syntax, frames, and semantics. In *Proceedings of the 53rd Annual Meeting of the Association for Computational Linguistics and the 7th International Joint*

Conference on Natural Language Processing (Volume 2: Short Papers), pages 700–706.

Dongfang Xu, Peter Jansen, Jaycie Martin, Zhengnan Xie, Vikas Yadav, Harish Tayyar Madabushi, Oyvind Tafjord, and Peter Clark. 2019. Multiclass hierarchical question classification for multiple choice science exams.

Zhilin Yang, Peng Qi, Saizheng Zhang, Yoshua Bengio, William W Cohen, Ruslan Salakhutdinov, and Christopher D Manning. 2018. Hotpotqa: A dataset for diverse, explainable multi-hop question answering. *arXiv preprint arXiv:1809.09600*.

7   Appendix

Annotation Workflow: The annotation workflow is as follows: The user selects a subset of questions to process (in this preliminary work, we select all *MATTER* questions in the WorldTree corpus). The user then switches to the Grid View, which displays one "grid" at a time, where each grid represents all the connections from a given table to another table in the tablestore (for example, all the connections from the *KINDOF* table to the *IF-THEN* table). The user then uses the Grid View to quickly verify that the automatic groupings are correct, and make adjustments or edits to these groupings. Here the user can also remove bad edges (two table rows that were automatically connected, but whose connection isn't meaningful), or remove subsets of the column links on edges that are partially correct (see Table 1). Once this is completed, the user then switches to the Graph View, where they click on each node group from the recently curated grid, highlight other nodes that contain similar rows, and make manual node merging decisions (by dragging and dropping nodes on top of each other). Notes can also be left on specific nodes or edges, to help describe what underlying concepts the nodes represent, and how they interconnect. Once this is completed, the user marks that grid completed, and moves on to the next grid. User-selectable filtering allows only nodes and edges from grids that have been completed to be displayed, greatly reducing clutter and visual search time.

Once the user has completed all grids, the graph is completed, and represents the interconnected knowledge of all of the explanations in the questions, typically itself clustered into a number of disconnected graphs that represent large high-level inference patterns (such as magnetic attraction, thermal transfer, or changes of state of matter). The user then manually inspects these, and highlights subgraphs of nodes to form a candidate inference pattern. These candidate patterns form a series of knowledge constraints for a series of tablestore rows that must be met in each node in order to satisfy the constraints. These constraints can then be run, debugged (as a whole, or as subsets of nodes or edges), and saved. During this process, missing knowledge or edits to existing knowledge in the tablestore that prevent generalization are often discovered – these edits can be immediately made to the Tablestore Google Sheet and the constraints rerun in seconds, to form a fast iteration cycle for debugging knowledge base and inference pattern constraint interactions.

7.1   Additional Resources

A full export of the inference patterns generated in this work, as well as example patterns from the knowledge base that satisfy their patterns of constraints, is available at `http://www.cognitiveai.org/explanationbank/`.

7.2   Additional Tables and Figures

Additional tables and figures are provided below.

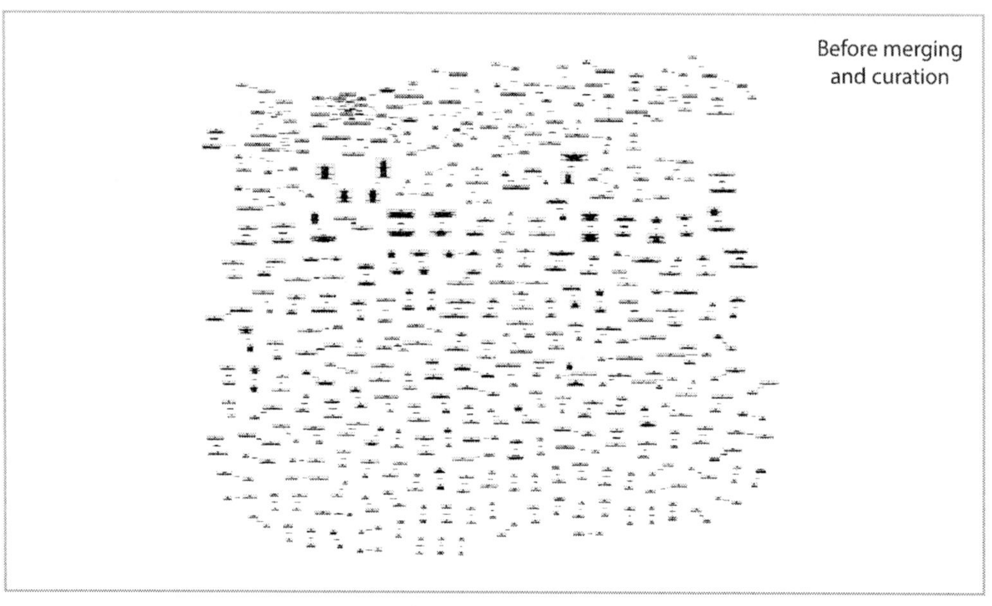

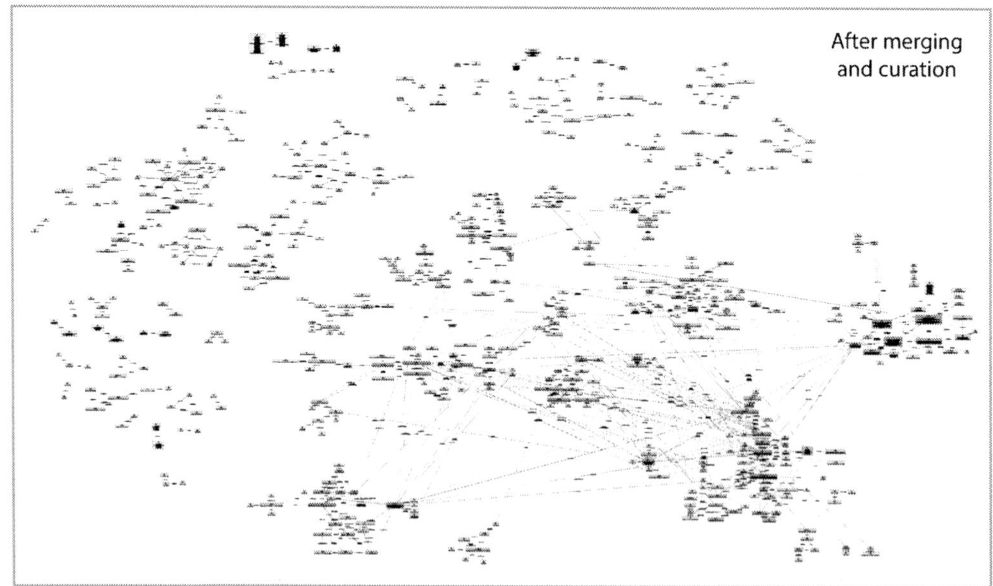

Figure 4: (top) the graph generated by the preprocessing tool, before manual curation and editing by the tool (step 2 in Figure 1). (bottom) the graph after manual curation and editing, and before inference patterns have been generated (step 3 in Figure 1). Clusters in the bottom graph approximately correspond to high-level inference patterns. The set of inference patterns is not shown for space, but each extracted pattern and it's enumerations are included as separate files in our supplementary material.

Inference Pattern	Nodes	Edges	Enumerated Instances in KB
Alloys	-	-	-
Alloy (Core)	3	2	27
Alloy (Composition)	5	6	8
Alloys (Single Elem Not Alloy)	3	2	6
Altitude *	8	10	6
Benefits of long lasting vs replacement	5	4	2
Building requires measuring - Study materials	-	-	-
Building requires measuring	6	7	19
Sturdy materials for building	6	7	3
Burning-Electrocution-Preventing Harm	-	-	-
Harm caused by burning	9	10	546
Harm caused by electrocution	7	7	324
Change of State	-	-	-
Change of State (Evaporating Liquids)	9	9	11
Phase Changes	4	3	7
State of Matter (changing between states of known substances)	8	13	3
Chemical Changes	-	-	-
Chemical Changes (Core+Grounding Specific Chemical Change)	4	3	2
Chemical Reactions (Core)	4	5	15
Chemical Reactions (Core + Substance Grounding)	6	7	363
Chemical Reactions (e.g., acids)	4	3	3
Containers contain things	-	-	-
Containers (Abstracted)	5	5	1000
Containers (Application)	6	6	15
Cooking Food	-	-	-
Cooking (Core)	6	6	26
Cooking a particular food	7	7	338
Cooking (Containers for cooking)	6	6	1
Electrical Conductivity	-	-	-
Dangers of Electric Shock	4	3	414
Electrical Insulation	15	23	46
Electrical Circuits in Devices	7	11	18
Friction	-	-	-
Friction (core)	16	31	3
General Motion *	3	3	6
Ice Wedging *	4	4	2
Magnetism	-	-	-
Magnetic Objects	5	4	10
Manufacturers use material for products	-	-	-
Manufacturers use materials for products (core)	4	3	19
Measurements	-	-	-
Measurement Tools	4	4	130
Observations (Celestial Bodies)	5	6	6
Observations (Distant Objects)	5	6	208
Observations (Microscopic Things)	6	6	4
Observations (Small Things)	6	6	94
Navigation-Direction-Being lost at sea	-	-	-
Navigation (core)	3	2	1
Navigation (being lost/boat)	6	7	2
Physical Changes	-	-	-
Physical Changes (Changing Shape)	9	10	832
Seeing	-	-	-
Things that can see and what they can see	6	6	1000
Soil erosion *	6	6	28
Solutions - Dissolving substances *	4	5	1
Sources of Heat *	3	2	6
Sunlight as a source of energy *	14	30	80
Sunlight location and shadow size *	7	7	312
Taste *	9	11	26
Taxonomic Inheritance	2	1	1000
Texture *	4	3	2
Thermal Conductivity	-	-	-
Thermal Conductivity (Core)	21	26	1000
Thermal Conductors 0	5	4	9
Thermal Conductors 1	5	4	8
Thermal Insulators	5	5	5
Touch-Hardness *	4	3	8

Table 5: An extended list of inference patterns discovered in the corpus of explanations for *Matter* science exam questions using this tool. Indented inference patterns represent a subset of smaller, more generic sub-patterns extracted from the larger pattern. "Enumerated instances in KB" represents the number of unique combinations of facts the pattern generates in our current KB (note that for speed, this currently has a hard upper limit of 1,000 patterns). An asterisk (*) represents patterns that are partial or otherwise limited in size because they overlap with questions (e.g. from Earth or Life Science) not examined in this preliminary study.

Commonsense Inference in Natural Language Processing (COIN)
—
Shared Task Report

Simon Ostermann
Saarland University /
Nuance Communications

simono@coli.uni-saarland.de

Sheng Zhang
Johns Hopkins
University

zsheng2@jhu.edu

Michael Roth
Stuttgart University/
Saarland University

rothml@ims.uni-stuttgart.de

Peter Clark
Allen Institute for
Artificial Intelligence

peterc@allenai.org

Abstract

This paper reports on the results of the shared tasks of the COIN workshop at EMNLP–IJCNLP 2019. The tasks consisted of two machine comprehension evaluations, each of which tested a system's ability to answer questions/queries about a text. Both evaluations were designed such that systems need to exploit commonsense knowledge, for example, in the form of inferences over information that is available in the common ground but not necessarily mentioned in the text. A total of five participating teams submitted systems for the shared tasks, with the best submitted system achieving 90.6% accuracy and 83.7% F1-score on task 1 and task 2, respectively.

1 Introduction

Due to the rise of powerful pre-trained word and sentence representations, automated text processing has come a long way in recent years, with systems that perform even better than humans on some datasets (Rajpurkar et al., 2016a). However, natural language understanding also involves complex challenges. One important difference between human and machine text understanding lies in the fact that humans can access commonsense knowledge while processing text, which helps them to draw inferences about facts that are not mentioned in a text, but that are assumed to be common ground.

(1)   *Max:* "It's 1 pm already, I think we should get lunch."
Dustin: "Let me get my wallet."

Consider the conversation in Example 1: Max will not be surprised that Dustin needs to get his wallet, since she knows that *paying* is a part of *getting lunch*. Also, she knows that a wallet is needed for paying, so Dustin needs to get a wallet

for lunch. This is part of the commonsense knowledge about getting lunch and should be known by both persons. For a computer system, inferring such unmentioned facts is a non-trivial challenge. The workshop on Commonsense Inference in NLP (COIN) is focused on such phenomena, looking at models, data, and evaluation methods for commonsense inference.

This report summarizes the results of the COIN shared tasks, an unofficial extension of the SemEval 2018 shared task 11, *Machine Comprehension using Commonsense Knowledge* (Ostermann et al., 2018b). The tasks aim to evaluate the commonsense inference capabilities of text understanding systems in two settings: Commonsense inference in everyday narrations (task 1) and commonsense inference in news texts (task 2). Framed as machine comprehension evaluations, the datasets used for both tasks contain challenging reading comprehension questions asking for facts that are not explicitly mentioned in the given reading texts.

Several teams participated in the shared tasks and submitted system description papers. All systems are based on Transformer architectures (Vaswani et al., 2017), some of them explicitly incorporating commonsense knowledge resources, whereas others only use pretraining on other machine comprehension data sets. The best submitted system achieves 90.6% accuracy and 83.7% F1-score on task 1 and task 2, respectively. Still, there are cases that remain elusive: Humans outperform this system by a margin of 7% (task 1) and 8% (task 2). Our results indicate that while Transformer models are able to perform extremely well on the data used in our shared task, there are still some remaining cases demonstrating that human level is not achieved yet. Still, we believe that our results also imply the need for more challenging data sets. In particular, we need data sets that

Proceedings of the First Workshop on Commonsense Inference in Natural Language Processing, pages 66–74
Hongkong, China, November 3, 2019. ©2019 Association for Computational Linguistics

make it harder to benefit from redundancy in the training data or large-scale pretraining on similar domains.

In the following, we briefly describe the data sets (§2), baselines and evaluation metrics of the shared tasks (§3) and we present a summary of the participating systems (§4), their results (§5) as well as a discussion thereof (§6).

2 Data and Tasks

Text understanding systems are often evaluated by means of a reading comprehension task, which is also referred to as machine (reading) comprehension (MC). The central idea is that a system has to process a text and then find a correct answer to a question that is asked on the text. Our shared tasks follow this paradigm and use machine comprehension settings to evaluate a model's capability to perform commonsense inferences. In contrast to most existing MC datasets, the two datasets that are used for our shared tasks, *MCScript2.0* (Ostermann et al., 2019) and ReCoRD (Zhang et al., 2018), are focused on questions that cannot be answered from the text alone, but that require a model to draw inference over unmentioned facts.

(2) *Text:* Camping is one of my favorite summer vacations. (...) Once I have all my gear and clothing I'll pack it into my car, making sure to leave room for myself, my dog and anything my friends want to bring. And then we are ready for our camping vacation.
Question: What do they put the drinks in?
a. Cooler
b. Sleeping bag

Example 2 illustrates the main idea of the shared tasks. It shows a reading text from MCScript2.0, together with a question and two candidate answers. For a human, it is trivial to find that the drinks are put into a cooler rather than the sleeping bag. This information is however not mentioned in the text, so a machine needs to have the capability to infer this fact from commonsense knowledge.

The reading texts of MCScript2.0 are narrations about everyday activities (task 1). Due to its domain, MCScript2.0 has a focus on evaluating script knowledge, i.e. knowledge about the events and participants of such everyday activities (Schank and Abelson, 1975). Task 2 utilizes the ReCoRD corpus (Zhang et al., 2018), which contains news texts, a more open domain. The inferences that are required for finding answers to the questions in ReCoRD are thus of a more general type.

2.1 Task 1: Commonsense Inference in Everyday Narrations

MCScript2.0 is a reading comprehension data set comprising 19,821 questions on 3,487 texts. Each of the questions has two answer candidates, one of which is correct. Questions in the data were annotated for reasoning types, i.e. according to whether the answer to a question can be found in the text or needs to be inferred from commonsense knowledge. Roughly half of the questions do require inferences over commonsense knowledge.

The texts in MCScript2.0 are short narrations (164.4 tokens on average) on a total of 200 different everyday activities. All texts were crowdsourced on Amazon Mechanical Turk[1], by asking crowd workers to tell a story about one of the 200 scenarios *as if talking to a child* (Modi et al., 2016; Ostermann et al., 2018a), resulting in simple texts which explicitly mention many details of a scenario. In the question collection, which was also conducted via crowdsourcing, turkers were then asked to write questions about noun or verb phrases that were highlighted in the texts. After collecting questions, the sentences containing the noun or verb phrases were deleted from the texts. During the answer collection, crowd workers thus had to infer the information required for finding an answer from background knowledge. Five turkers wrote correct and incorrect answer candidates for each question, and the most difficult incorrect candidates were selected via adversarial filtering (Zellers et al., 2018).

For our shared task, we use the same data split as Ostermann et al. (2019): 14,191 questions on 2,500 texts for the training set, 2,020 questions on 355 texts for the development set and 3,610 questions on 632 texts for the test set. All texts for five scenarios were reserved for the test set only to increase difficulty.

2.2 Task 2: Commonsense Inference in News Articles

ReCoRD is a large-scale dataset for reading comprehension, which consists of over 120,000 ex-

---

[1] https://www.mturk.com/

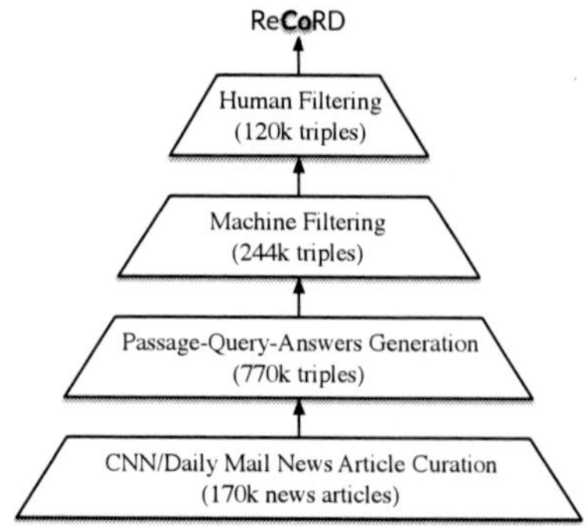

Figure 1: ReCoRD data collection procedure.

	Train	Dev.	Test	Overall
queries	100,730	10,000	10,000	120,730
unique passages	65,709	7,133	7,279	80,121
passage vocab.	352,491	93,171	94,386	395,356
query vocab.	119,069	30,844	31,028	134,397
tokens / passage	169.5	168.6	168.1	169.3
entities / passage	17.8	17.5	17.3	17.8
tokens / query	21.3	22.1	22.2	21.4

Table 1: Statistics of ReCoRD

amples, most of which require commonsense reasoning. ReCoRD was collected in a four-stage process (Figure 1): (1) curating CNN/Daily Mail news articles, (2) generating passage-query-answers triples based on the news articles, (3) filtering out the queries that can be easily answered by state-of-the-art machine comprehension (MC) models, and (4) filtering out the queries ambiguous to human readers. All named entities in the passages are possible answers to the queries. Table 1 summarizes the data statistics.

3 Shared Task Setup

The baselines for our shared tasks were adapted from Ostermann et al. (2019) and Zhang et al. (2018), respectively.

3.1 Task 1 Baselines

Following Ostermann et al. (2019), we present results of three baseline models.

Logistic Regression Model. Merkhofer et al. (2018) presented a logistic regression classifier for the SemEval 2018 shared task 11, which used simple overlap features and word patterns on *MC-Script*, a predecessor of the dataset used for this task. Their model outperformed many neural networks in spite of its simplicity.

Attentive Reader. The second baseline model is an attentive reader network (Hermann et al., 2015). GRU units (Cho et al., 2014) are used to process text, question and answer. A question-aware text representation is computed based on a bilinear attention function, which is then combined with a GRU-based answer representation for prediction. For details, we refer to Ostermann et al. (2019), Ostermann et al. (2018a) and Chen et al. (2016)

TriAN. As last model, we use the three-way attentive network (TriAN) (Wang et al., 2018), a recurrent neural network that scored the first place in the SemEval 2018 task. They use LSTM units (Hochreiter and Schmidhuber, 1997), several attention functions, and self attention to compute representations for text, question and answer. ConceptNet (Speer et al., 2017), a large commonsense knowledge base containing thousands of entities and commonsense relations between them, is used to enhance text representations with commonsense information, by computing relation embeddings and appending them to the text representations. For more information we refer to Wang et al. (2018).

3.2 Task 2 Baselines

We present five baselines for ReCoRD:

BERT (Devlin et al., 2019) is a new language representation model. Recently fine-tuning the pre-trained BERT with an additional output layer has created state-of-the-art models on a wide range of NLP tasks. We formalized ReCoRD as an extractive QA task like SQuAD, and then reused the fine-tuning script for SQuAD to fine-tune BERT for ReCoRD.

KT-NET (Yang et al., 2019a) employs an attention mechanism to adaptively select desired knowledge from knowledge bases, and then fuses selected knowledge with BERT to enable context- and knowledge-aware predictions for machine reading comprehension.

SAN (Liu et al., 2018) is a top-ranked MC model. It shares many components with other MC models, and employs a stochastic answer module. As we used SAN to filter out queries in the data collection, it is necessary to verify that the collected queries are hard for not only SAN but also other MC architectures.

Rank	Team Name	Architecture	Commonsense	Other Resources	Tasks
1	PSH–SJTU	Transformer (XLNet)	-	RACE, SWAG	1, 2
2	IIT-KGP	Transformer (BERT + XLNet)	-	RACE	1
3	BLCU-NLP	Transformer (BERT)	-	ReCoRD, RACE	1
4	JDA	Transformer (BERT)	ConceptNet, Atomic, Webchild	Wikipedia	1
5	KARNA	Transformer (BERT)	ConceptNet	-	1

Table 2: Overview of participating systems

DocQA (Clark and Gardner, 2018) is a strong baseline model for extractive QA. It consists of components such as bi-directional attention flow (Seo et al., 2016) and self-attention, both of which are widely used in MC models. We also evaluated a variant of DocQA with ELMo (Peters et al., 2018) to analyze the impact of ELMo on this task.

Random Guess acts as the lower bound of the evaluated models, which randomly picks a named entity from the passage as the answer. The reported results are averaged over 5 runs.

3.3 Evaluation

Task 1. The evaluation measure for task 1 is accuracy, computed as the number of correctly answered questions divided by the number of all questions. We also report accuracy values on questions that crowd workers explicitly annotated as requiring commonsense as well as performance on the five held-out scenarios.

Task 2. We use two evaluation metrics, EM and F1, similar to those used by SQuAD (Rajpurkar et al., 2016b). Exact Match (EM) measures the percentage of predictions that match a reference answer exactly. (Macro-averaged) F_1 measures the average overlap between model predictions and reference answers. For computing F_1, we treat prediction and reference answers as bags of tokens. We take the maximum F_1 over all reference answers for a given query, and then average over all queries.

4 Participants

In total, five teams submitted systems in task 1, and one team participated in task 2. All submitted models were neural networks, and all made use of pretrained Transformer language models such as *BERT* (Devlin et al., 2019). The participants used a wide range of external corpora and resources to augment their models, ranging from other machine comprehension data sets such as *RACE* (Lai et al., 2017) or *MCScript* (Ostermann et al., 2018a), up to commonsense knowledge databases such as *ConceptNet* (Speer et al., 2017), *WebChild* (Tandon et al., 2017) or ATOMIC (Sap et al., 2019). Table 2 gives a summary of the participating systems.

- **PSH–SJTU** (Li et al., 2019) participated in both tasks with a Transformer model based on *XLNet* (Yang et al., 2019b). For task 1, they pretrain the model in several steps, first on the RACE data (Lai et al., 2017) and then on SWAG (Zellers et al., 2018). For task 2, they do not conduct specific pretraining steps, but implement a range of simple rule-based answer verification strategies to verify the output of the model.

- **IIT-KGP** (Sharma and Roychowdhury, 2019) present an ensemble of different pretrained language models, namely BERT and XLNet. Both models are pretrained on the RACE data (Lai et al., 2017), and their output is averaged for a final prediction.

- **BLCU-NLP** (Liu et al., 2019) use a Transformer model based on BERT, which is fine-tuned in two stages: they first tune the BERT-based language model on the RACE and ReCoRD datasets and then (further) train the model for the actual machine comprehension task.

- **JDA** (Da, 2019) use three different knowledge bases, namely ConceptNet (Speer et al., 2017), ATOMIC (Sap et al., 2019) and WebChild (Tandon et al., 2017). They extract relevant edges from the knowledge bases and compute relation embeddings, which are combined with BERT-based word representations with a diadic multiplication operation.

- **KARNA** (Jain and Singh, 2019) use a BERT model, but they enhance the text representation with edges that are extracted from ConceptNet. Following Wang et al. (2018), they extract relations between words in the text and the question/answer, and append them to the text representation. Instead of computing relational embeddings, they append a specific string that describes the relation.

5 Results

Table 3 shows the performance of the participating systems and the baselines on the task 1 data. We tested for significance using a pairwise approximate randomization test (Yeh, 2000) over questions. Except for the two top scoring systems, each system performs significantly better than the next in rank. All systems significantly outperform the baselines. All systems show a lower performance on commonsense-based questions as compared to the average on all questions, with the difference for the two top-scoring systems being smallest. Surprisingly, all models are able to perform better on the questions from held-out scenarios as compared to their performance on all questions. This indicates that all models are able to generalize well from the training material.

Table 5 shows the systems' performance on single question types for task 1. Question types are determined automatically, as described in (Ostermann et al., 2019). As can be seen, both top-scoring systems perform well over all different question types, indicating that both systems are able to model a wide range of phenomena. Interestingly, *when* questions seem to be the most challenging question type for all systems, indicating difficulties when it comes to model event ordering information. Also, *where* questions seem to be challenging, at least for some systems.

Table 4 shows EM (%) and F_1 (%) of human performance, the PSH-SJTU system as well as baselines on the development and test sets of task 2. Compared with the best baseline, KT-NET (Yang et al., 2019a), PSH-SJTU achieves significantly better scores. On the hidden test set, they improve EM by 10.08%, and F_1 by 8.98%.

#	Team Name	acc	acc_{cs}	acc_{OOD}
1	PSH–SJTU	**0.906**	**0.903**	0.915
2	IIT-KGP	0.905*	0.894	**0.931**
3	BLCU-NLP	0.842*	0.812	0.838
4	JDA	0.807*	0.775	0.796
5	KARNA	0.733*	0.697	0.729
-	TriAN	0.715	0.666	0.673
-	Attentive Reader	0.651	0.634	0.619
-	Logistic	0.608	0.562	0.544
-	*Human*	0.97		

Table 3: Performance of participating systems and baselines for **task 1**, in total (acc), on commonsense-based questions (acc_{cs}), and on out-of-domain questions that belong to the five held-out scenarios (acc_{OOD}). Significant differences in results between two adjacent lines are marked by an asterisk (* p<0.05) in the upper line. The best model performance per column is marked in **bold print**.

	Dev.		Test	
	EM(%)	F_1(%)	EM(%)	F_1(%)
Human	**91.28**	**91.64**	**91.31**	**91.69**
PSH-SJTU	**82.72**	**83.38**	**83.09**	**83.74**
KT-NET	71.60	73.61	73.01	74.76
BERT-Large	66.11	68.49	67.61	70.01
SAN	48.86	50.08	50.43	51.41
DocQA	44.13	45.39	45.44	46.65
Random	18.41	19.06	18.55	19.12

Table 4: Performance (EM and F_1) of human, participating systems and baselines for **task 2**.

Consequently, PSH-SJTU has reduced the gap between human and machine performance, with human performance being only 8% higher than PSH-SJTU.

6 Discussion

Pretrained Transformer language models. A main finding of our shared tasks is that large pretrained Transformer language models such as BERT or XLNet perform well even on challenging commonsense inference data. Strikingly, all models generalize well, as can be seen from the good performance on held-out scenarios. On task 1, XLNet-based systems perform best. The difference to the models purely based on BERT

#	Team Name	what	when	where	who	how
1	PSH–SJTU	0.918	0.891	0.890	0.921	0.890
2	IIT-KGP	0.915	0.897	0.890	0.921	0.925
3	BLCU-NLP	0.874	0.800	0.815	0.857	0.870
4	JDA	0.844	0.777	0.744	0.794	0.829
5	KARNA	0.755	0.683	0.734	0.750	0.788
-	TriAN	0.749	0.647	0.712	0.730	0.801
-	AttentiveReader	0.700	0.578	0.620	0.659	0.726
-	Logistic	0.644	0.546	0.573	0.663	0.685

Table 5: Performance of participating systems and baselines for **task 1** on the 5 most common question types.

can mostly be attributed to the performance on commonsense-based questions: While the performance of XLNet-based models on such questions is almost on par with their average performance, models based on BERT underperform on commonsense questions. An interesting observation was made by Li et al. (2019), who found that including WordNet into a BERT model boosts performance, while there is no such boost for an XLNet model. This seems to indicate that XLNet is able to cover (at least partially) some form of lexical background knowledge, as encoded in WordNet, without explicitly requiring access to such a resource.

Still, when inspecting questions that were not answered correctly by the best scoring model, we found a large number of commonsense-based *when* questions that ask for the typical order of events. This indicates that XLNet-based models are only to a certain extent able to model complex phenomena such as temporal order.

Commonsense knowledge databases. Only two participants made use of commonsense knowledge, in the form of knowledge graphs such as ConceptNet. Both participants conducted ablation tests indicating the importance of including commonsense knowledge. In comparison to ATOMIC and WebChild, Da (2019) report that ConceptNet is most beneficial for performance on the task 1 data, which can be explained with its domain: The OMCS (Singh et al., 2002) data are part of the ConceptNet database, and OMCS scenarios were also used to collect texts for the task 1 data.

All in all, powerful pretrained models such as XLNet still outperform approaches that make use of structured knowledge bases, which indicates that they are (at least to some extent) capable of performing commonsense inference without explicit representations of commonsense knowledge.

Pretraining and finetuning on other data. Several participants reported effects of pretraining/finetuning their models on related tasks. For instance, Liu et al. (2019) experimented with different pretraining corpora and found results to be best when pretraining the encoder of their BERT model on RACE and ReCoRD. Similarly, Li et al. (2019) report improved results when using larger data sets from other reading comprehension (RACE) and commonsense inference tasks (SWAG) for training before fine-tuning the model with the actual training data from the shared task.

7 Related Work

Evaluating commonsense inference via machine comprehension has recently moved into the focus of interest. Existing datasets cover various domains:

Web texts. *TriviaQA* (Joshi et al., 2017) is a corpus of webcrawled trivia and quiz-league websites together with evidence documents from the web. A large part of questions requires a system to make use of factual commonsense knowledge for finding an answer. *CommonsenseQA* (Talmor et al., 2018) consists of 9,000 crowdsourced multiple-choice questions with a focus on relations between entities that appear in ConceptNet (Speer et al., 2017). Evidence documents were webcrawled based on the question and added after the crowdsourcing step.

Fictive texts. *NarrativeQA* (Kočiský et al., 2018) provides full novels and other long texts as evidence documents and contains approx. 30 crowdsourced questions per text. The questions require a system to understand the whole plot of the text and to conduct many successive complicated inference steps, under the use of various types of background knowledge.

News texts. NewsQA (Trischler et al., 2017) provides news texts with crowdsourced questions and answers, which are spans of the evidence documents. The question collection procedure for NewsQA resulted in a large number of questions that require factual commonsense knowledge for finding an answer.

Other tasks. There have been other attempts at evaluating commonsense inference apart from machine comprehension. One example is the Story cloze test and the *ROC* dataset (Mostafazadeh et al., 2016), where systems have to find the correct ending to a 5-sentence story, using different types of commonsense knowledge. *SWAG* (Zellers et al., 2018) is a natural language inference dataset with a focus on difficult commonsense inferences.

8 Conclusion

This report presented the results of the shared tasks at the Workshop for Commonsense Inference in NLP (COIN). The tasks aimed at evaluating the capability of systems to make use of commonsense knowledge for challenging inference questions in a machine comprehension setting, on everyday narrations (task 1) and news texts (task 2). In total, 5 systems participated in task 1, and one system participated in task 2. All submitted models were Transformer models, pretrained with a language modeling objective on large amounts of textual data. The best system achieved 90.6% accuracy and 83.7% F1-score on task 1 and 2, respectively, leaving a gap of 7% and 8% to human performance.

The results of our shared tasks suggest that existing models cover a large part of the commonsense knowledge required for our data sets in the domains of narrations and news texts. This does however not mean that commonsense inference is solved: We found a range of examples in our data that are not successfully covered. Furthermore, data sets such as *HellaSWAG* (Zellers et al., 2019) show that commonsense inference tasks can be specifically tailored to be hard for Transformer models. We believe that modeling true language understanding requires a shift towards text types and tasks that test commonsense knowledge going beyond information that can be obtained by exploiting the redundancy of large-scale corpora and/or pretraining on related tasks.

References

Danqi Chen, Jason Bolton, and Christopher D. Manning. 2016. A Thorough Examination of the CNN/Daily Mail Reading Comprehension Task. In *Proceedings of the 54th Annual Meeting of the Association for Computational Linguistics (Volume 1: Long Papers)*, volume 1, pages 2358–2367.

Kyunghyun Cho, Bart Van Merriënboer, Caglar Gulcehre, Dzmitry Bahdanau, Fethi Bougares, Holger Schwenk, and Yoshua Bengio. 2014. Learning phrase representations using rnn encoder-decoder for statistical machine translation. *arXiv preprint arXiv:1406.1078*.

Christopher Clark and Matt Gardner. 2018. Simple and effective multi-paragraph reading comprehension. In *Proceedings of the 56th Annual Meeting of the Association for Computational Linguistics (Volume 1: Long Papers)*, pages 845–855. Association for Computational Linguistics.

Jeffrey Da. 2019. Jeff Da at COIN - Shared Task. In *Proceedings of the 2019 EMNLP Workshop COIN: Commonsense Inference in NLP*.

Jacob Devlin, Ming-Wei Chang, Kenton Lee, and Kristina Toutanova. 2019. Bert: Pre-training of deep bidirectional transformers for language understanding. In *Proceedings of the 2019 Conference of the North American Chapter of the Association for Computational Linguistics: Human Language Technologies, Volume 1 (Long and Short Papers)*, pages 4171–4186.

Karl Moritz Hermann, Tomáš Kočiský, Edward Grefenstette, Lasse Espeholt, Will Kay, Mustafa Suleyman, and Phil Blunsom. 2015. Teaching machines to read and comprehend. In *Advances in Neural Information Processing Systems*, pages 1693–1701.

Sepp Hochreiter and Jürgen Schmidhuber. 1997. Long short-term memory. *Neural computation*, 9(8):1735–1780.

Yash Jain and Chinmay Singh. 2019. KARNA at COIN - Shared Task: Bidirectional Encoder Representations from Transformers with relational knowledge for machine comprehension with common sense . In *Proceedings of the 2019 EMNLP Workshop COIN: Commonsense Inference in NLP*.

Mandar Joshi, Eunsol Choi, Daniel S. Weld, and Luke Zettlemoyer. 2017. TriviaQA: A Large Scale Distantly Supervised Challenge Dataset for Reading Comprehension. In *Proceedings of the 55th Annual Meeting of the Association for Computational Linguistics*, pages 1601–1611. Association for Computational Linguistics.

Tomáš Kočiský, Jonathan Schwarz, Phil Blunsom, Chris Dyer, Karl Moritz Hermann, Gáabor Melis, and Edward Grefenstette. 2018. The NarrativeQA Reading Comprehension Challenge. *Transactions of the Association of Computational Linguistics*, 6:317–328.

Guokun Lai, Qizhe Xie, Hanxiao Liu, Yiming Yang, and Eduard Hovy. 2017. RACE: Large-scale ReAding Comprehension Dataset From Examinations. In *Proceedings of the 2017 Conference on Empirical Methods in Natural Language Processing*, pages 785–794.

Xiepeng Li, Zhexi Zhang, Wei Zhu, Yuan Ni, Peng Gao, Junchi Yan, and Guotong Xie. 2019. Pingan Smart Health and SJTU at COIN - Shared Task: Utilizing Pre-trained Language Models and Commonsense Knowledge in Machine Reading Tasks. In *Proceedings of the 2019 EMNLP Workshop COIN: Commonsense Inference in NLP*.

Chunhua Liu, Shike Wang, Bohan Li, and Dong Yu. 2019. BLCU-NLP at COIN - Shared Task: Stagewise Fine-tuning BERT for Commonsense Inference in Everyday Narrations. In *Proceedings of the 2019 EMNLP Workshop COIN: Commonsense Inference in NLP*.

Xiaodong Liu, Yelong Shen, Kevin Duh, and Jianfeng Gao. 2018. Stochastic answer networks for machine reading comprehension. In *Proceedings of the 56th Annual Meeting of the Association for Computational Linguistics (Volume 1: Long Papers)*, pages 1694–1704. Association for Computational Linguistics.

Elizabeth M. Merkhofer, John Henderson, David Bloom, Laura Strickhart, and Guido Zarrella. 2018. MITRE at SemEval-2018 Task 11: Commonsense Reasoning without Commonsense Knowledge. In *Proceedings of the 12th International Workshop on Semantic Evaluations (SemEval-2018)*, pages 1078–1082.

Ashutosh Modi, Tatjana Anikina, Simon Ostermann, and Manfred Pinkal. 2016. InScript: Narrative texts annotated with script information. In *Proceedings of the Tenth International Conference on Language Resources and Evaluation (LREC 2016)*, pages 3485–3493. European Language Resources Association (ELRA).

Nasrin Mostafazadeh, Nathanael Chambers, Xiaodong He, Devi Parikh, Dhruv Batra, Lucy Vanderwende, Pushmeet Kohli, and James Allen. 2016. A corpus and cloze evaluation for deeper understanding of commonsense stories. In *Proceedings of the 2016 Conference of the North American Chapter of the Association for Computational Linguistics: Human Language Technologies*, pages 839–849, San Diego, California. Association for Computational Linguistics.

Simon Ostermann, Ashutosh Modi, Michael Roth, Stefan Thater, and Manfred Pinkal. 2018a. MCScript: A Novel Dataset for Assessing Machine Comprehension Using Script Knowledge. In *Proceedings of the 11th International Conference on Language Resources and Evaluation (LREC 2018)*, pages 3567–3574.

Simon Ostermann, Michael Roth, Ashutosh Modi, Stefan Thater, and Manfred Pinkal. 2018b. SemEval-2018 Task 11: Machine Comprehension using Commonsense Knowledge. In *Proceedings of The 12th International Workshop on Semantic Evaluation*, pages 747–757.

Simon Ostermann, Michael Roth, and Manfred Pinkal. 2019. MCScript2.0: A Machine Comprehension Corpus Focused on Script Events and Participants. In *Proceedings of the Eighth Joint Conference on Lexical and Computational Semantics (* SEM 2019)*, pages 103–117.

Matthew Peters, Mark Neumann, Mohit Iyyer, Matt Gardner, Christopher Clark, Kenton Lee, and Luke Zettlemoyer. 2018. Deep contextualized word representations. In *Proceedings of the 2018 Conference of the North American Chapter of the Association for Computational Linguistics: Human Language Technologies, Volume 1 (Long Papers)*, pages 2227–2237. Association for Computational Linguistics.

Pranav Rajpurkar, Jian Zhang, Konstantin Lopyrev, and Percy Liang. 2016a. SQuAD: 100,000+ Questions for Machine Comprehension of Text. In *Proceedings of the 2016 Conference on Empirical Methods in Natural Language Processing*, pages 2383–2392.

Pranav Rajpurkar, Jian Zhang, Konstantin Lopyrev, and Percy Liang. 2016b. Squad: 100,000+ questions for machine comprehension of text. In *Proceedings of the 2016 Conference on Empirical Methods in Natural Language Processing*, pages 2383–2392, Austin, Texas. Association for Computational Linguistics.

Maarten Sap, Ronan Le Bras, Emily Allaway, Chandra Bhagavatula, Nicholas Lourie, Hannah Rashkin, Brendan Roof, Noah A Smith, and Yejin Choi. 2019. Atomic: an atlas of machine commonsense for if-then reasoning. In *Proceedings of the AAAI Conference on Artificial Intelligence*, volume 33, pages 3027–3035.

Roger C Schank and Robert P Abelson. 1975. Scripts, Plans, and Knowledge. In *Proceedings of the 4th international joint conference on Artificial intelligence-Volume 1*, pages 151–157. Morgan Kaufmann Publishers Inc.

Minjoon Seo, Aniruddha Kembhavi, Ali Farhadi, and Hannaneh Hajishirzi. 2016. Bidirectional attention flow for machine comprehension. *arXiv preprint arXiv:1611.01603*.

Prakhar Sharma and Sumegh Roychowdhury. 2019. IIT-KGP at COIN - Shared Task: Using pre-trained Language Models for modeling Machine Comprehension. In *Proceedings of the 2019 EMNLP Workshop COIN: Commonsense Inference in NLP*.

Push Singh, Thomas Lin, Erik T. Mueller, Grace Lim, Travell Perkins, and Wan Li Zhu. 2002. Open Mind Common Sense: Knowledge Acquisition from the General Public. In *On the move to Meaningful Internet Systems 2002: CoopIS, DOA, and ODBASE*, pages 1223–1237. Springer.

Robyn Speer, Joshua Chin, and Catherine Havasi. 2017. Conceptnet 5.5: An open multilingual graph of general knowledge. In *Proceedings of the Thirty-First AAAI Conference on Artificial Intelligence (AAAI-17)*, pages 4444–4451.

Alon Talmor, Jonathan Herzig, Nicholas Lourie, and Jonathan Berant. 2018. CommonsenseQA: A Question Answering Challenge Targeting Commonsense Knowledge. *arXiv preprint arXiv:1811.00937*.

Niket Tandon, Gerard de Melo, and Gerhard Weikum. 2017. Webchild 2.0: Fine-grained commonsense knowledge distillation. In *The 55th Annual Meeting of the Association for Computational Linguistics*, pages 115–120. ACL.

Adam Trischler, Tong Wang, Xingdi Yuan, Justin Harris, Alessandro Sordoni, Philip Bachman, and Kaheer Suleman. 2017. NewsQA: A Machine Comprehension Dataset. In *Proceedings of the 2nd Workshop on Representation Learning for NLP*, pages 191–200.

Ashish Vaswani, Noam Shazeer, Niki Parmar, Jakob Uszkoreit, Llion Jones, Aidan N Gomez, Łukasz Kaiser, and Illia Polosukhin. 2017. Attention is all you need. In *Advances in Neural Information Processing Systems*, pages 5998–6008.

Liang Wang, Meng Sun, Wei Zhao, Kewei Shen, and Jingming Liu. 2018. Yuanfudao at SemEval-2018 Task 11: Three-way Attention and Relational Knowledge for Commonsense Machine Comprehension. In *Proceedings of the 12th International Workshop on Semantic Evaluations (SemEval-2018)*, pages 758–762.

An Yang, Quan Wang, Jing Liu, Kai Liu, Yajuan Lyu, Hua Wu, Qiaoqiao She, and Sujian Li. 2019a. Enhancing pre-trained language representations with rich knowledge for machine reading comprehension. In *Proceedings of the 57th Annual Meeting of the Association for Computational Linguistics*, pages 2346–2357, Florence, Italy. Association for Computational Linguistics.

Zhilin Yang, Zihang Dai, Yiming Yang, Jaime Carbonell, Ruslan Salakhutdinov, and Quoc V Le. 2019b. Xlnet: Generalized autoregressive pretraining for language understanding. *arXiv preprint arXiv:1906.08237*.

Alexander Yeh. 2000. More accurate tests for the statistical significance of the result differences. In *Proc. 17th International Conf. on Computational Linguistics*, pages 947–953, Saarbruken, Germany.

Rowan Zellers, Yonatan Bisk, Roy Schwartz, and Yejin Choi. 2018. SWAG: A Large-Scale Adversarial Dataset for Grounded Commonsense Inference. In *Proceedings of the 2018 Conference on Empirical Methods in Natural Language Processing*, pages 93–104.

Rowan Zellers, Ari Holtzman, Yonatan Bisk, Ali Farhadi, and Yejin Choi. 2019. Hellaswag: Can a machine really finish your sentence? In *Proceedings of the 57th Annual Meeting of the Association for Computational Linguistics*.

Sheng Zhang, Xiaodong Liu, Jingjing Liu, Jianfeng Gao, Kevin Duh, and Benjamin Van Durme. 2018. ReCoRD: Bridging the Gap between Human and Machine Commonsense Reading Comprehension. *arXiv preprint arXiv:1810.12885*.

KARNA at COIN Shared Task 1: Bidirectional Encoder Representations from Transformers with relational knowledge for machine comprehension with common sense

Yash Jain
IIT Kharagpur
Kharagpur, India
yoyo1704@iitkgp.ac.in

Chinmay Singh
IIT Kharagpur
Kharagpur, India
chinmaysingh@iitkgp.ac.in

Abstract

This paper describes our model for COmmonsense INference in Natural Language Processing (COIN) shared task 1: Commonsense Inference in Everyday Narrations. This paper explores the use of Bidirectional Encoder Representations from Transformers(BERT) along with external relational knowledge from ConceptNet to tackle the problem of commonsense inference. The input passage, question and answer are augmented with relational knowledge from ConceptNet. Using this technique we are able to achieve an accuracy of 73.3 % on the official test data.

1 Introduction

Commonsense refers to the skill of making presumptions regarding the physical form, use, behaviour, interaction with other objects etc. that is derived from the naive physics as well as the humans' folk psychology that develops because of the frequent experience that we have as a result of our day to day interaction with these entities.

The task of making commonsense inferences about everyday world is an unsolved and worked upon milestone in the path of Artificial General Intelligence. The approach of attaining this task in the field of Natural Language Processing has seen some advancement in the recent times with the advent of standard Data sets and Tasks like SWAG, Event2Mind and Winograd Schema Challenge.

The general approach followed in natural language processing to judge performance in commonsense inference task is to provide a excerpt of the situation/ event and then some questions are asked relating to the aforementioned paragraph. The model is expected to answer the question which is of the form that cannot be answered by simple extraction of text from the passage but requires certain information that has to be inferred from outside general commonsense resources *i.e.* by the use of commonsense.

Commonsense knowledge is usually exploited by the use of explicit relations (positional, of form etc.) stored in the form of knowledge graphs or binary entity wise relations. Some examples of these databases include Never Ending Language Learner (NELL)(T. Mitchell, 2015), ConceptNet(Liu and Singh, 2004), WebChild(Tandon et al., 2017) etc.

2 Previous Work

Work in development of N.L.P. models that can go beyond simple pattern recognition and use the world knowledge has made progress lately.
Following are some of the major Corpus which have helped make significant progress towards this task:

- **Event2Mind**: (Rashkin et al., 2018) which has 25,000 narrations about everyday activities and situations has been. The best performing model is *ConvNet (Rashkin et al., 2018)*

- **SWAG**: (Zellers et al., 2018) It is a dataset of 113k highly varied grounded situations for commonsense application. BERT Large (Devlin et al., 2018) gives 86.3 percent accuracy on it, which is the current state of the art

- **Winograd and Winograd NLI schema Challenge**: (Mahajan, 2018) Employs Winograd Schema questions that require the resolution of anaphora *i.e.* the model should identify the antecedent of an ambiguous pronoun.

The commonsense information in the form of

Proceedings of the First Workshop on Commonsense Inference in Natural Language Processing, pages 75–79
Hongkong, China, November 3, 2019. ©2019 Association for Computational Linguistics

various relations is stored in the form of the following knowledge bases:

- **ConceptNet**: It is a freely-available multilingual language base from crowd sourced resources like Wikitionary and Open Mind Common Sense. It is a knowledge graph with words and phrases as the nodes and relation between them as the edges.

- **WebChild**: It is a large collection of commonsense knowledge, automatically extracted from Web contents. WebChild contains triples that connect nouns with adjectives via fine-grained relations. The arguments of these assertions, nouns and adjectives, are disambiguated by mapping them onto their proper WordNet senses.

- **Never Ending Language Learner**:It is C.M.U.'s learning agent that actively learns relations from the web and keeps expanding it's knowledge base 24/7 since 2010. It has about 80 million facts from the web with varying confidences. It continuously learns facts and also keeps improving it's reading competence and thus learning accuracy.

3 Model

Before getting into the details of our model we first briefly describe the problem statement. Given a scenario, a short context about the narrative texts and several questions about the context, we are required to build a system to solve the question by choosing the correct answer from the choices. We are allowed to use external knowledge to improve our model's common sense inference. For more details, please refer. (Ostermann et al., 2018)

. In our system, we have used BERT(Devlin et al., 2018), a pre-trained representation of unlabelled text conditioned on both right and left sequences. To incorporate commonsense in our model we have used relation knowledge between phrases and words from ConceptNet(Liu and Singh, 2004), a knowledge graph that connects words and phrases of natural language (terms) with labeled, weighted edges (assertions).

Passage, questions and answers were extracted from XML files. Each training example contains a passage $\{P_i\}_{i=1}^{|P|}$, a question $\{Q_i\}_{i=1}^{|Q|}$ and an answer $\{A_i\}_{i=1}^{|A|}$. Each passage is concatenated with

Edge Relation	Event Phrase
RelatedTo	A is related to B
FormOf	A is a form of B
PartOf	A is a part of B
UsedFor	A is used for B
AtLocation	A is at B
Causes	A causes B
Synonym	A is synonym of B
Antonym	A is antonym of B
DerivedFrom	A is derived from B

Table 1: Event Phrases

edge relation from ConceptNet. Method of querying from ConceptNet is inspired from (Wang, 2018), but instead of using a relational vector we convert those relations into event phrases and append them to the passage. The conversion from edge relation to event phrases is given in Table 1. This step is important as edge relations in ConceptNet are not present in vocabulary of pre-trained BERT(Devlin et al., 2018). Event phrases convert the intent of edge relation into words that are present in the vocabulary of pre-trained BERT

Since it is a multiple choice task, every training sample, after augmenting with relational knowledge from ConceptNet is formatted as proposed in (Radford, 2018). Each choice will correspond to a sample on which we run the inference. For a given Swag example, we will create the 4following inputs:

$-[CLS]context[SEP]choice_1[SEP]$
$-[CLS]context[SEP]choice_2[SEP]$
$-[CLS]context[SEP]choice_3[SEP]$
$-[CLS]context[SEP]choice_4[SEP]$

$context$ contains passage concatenated with question and relational knowledge from ConceptNet The model outputs a single value for each input. To get the final decision of the model, we run a softmax over these 4 outputs.

4 Experiments

The training data includes 2500 passages with 14,190 questions while development data has 355 passages and 2019 questions in total. We have used (Pyt) along with Pytorch to read and fine tune pretrained BERT. We have listed the hyperparameters in Table 2. We have tried model and selected the one with best score in development data. We have pretrained the model with Race Dataset (Lai et al., 2017) for 1 epoch. The model is trained on

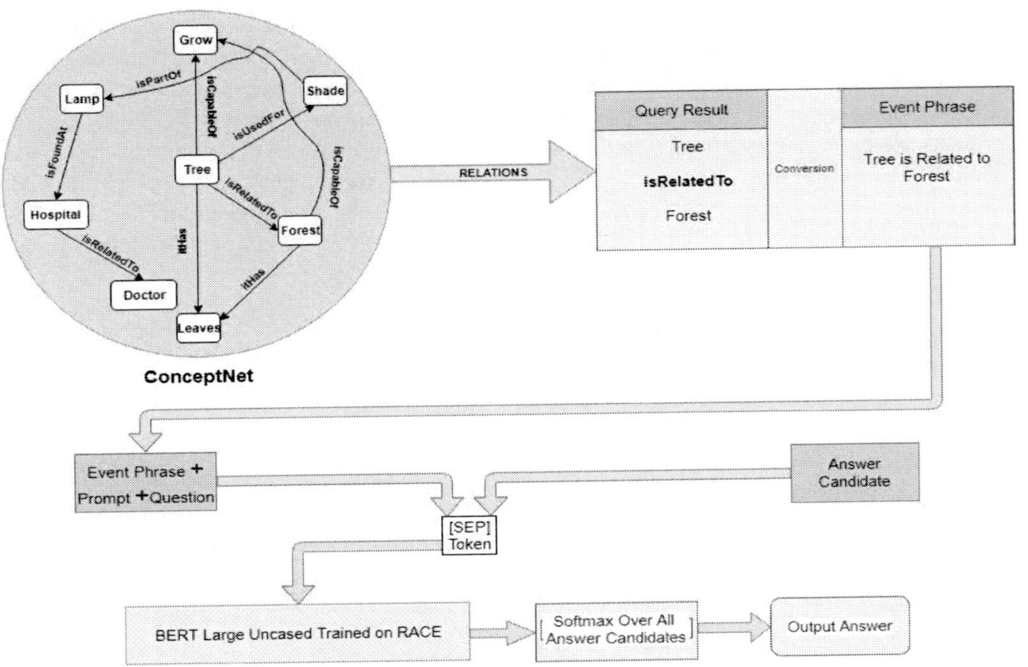

Figure 1: Model Overview

Paramter	Value
$learning rate$	2e-5
$max seq length$	210
$batch size$	4
$epochs$	3
$Optimizer$	ADAM

Table 2: Hyperparameters

Model	Dev-set	Test-set
$w/o\,Q$	**83.6%**	73.3%
$w/o\,RACE$	81.2%	-
$w/o\,Q\,and\,PA\,Rel$	76.7%	-
$w/o\,Q\,and\,QA\,Rel$	79.8%	-
$w/o\,PA\,Rel\,and\,QA\,Rel$	74.1%	-

Table 3: Results

Google Colab GPU for 2 epochs. We have used BERT uncased base pretrained model. Gradients are clipped to have a maximum L2 norm of 10.

5 Results

The experimental results are shown in Table 3. The evaluation metric used is accuracy. We have experimented with different variants of *context*. Description of models are given below:

- $w/o\,RACE$: Model without pretraining with RACE and *context* contains passage, question , relation between passage and answer and relation between question and answer.

- $w/o\,Q$: Model with *context* containing passage, relation between passage and answer and relation between question and answer.

- $w/o\,Q\,and\,PA\,Rel$: Model with *context* containing passage and relation between question and answer.

- $w/o\,Q\,and\,QA\,Rel$: Model with *context* containing passage and relation between question and answer.

- $w/o\,PA\,Rel\,and\,QA\,Rel$: Model with *context* containing only passage and question.

6 Error Analysis

The reason for difference in accuracy of test set and dev set might be due to the fact that we are using a subset of ConceptNet. The subset was selected based on the vocabulary of training data and development data. The vocabulary

77

of test data might not be in the selected subset of ConceptNet. There might be few or even no edges for the test data in the selected subset. Thus the accuracy of test data for model $w/o\,Q$ is pretty close to accuracy of dev data for model $w/o\,PA\,Rel\,and\,QA\,Rel$.

7 Conclusion

We conculde from our experiments that:

- Pre-Trained Models work better with fine-tuning when the target task for which we are training for is brought into the same domain as the training task. We thus tried with out approach to convert the COIN task as the question anwering task for which BERT was pre trained.

- The addition of ConceptNet derived event phrases increased the model accuracy on the dev set by 9 percent. This is a positive feedback towards the exploitation of the various Knowledge Graphs and Corpora (as mentioned in the introduction). The improvement of accuracy of this method of use of commonsense relations would improve along the the progress of Natural Language Understanding.

- We were not able to use the event phrases on the test set as the edges that we had extracted out of ConceptNet were not inclusive of the test dataset. This problem could be solved if there were enough compute power made available to build and use the whole of ConceptNet or call it from it's web API in the presence of an active internet connection during model evaluation and with sufficient number of call instances of the API available.

8 Scope and Future Work

The Development in Commonsense Inference is detrimental to the progress towards truly general purpose A.I. It's application can be easily be found in development of smarter chat bots and search engines. It delimits the inference systems from using only the provided contextual information from the question asked and hence makes the system more human-like.

Possible developments in this task can come with the use of word embeddings made from ConceptNet and other commonsense corporas and graphs (cite) like Conceptnet Numberbatch embeddings. The accuracy can further be improved by making more grammatically correct and composite sentences from the relations. Further tuning of the Hyperparameters of the model and larger training sample collection would also go long way in helping this field develop.

References:

References

Pytorchtransformer. `https://github.com/huggingface/pytorch-transformers`.

Jacob Devlin, Ming-Wei Chang, Kenton Lee, and Kristina Toutanova. 2018. BERT: pre-training of deep bidirectional transformers for language understanding. *CoRR*, abs/1810.04805.

Guokun Lai, Qizhe Xie, Hanxiao Liu, Yiming Yang, and Eduard Hovy. 2017. Race: Large-scale reading comprehension dataset from examinations. pages 785–794.

H. Liu and P. Singh. 2004. Conceptnet — a practical commonsense reasoning tool-kit. *BT Technology Journal*, 22(4):211–226.

Vatsal Mahajan. 2018. Winograd schema - knowledge extraction using narrative chains. *CoRR*, abs/1801.02281.

Simon Ostermann, Michael Roth, Ashutosh Modi, Stefan Thater, and Manfred Pinkal. 2018. Semeval-2018 task 11: Machine comprehension using commonsense knowledge. pages 747–757.

Alec Radford. 2018. Improving language understanding by generative pre-training.

Hannah Rashkin, Maarten Sap, Emily Allaway, Noah A. Smith, and Yejin Choi. 2018. Event2mind: Commonsense inference on events, intents, and reactions. *CoRR*, abs/1805.06939.

Et al. T. Mitchell. 2015. Never-ending learning. In *Proceedings of the Twenty-Ninth AAAI Conference on Artificial Intelligence (AAAI-15)*.

Niket Tandon, Gerard de Melo, and Gerhard Weikum. 2017. WebChild 2.0 : Fine-grained commonsense knowledge distillation. In *Proceedings of ACL 2017, System Demonstrations*, pages 115–120, Vancouver, Canada. Association for Computational Linguistics.

Liang Wang. 2018. Yuanfudao at semeval-2018 task 11: Three-way attention and relational knowledge for commonsense machine comprehension. *CoRR*, abs/1803.00191.

Rowan Zellers, Yonatan Bisk, Roy Schwartz, and Yejin Choi. 2018. SWAG: A large-scale adversarial dataset for grounded commonsense inference. In *Proceedings of the 2018 Conference on Empirical Methods in Natural Language Processing*, pages 93–104, Brussels, Belgium. Association for Computational Linguistics.

IIT-KGP at COIN - Shared Task: Using pre-trained Language Models for modeling Machine Comprehension

Prakhar Sharma, Sumegh Roychowdhury
Indian Institute of Technology Kharagpur,
India
`{prakharsharma, sumegh01}@iitkgp.ac.in`

Abstract

In this paper, we describe our system for *COIN 2019 Shared Task 1: Commonsense Inference in Everyday Narrations* Ostermann et al. (2019). We show the power of leveraging state-of-the-art pre-trained language models such as **BERT** (Bidirectional Encoder Representations from Transformers) Devlin et al. (2018) and **XLNet** Yang et al. (2019) over other Commonsense Knowledge Base Resources such as ConceptNet Speer et al. (2018) and NELL Mitchell et al. (2015) for modeling machine comprehension. We used an ensemble of $BERT_{Large}$ and $XLNet_{Large}$. Experimental results show that our model gives substantial improvements over the baseline and other systems incorporating knowledge bases and got the **2nd position** on the final test set leaderboard with an accuracy of 90.5%.

1 Introduction

Machine Reading Comprehension (MRC) recently has been one of the most explored topics in the field of natural language processing. MRC consists of various sub-tasks Chen et al. (2018), such as cloze-style reading comprehension Hermann et al. (2015); Hill et al. (2015); Cui et al. (2018), span-extraction reading comprehension Rajpurkar et al. (2016) and open-domain reading comprehension Chen et al. (2017), etc. Earlier approaches to machine reading and comprehension have been based on either hand engineered grammars Riloff and Thelens (2000), or information extraction methods of detecting predicate argument triples that can later be queried as a relational database Poon et al. (2010). These methods show effectiveness, but they rely on feature extraction and language tools. Recently, with the advances and huge success of neural networks over traditional feature based models, there have been great interests in building neural architectures for

various NLP task Li and Zhou (2018), including several pieces of work on machine comprehension Hermann et al. (2015); Hill et al. (2015); Yin et al. (2016); Kadlec et al. (2016); Cui et al. (2018), which have gained significant performance in machine comprehension domain.

Machine comprehension using commonsense reasoning is required to answer multiple-choice questions based on narrative texts about daily activities of human beings Yuan et al. (2018). The answer to many questions does not appear directly in the text, but requires simple reasoning to achieve. In terms of the nature of the problem, this task can be considered as a binary classification. That is, for each question, the candidate answers are divided into two categories: the correct answers and the wrong answers.

In this paper, we show that pretrained Language Models alone can model commonsense reasoning better than the other models incorporating commonsense knowledge base resources like ConceptNet, NELL, etc integrated with deep neural architectures. We propose to use an ensemble architecture consisting of *BERT* and *XLNet* for this task which achieves an accuracy of 91.0% on the dev set and 90.5% on the test set outperforming the *Attentive Reader* baseline by a large margin of 25.4%.

2 Task Description & Dataset

Formally, this Shared Task: Commonsense Inference in Everyday Narrations Ostermann et al. (2019), organized within COIN 2019 is a multiple-choice machine comprehension task that can be expressed as a quadruple: $< D, Q, A, a >$ Sheng et al. (2018). Where D represents a narrative text about everyday activities, Q represents a question for the content of the narrative text, A is the candidate answer choice set to the question(this task

Proceedings of the First Workshop on Commonsense Inference in Natural Language Processing, pages 80–84
Hongkong, China, November 3, 2019. ©2019 Association for Computational Linguistics

T	My backyard was looking a little empty, so I decided I would plant something. I went out and bought tree seeds. I found a spot in my yard that looked like it would get enough sunshine. There, I dug a hole for the seeds. Once that was done, I took my watering can and watered the seeds .
Q1	*Why was the tree planted in that spot?*
	to get enough sunshine ✓
	there was no other space ✗
Q2	*What was used to dig the hole?*
	a shovel ✓
	their bare hands ✗
Q3	*Who took the watering can?*
	the grandmother ✗
	the gardener ✓

Figure 1: Example text from SemEval '18 Task 11

contains two candidate answers choice a0 and a1) and a represents the correct answer. The system is expected to select an answer from A that best answers Q according to the evidences in document D or commonsense knowledge.

This task assesses how the inclusion of commonsense knowledge in the form of script knowledge would benefit machine comprehension systems. Script knowledge is defined as the knowledge about everyday activities, i.e. sequences of events describing stereotypical human activities (also called scenarios), for example baking a cake, taking a bus, etc. In addition to what is mentioned in the text, a substantial number of questions require inference using script knowledge about different scenarios, i.e. answering the questions requires knowledge beyond the facts mentioned in the text.

Answers are short and limited to a few words. The texts used in this task cover more than 100 everyday scenarios, hence include a wide variety of human activities. While for question A, it is easy to find the correct answer ("to get enough sunshine") from the text, questions B and C are more complicated to answer. For a person, it is clear that the most plausible answers are "a shovel" and "the gardener", although both are not explicitly mentioned in the texts.

Recently, a number of datasets have been proposed for machine comprehension. One example is MCTest Richardson et al. (2013), a small curated dataset of 660 stories, with 4 multiple choice questions per story. The stories are crowdsourced and not limited to a domain. Answering questions in MCTest requires drawing inferences from multiple sentences from the text passage. Another recently published multiple choice dataset is RACE Lai et al. (2017), which contains more than 28,000 passages and nearly 100,000 questions. The dataset is collected from English examinations in China, which are designed for middle school and high school students.

3 System Overview

We created an ensemble of two systems **BERT** Devlin et al. (2018) and **XLNet** Yang et al. (2019), each of which independently calculates the probabilities of all options for a correct answer.

3.1 Finetuned BERT

BERT is designed to train deep bidirectional representations by jointly conditioning on both left and right context in all layers. We chose $BERT_{Large, uncased}$ as our underlying BERT model. It consists of 24-layers, 1024-hidden, 16-heads, and 340M parameters. It was trained on the Book-Corpus (800M words) and the English Wikipedia (2,500M words). The context, questions and options were first tokenized with *BertTokenizer* to perform punctuation splitting, lower casing and invalid characters removal. The sequence which is fed into the model is generated in form of [CLS] + context + [SEP] + question + answer + [SEP] for every possible answer and sequence was assigned label 1 for correct answer and 0 otherwise. The maximum sequence length was set as 500 on COIN dataset, with shorter sequences padded and in longer sequences context were truncated to adjust context + question + answer to this length. We first fine-tuned BERT on the RACE dataset using a maximum sequence length of 350 for 2 epochs.

We used the PyTorch implementation of BERT from *transformers*[1] which had the BERT tokenizer, positional embeddings, and pre-trained BERT model. Following the recommendation for fine-tuning in the original BERT approach Devlin et al. (2018), we trained our model with a batch size of 8 for 8 epochs. The dropout probability was set to 0.1 for all layers, and Adam optimizer was used with a learning rate of 1e-5.

---

[1] https://github.com/huggingface/transformers

3.2 Semi-Finetuned XLNet

Both RACE and COIN dataset contains relatively long passages with average sequence length greater than 300. Since the use of the Transformer-XL architecture improves the capability of modeling long sequences besides the AR objective as mentioned in Yang et al. (2019). Hence we focused our attention on XLNet model which is a pre-trained language model built upon the Transformer-XL architecture. We used the XLNet$_{Large, Cased}$ model which has 24-layer, 1024-hidden and 16-heads. The input to XLNet model is similar to BERT : [A, SEP, B, SEP, CLS], with a small difference that [CLS] token is used at the end instead of the beginning. Here A and B are the two segments, A represents the context and B represents the question + answer. We call our model **semi-finetuned** because we used the *Google Colab TPU* for fine-tuning XLNet but we had to limit the maximum sequence length to 312 owing to the huge computational capacity required by XLNet$_{Large, Cased}$. We used the Tensorflow implementation of XLNet from *zihangdai/xlnet*[2]. So we couldn't properly fine-tune XLNet on RACE. After fine-tuning on RACE dataset for a few epochs, we fine-tuned further on the COIN dataset keeping maximum sequence length close to 400. The maximum train steps was set to 12000, batch size as 8 and Adam optimizer was used with a learning rate of 1e-5.

3.3 Ensemble

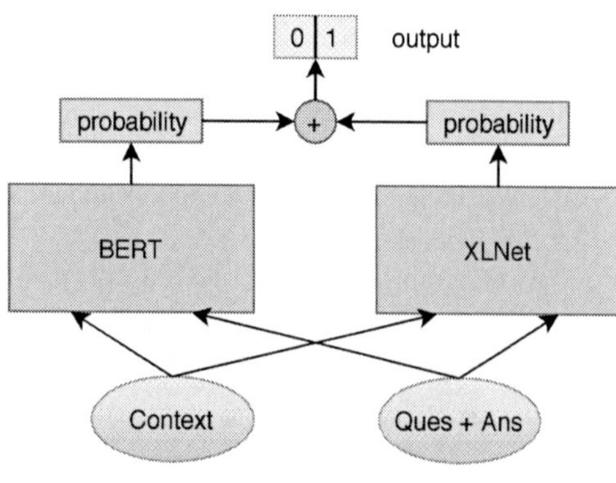

Figure 2: Ensemble Model

Ensemble learning is an effective approach to improve model generalization, and has been used

---

to achieve new state-of-the-art results in a wide range of natural language understanding (NLU) tasks Devlin et al. (2018); Liu et al. (2019b, 2018). For the COIN 2019 shared task, we adopt a simple ensemble approach, that is, **averaging** the softmax outputs from both BERT$_{Large, uncased}$ and XLNet$_{Large, cased}$, and make predictions based on these averaged class probabilities. Our final submission follow this ensemble strategy.

4 Additional Experiments

We applied several approaches to the problem that did not generalize as well to the development data and were not included in the final ensemble. Due to space constraints we don't describe the simpler models which include simple rule-based, feature-based classification models, etc.

TriAN: We started with the previous state-of-the-art model for SemEval '18 Task-11 : *TriAN* Wang et al. (2018) as our baseline. We used both SemEval'18 Task 11 and COIN 2019 datasets for training. The Input layer uses GloVe word embeddings concatenated with the part-of-speech tag, named-entity and relation embeddings. It then consists of a Attention Layer which models three way attention between context, question and answer. Question-aware passage representation $\{\mathbf{w}^q_{P_i}\}_{i=1}^{|P|}$ can be calculated as: $\mathbf{w}^q_{P_i} = Att_{seq}(\mathbf{E}^{glove}_{P_i}, \{\mathbf{E}^{glove}_{Q_i}\}_{i=1}^{|Q|})$. Similarly, we can get passage-aware answer representation $\{\mathbf{w}^p_{A_i}\}_{i=1}^{|A|}$ and question-aware answer representation $\{\mathbf{w}^q_{A_i}\}_{i=1}^{|A|}$. These Question-aware passage representation, Passage-aware answer representation and Question-aware answer representation obtained from above are concatenated and fed into 3 BiLSTMs to model the temporal dependency. Then three BiLSTMs are applied to the concatenation of those vectors to model the temporal dependency:

$$h^q = \text{BiLSTM}(\{\mathbf{w}_{Q_i}\}_{i=1}^{|Q|})$$

$$h^p = \text{BiLSTM}(\{[\mathbf{w}_{P_i}; \mathbf{w}^q_{P_i}]\}_{i=1}^{|P|})$$

$$h^a = \text{BiLSTM}(\{[\mathbf{w}_{A_i}; \mathbf{w}^p_{A_i}; \mathbf{w}^q_{A_i}]\}_{i=1}^{|A|})$$

$\mathbf{h}^p, \mathbf{h}^q, \mathbf{h}^a$ are the new representation vectors that incorporates more context information. Then we have question representation $\mathbf{q} = Att_{self}(\{\mathbf{h}^q_i\}_{i=1}^{|Q|})$, answer representation $\mathbf{a} = Att_{self}(\{\mathbf{h}^a_i\}_{i=1}^{|A|})$ and passage representation $\mathbf{p} =$

---

[2]https://github.com/zihangdai/xlnet

$Att_{seq}(\mathbf{q}, \{\mathbf{h}_i^p\}_{i=1}^{|P|})$. The final output y is based on their bilinear interactions:

$$y = \sigma(\mathbf{p}^T \mathbf{W}_3 \mathbf{a} + \mathbf{q}^T \mathbf{W}_4 \mathbf{a}) \tag{1}$$

Question sequence and answer sequence representation are summarized into fixed-length vectors with self-attention

5 Results and Discussion

This section discusses regarding the results of various approaches we applied in this task. First, as a starting point we ran the best performing model on the SemEval '18 Task 11 - *TriAN* using the same hyper-parameters settings as stated in the paper (Wang et al., 2018). It achieved an accuracy close to 69.0%. We fine-tuned the single BERT$_{\text{Large, uncased}}$ model on the COIN + SemEval '18 Task 11 dataset and that achieved an accuracy of 83.4% on the dev set. We further fine-tuned it on the commonsense dataset RACE for a few epochs which increased the accuracy by 1%. We also fine-tuned the XLNet$_{\text{Large, cased}}$ model on the COIN + SemEval '18 dataset which alone achieved an accuracy of 90.6% on the dev set. But we couldn't fully fine-tune it on the RACE dataset as mentioned earlier in *Section 3.2*. We finally submitted our ensemble system which achieves an accuracy of 91.0% on the dev set and 90.5% on the hidden test set.

We can see there isn't much difference in the accuracy of our final ensemble model on the hidden Test set compared to the Dev set which shows that our model generalizes well to new/unseen data.

Model	Dev Accuracy
TriAN	69.0
BERT$_{\text{large, uncased}}$	84.4
XLNet$_{\text{large, cased}}$	90.6
Ensemble	**91.0**

Table 1: Accuracy results for various models.

The main problem with commonsense knowledge bases is that they are hard-coded Wang et al. (2018) and they do not generalize well to hidden dataset. This is also evident from *Table 2* as the top 3 systems (*unofficial leaderboard*)[3] do not use any kind of commonsense knowledge bases.

Rank	Team	Acc.	Knowledge Base
1	PSH-SJTU (Li et al., 2019)	90.6	No
2	**IIT-KGP (ours)**	**90.5**	**No**
3	BLCU-NLP (Liu et al., 2019a)	84.2	No
4	JDA (Da, 2019)	80.7	Yes
5	KARNA (Jain and Singh, 2019)	73.3	Yes

Table 2: Performance comparison among participants of the COIN Shared Task 1, depicting use of commonsense knowledge bases.

6 Conclusion & Future Work

In this paper, we present our system for the *Commonsense Inference in Everyday Narrations Shared Task* at *COIN 2019*. We built upon the recent success of pre-trained language models and apply them for reading comprehension. Our System achieves close to state-of-art performance on this task.

As future work, we will try to explore the in-depth layer by layer analysis of BERT and XLNet attention similar to Clark et al. (2019) and how the attention helps in commonsense reasoning.

Acknowledgments

We would like to thank the **Computer Science and Engineering Department** of **Indian Institute of Technology, Kharagpur** for providing us the computational resources required for performing various experiments. Also, we would like to thank Google for providing us **Google Colab**[4] and free **TPU (Tensor Processing Unit)** access which was extremely crucial for us in fine-tuning XLNet.

References

Danqi Chen, Adam Fisch, Jason Weston, and Antoine Bordes. 2017. Reading wikipedia to answer open-domain questions.

Zhipeng Chen, Yiming Cui, Wentao Ma, Shijin Wang, Ting Liu, and Guoping Hu. 2018. Hfl-rc system at semeval-2018 task 11: Hybrid multi-aspects model for commonsense reading comprehension.

---

[3] https://coinnlp.github.io/task1.html

[4] https://colab.research.google.com/

Kevin Clark, Urvashi Khandelwal, Omer Levy, and Christopher D. Manning. 2019. What does bert look at?an analysis of berts attention.

Yiming Cui, Ting Liu, Zhipeng Chen, Wentao Ma, Shijin Wang, and Guoping Hu. 2018. Dataset for the first evaluation on chinese machine reading comprehension.

Jeff Da. 2019. Jeff da at coin - shared task.

Jacob Devlin, Ming-Wei Chang, Kenton Lee, and Kristina Toutanova. 2018. Bert: Pre-training of deep bidirectional transformers for language understanding.

Karl Moritz Hermann, Tomas Kocisky, Edward Grefenstette, Lasse Espeholt, Will Kay, Mustafa Suleyman, and Phil Blunsom. 2015. Teaching machines to read and comprehend.

Felix Hill, Antoine Bordes, Sumit Chopra, and Jason Weston. 2015. The goldilocks principle: Reading childrens books with explicit memory representations.

Yash Jain and Chinmay Singh. 2019. Karna at coin - shared task: Bidirectional encoder representations from transformers with relational knowledge for machine comprehension with common sense.

Rudolf Kadlec, Martin Schmid, Ondrej Bajgar, and Jan Kleindienst. 2016. Text understanding with the attention sum reader network.

Guokun Lai, Qizhe Xie, Hanxiao Liu, Yiming Yang, and Eduard Hovy. 2017. Race: Large-scale reading comprehension dataset from examinations.

Xiepeng Li, Zhexi Zhang, Wei Zhu, Yuan Ni, Peng Gao, Junchi Yan, and Guotong Xie. 2019. Pingan smart health and sjtu at coin - shared task: Utilizing pre-trained language models and commonsense knowledge in machine reading tasks.

Yongbin Li and Xiaobing Zhou. 2018. Zmu at semeval-2018 task 11: Machine comprehension task using deep learning models.

Chunhua Liu, Shike Wang, , Bohan Li, and Dong Yu. 2019a. Blcu-nlp at coin - shared task: Stagewise fine-tuning bert for commonsense inference in everyday narrations.

Xiaodong Liu, Pengcheng He, Weizhu Chen, and Jianfeng Gao. 2019b. Improving multi-task deep neural networks via knowledge distillation for natural language understanding.

Xiaodong Liu, Yelong Shen, Kevin Duh, and Jianfeng Gao. 2018. Stochastic answer networks for machine reading comprehension.

T. Mitchell, W. Cohen, and E. Hruschka. 2015. Neverending learning.

Simon Ostermann, Sheng Zhang, Michael Roth, and Peter Clark. 2019. Commonsense Inference in Natural Language Processing (COIN) Shared Task Report. In *Proceedings of the 2019 EMNLP Workshop COIN: Commonsense Inference in NLP*.

Hoifung Poon, Janara Christensen, Pedro Domingos, Oren Etzioni, Raphael Hoffmann, Chloe Kiddon, Thomas Lin, Xiao Ling, Alan Ritter, and et al Stefan Schoenmackers. 2010. Machine reading at the university of washington.

Pranav Rajpurkar, Jian Zhang, Konstantin Lopyrev, and Percy Liang. 2016. A span-extraction dataset for chinese machine reading comprehension.

Matthew Richardson, Christopher J.C. Burges, and Erin Renshaw. 2013. MCTest: A challenge dataset for the open-domain machine comprehension of text.

Ellen Riloff and Michael Thelens. 2000. A rule-based question answering system for reading comprehension tests.

Yixuan Sheng, Man Lan, and Yuanbin Wu. 2018. Ecnu at semeval-2018 task 11: Using deep learning method to address machine comprehension task.

Robyn Speer, Joshua Chin, and Catherine Havasi. 2018. Conceptnet 5.5: An open multilingual graph of general knowledge.

Liang Wang, Meng Sun, Wei Zhao, Kewei Shen, and Jingming Liu. 2018. Yuanfudao at semeval-2018 task 11: Three-way attention and relational knowledge for commonsense machine comprehension.

Zhilin Yang, Zihang Dai, Yiming Yan, Jaime Carbonell, Ruslan Salakhutdinov, and Quoc V. Le. 2019. Xlnet: Generalized autoregressive pretraining for language understanding.

Wenpeng Yin, Sebastian Ebert, and Hinrich Schutze. 2016. Attention-based convolutional neural network for machine comprehension.

Hang Yuan, Jin Wang, and Xuejie Zhang. 2018. Ynuhpcc at semeval-2018 task 11: Using an attention-based cnn-lstm for machine comprehension using commonsense knowledge.

Jeff Da at COIN - Shared Task: BIG MOOD: Relating Transformers to Explicit Commonsense Knowledge

Jeff Da

Paul G. Allen School of Computer Science & Engineering,
University of Washington, Seattle, WA, USA
`jzda@cs.washington.edu`

Abstract

We introduce a simple yet effective method of integrating contextual embeddings with commonsense graph embeddings, dubbed BERT Infused Graphs: Matching Over Other embeDdings. First, we introduce a preprocessing method to improve the speed of querying knowledge bases. Then, we develop a method of creating knowledge embeddings from each knowledge base. We introduce a method of aligning tokens between two misaligned tokenization methods. Finally, we contribute a method of contextualizing BERT after combining with knowledge base embeddings. We also show BERTs tendency to correct lower accuracy question types. Our model achieves a higher accuracy than BERT, and we score fifth on the official leaderboard of the shared task and score the highest without any additional language model pretraining.

1 Introduction

Recently, wide-scale pre-training and deep contextual representations have taken the world by storm. Peters et al. (2018) underscored the importance of bidirectional contextual representations by using traditional neural networks trained on a large corpus of text. Devlin et al. (2018) used transformers (Vaswani et al., 2017) and word masking to pre-train on another large corpus of data, reporting human-level performance on one commonsense dataset (Zellers et al., 2018). Yang et al. (2019) achieves state-of-the-art on RACE (Lai et al., 2017) with a Transformer-XL based model (Dai et al., 2019).

The key to success in the performance of many of these models is their ability to train on extremely large datasets. BERT (Devlin et al., 2018), for example, trains on the BooksCorpus (Zhu et al., 2015) and English Wikipedia, for a combined 3,200M words. Other iterations increased the amount of knowledge used during pre-training, such as RoBERTa (Liu et al., 2019). Training large-scale models on these massive datasets has drawbacks, such as significantly increased carbon pollution and harm to the environment (Schwartz et al., 2019; Strubell et al., 2019).

We present a methodology of combining queries from commonsense knowledge bases with contextual embeddings, **BIG MOOD** - BERT Infused Graphs: Matching Over Other embeDdings, and abbreviated for its relationship to human knowledge awareness. Our methodology achieves a increase without significant additional fine-tuning or pre-training. Instead, it learns a separate representation from commonsense graphical knowledge bases, and augments the BERT representation with this learned explicit representation. We introduce several methods of combining and querying knowledge base embeddings to introduce them to the BERT embedding layers.

2 Related Work

2.1 Knowledge Graphs

Significant research has been put into representing human knowledge in various ways (Lenat and Guha, 1989; Auer et al., 2007; Chambers and Jurafsky, 2008). ConceptNet (Speer and Havasi, 2013) contains various aspects of commonsense knowledge through a knowledge graph.The knowledge is collected from crowedsourced resources (Meyer and Gurevych, 2012; Havasi et al., 2010; von Ahn et al., 2006) and expert-created resources (Miller, 1992; Breen, 2004). WebChild (Tandon et al., 2017) is a collection of commonsense knowledge automatically extracted from web contents. The database is constructed similarly to ConceptNet, and intended to cover concepts that ConceptNet does not cover. ATOMIC (Sap et al., 2018) focuses on inferential

Proceedings of the First Workshop on Commonsense Inference in Natural Language Processing, pages 85–92
Hongkong, China, November 3, 2019. ©2019 Association for Computational Linguistics

Passage: I had decided that I wanted to visit my friend Paul whom lives quite a distance away. With this and my fear of air travel in mind I decided to take a train. After researching and finding one online I was well on my way to going to see my friend Paul. I drive to the station and decide that I am going to purchase a round trip ticket as this would be cheaper than just buying both tickets separately. Whenever my train arrives I have to get in line as they process our tickets. After all this is done I decide to take a seat by the window. I sit and fall asleep a bit as I ride on the train for hours. After a couple hours we finally reach the destination and I get off the train, excited to see my friend.

When did they wait for their train?
a) before buying the ticket
b) after buying a ticket

Table 1: Example of a prompt from the shared task dataset, an everyday commonsense reasoning dataset. Questions often require script knowledge that extends beyond referencing the text.

$If - Then$ relations, built for everyday commonsense reasoning.

2.2 Knowledge Integration

Knowledge graphs have been applied in various natural language processing applications, such as reading comprehension (Lin et al., 2017; Yang and Mitchell, 2017) and machine translation (Zhang et al., 2017). ERNIE: Enhanced Representation through Knowledge Integration (Sun et al., 2019) appends knowledge to the input of the model and learns via knowledge masking, as well as entity-level masking and phrase-level masking. TriAN (Wang, 2018), the top public model on the MC-Script (Ostermann et al., 2018) shared task, uses ConceptNet embeddings to highlight relationships between the question, text, and answer.

3 Model

We present our model for this shared task. Our model has three major components: language model adaptation, knowledge graph embeddings, and attention for classification.

3.1 Data Preprocessing

Before model usage, we preprocess the data in two ways to make it easier for the model to un-

derstand. For language modeling, we create training data similar to those in BERT (Devlin et al., 2018). For knowledge graph use, we preprocess language to create commonsense object and relationship vocabulary and to match as many related commonsense objects as possible.

3.1.1 Language Model Preprocessing

We prepossess each passage for training. We use this process for each training epoch, since it allows for the most dense pretraining framework.

Commonly known as a *cloze task*, Devlin et al. (2018) introduced a framework that pretrained transformers (Vaswani et al., 2017) based on masked token prediction. First, we preprocess the tokens with WordPiece embeddings (Wu et al., 2016). Then, we append special $[CLS]$ and $[SEP]$ to each datum. We append $[CLS]$ to the beginning of each datum, and $[SEP]$ to separate the question with the answer, as such:

$$[CLS] \; passage \; question \; [SEP] \; ans. \; [SEP]$$

Then, we randomly mask 15% of all WordPiece embeddings. Unlike Devlin et al. (2018), we run the randomization script once per each training epoch. Otherwise, we follow the procedure in Devlin et al. (2018). 80% of the time, we replace the word with the $[MASK]$ prediction, to be replaced through cloze task prediction. 10% of the time, we replace the word with a random word. 10% of the time, we keep the word unchanged.

Combined with the above cloze task, we process the data for next sentence prediction. We do this process after the cloze task masking, similar to Devlin et al. (2018). For each datum, we randomly pick either a sentence labeled correctly as the next sentence 50% of the time, or a random sentence 50% of the time. We ensure that the random sentence is not the next sentence.

3.1.2 Knowledge Graph Processing

We preprocess the data in the shared task along with knowledge graph preprocessing. The purpose of this procedure is to reduce the number of items in the knowledge graph, to speed up fine-tuning since the knowledge graphs are extremely large, and also to ensure matching between as many different types of knowledge graph edges that are relevant as possible.

First, we create an index of *(start, end, edge)* relationships that match vocabulary within the shared task prompt. For each *(start, end, edge)*, we

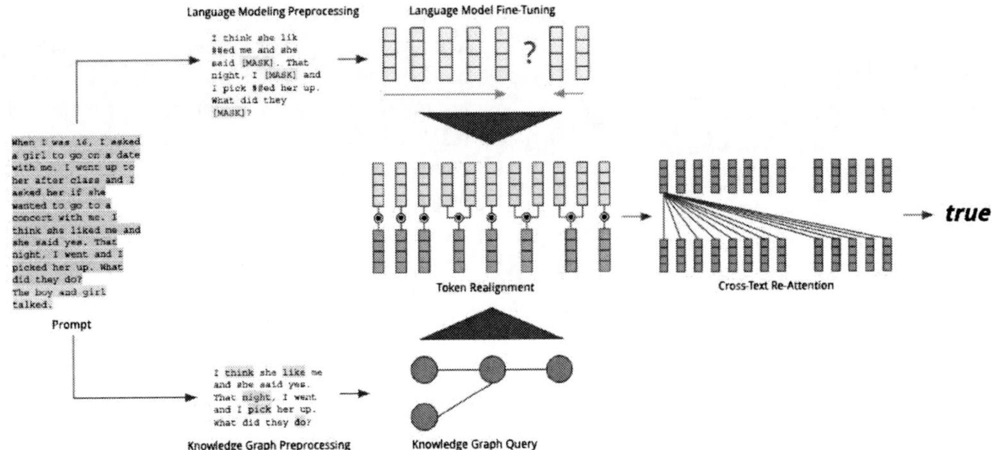

Figure 1: Our model architecture. Our design mimics (Vaswani et al., 2017). Since the queries work on whole words only, one knowledge base embeddings may be integrated with one or more language embedding. Several self-attention encoding layers are used.

Algorithm 1: Knowledge Graph Vocab Creation

for *prompt in dataset* **do**
    for *KG in knowledge_graphs* **do**
        for *(start, end, edge) in KG* **do**
            if *start in prompt & end in prompt*
            then
                add((start, end, edge))
                index_as_relationship(edge)
            end if
        end for
    end for
end for

---

check to see if there are any matching prompts in which *start* is present in the text and *end* is present in the text. If so, we store the *(start, end, edge)*, and note the edge as a relationship. We also index the relationship (edge), giving an index for each unique relationship.

For longer sequences, we allow matches between any trigram, and store an index for each trigram matched. In addition, we stem words beforehand, to ensure that the different word endings do not effect the result of the matches. We use the Porter Stemmer (Porter, 1980) to stem each word in both the text and the knowledge graph. Note that we only use the stemming to match different words, and do not keep the stemmed words for later use in the process, as to keep comparability between embedding types. We also stem words in knowledge bases, to allow for comprasion. Algorithm 1 shows our process for matching sequences.

3.2 Knowledge Graph Usage

We query each of three knowledge bases to create an embedding layer, for each word, for each knowledge graph. Here, we describe our procedure for querying each knowledge graph. We stem words beforehand, to allow for matches agnostic of linguistic postfixes (Merkhofer et al., 2018).

3.2.1 ConceptNet

ConceptNet (Speer and Havasi, 2013) represents everyday words and phrases, with edges between the commonsense relationships between them. We first preprocess ConceptNet, keeping only the vocabulary present in the shared task. Then, for each edge, we store a tuple *(agent, dependent, relationship)* that describes the commonsense relationship mentioned in the knowledge graph.

During fine-tuning, we check the text for any present *agent, dependent* pairs. If any word in the text is an *agent*, and the *dependent* is present in the text, we add that *relationship* index as input into the embedding layer. (For *agents* that span more than one word, such as the phrase "apple pie", we apply the index to the first word, as long as the entire phrase is found in the text). We randomly generate a length 10 embedding for each relationship, and if more than one relationship is matched, we randomly pick one.

3.2.2 WebChild

WebChild (Tandon et al., 2017) is a large collection of commonsense knowledge collected from various sources on the web. The format is similar to ConceptNet, which allows us to follow a similar process. WordNet instances are split into categories $part - whole$, $comparative$, $property$, $activity$, and $spatial$. For each category, we capture the $(agent, dependent, relationship)$ tuple, which is usually defined as properties such as $x_{disambi}$, $y_{disambi}$, and $sub - relation$, but is slightly different for each category. We ignore the WordNet (Miller, 1992) relation (some categories will contain subjects such as $bike\#n\#1$, and take only the stemmed word. For fine-tuning, we follow the same procedure as ConceptNet, creating an additional 10-length embedding for each word.

3.2.3 ATOMIC

ATOMIC (Sap et al., 2018) is a resource that focuses on inferential knowledge via $If - Then$ relations. ATOMIC separates its relationships into nine different types ($xNeed$, $xIntent$, $xAttr$, $xEffect$, $xReact$, $xWant$, $oEffect$, $oWant$). For each of the nine categories, for each datum in the given category, we search our text for relationships that match the defined $If - Then$ relationship. Since each relationship is nearly a full sentence, we allow a match to be any trigram matched between the given datum and the text. Then, we append an index $[0, 8]$ to the embedding layer of the first word in the selected trigram based on the type of relationship matched. For fine-tuning, we follow the same procedure as ConceptNet and WebChild, creating an additional 10-length embedding for each word.

3.3 Architecture

Out modeling procedure consists of three parts. First, we query each knowledge graph, allowing us to create embeddings for each specific graph. Then, we describe our word-level knowledge fusion procedure, creating augmented embeddings for each word. Finally, we describe our fine-tuning procedure for the shared task dataset. We modify pytorch-transformers[1].

3.3.1 Language Model Fine-Tuning

Contrary to Devlin et al. (2018), we do language model fine-tuning in addition to classification fine-tuning. We find that this generally provides better results, and allows for more stable accuracy since the shared task involves a small dataset. For each prompt, we use the previous preprocessed data to create tasks for our model to predict. We do this before token realignment, so this happens before any extra knowledge graph embeddings are added to the model architecture. For masked tokens, we predict that token through bidirectional context, the same as Devlin et al. (2018). For next sentence prediction, we use the unbiased method previously introduced as well as in Devlin et al. (2018).

3.3.2 Token Realignment

We do a word-level fusion to incorporate knowledge embeddings into the BERT model. First, we collect word embeddings from BERT. We sum the last four layer of BERT together, as suggested by "The Illustrated BERT, ELMo, and co."[2]. We fuse these embeddings with the embeddings gathered from querying each of the three databases. For each word, we take the dyadic product, or linear fusion, of the contextual BERT embeddings with the concatenation of the three graph embeddings. When there is no related embedding (if the word did not match any edges during querying, or if the word is a BERT-specific token such as $[CLS]$, we do not do any dyadic fusion. Finally, to get a single linear layer, we concatenate each dimension of the result of the dyadic fusion with the original BERT embedding. Algorithm 2 shows a detailed explanation of our token realignment process.

3.3.3 Re-Attention

To get a final result, we do a few more necessary steps. First, we do a single layer of self-attention over the text, allowing each of the word-level embeddings to interact with one another. For this self-attention, we follow the same process as in (Vaswani et al., 2017). We compare each token with each other and do token-level fusion with each other to learn an attention embedding layer. Then, we use the sequence embedding for classification. We add a simple linear layer over the sequence embedding for classification, and softmax over the given choices. Note that we do not freeze any weights along the process, allowing the transformer and perceptron to

---

Algorithm 2: Psuedocode for the token realignment algorithm, a method of finding token alignments between two different sequences.

```
token_realignment(seq_1, seq_2):
alignment_dict = dict
seq_1_i = 0
seq_2_i = 0
while seq_1_i < len(seq_1) & seq_2_i < len(seq_2) do
    if seq_1[seq_1_i] is seq_2[seq_2_i] then
        alignment_dict[seq_1_i].append(seq_2_i)
        seq_1_i++
        seq_2_i++
    end if
    if seq_1[seq_1_i] in seq_2[seq_2_i] then
        alignment_dict[seq_1_i].append(seq_2_i)
        seq_1_i++
    end if
    if seq_2[seq_2_i] in seq_1[seq_1_i] then
        alignment_dict[seq_1_i].append(seq_2_i)
        seq_2_i++
    end if
end while
return alignment_dict
```

be fine-tuned during this process. We also allow the knowledge embeddings to be modified through this back-propagation. Hyperparameters are noted in Section 4.1. We also ablate our use of this extra attention layer, showing that it is important to learn comparisons between knowledge embeddings. For BERT baselines, we use the process in Devlin et al. (2018), and use the $[CLS]$ token, without attention, for classification.

4 Analysis

4.1 Hyperparameter Tuning

For hyperparameter tuning with BERT, we find that grid search is the best method. We tune various hyperparameters, including batch size, learning rate, warmup, and epoch count (for hyperparameter details, see appendix). Graph 2 shows the results of several hyperparameters on BERT with our additional knowledge bases. We find that B. MOOD seems to correct its deficiencies as it gets closer to the maxima. Interestingly, B. MOOD seems to be naturally good "What" questions, which commonly require commonsense inference. This could be explained by the effect of the commonsense knowledge graphs, showing that is picking up on commonsense attributes. How-

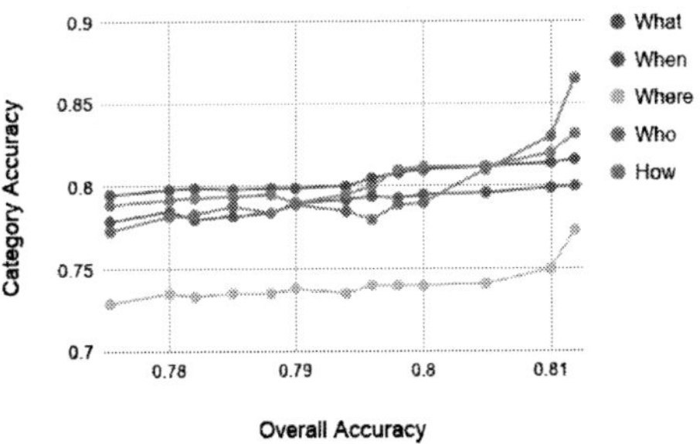

Figure 2: Example of B. MOOD accuracy across categories during hyperparameter turning. Values to the right are closer to the maxima.

ever, for "Where" questions, which it requires more information from the text, B. MOOD needs to learn and thus experiences a greater gain as the accuracy gets closer to its maxima.

We also compare to TriAN (Wang, 2018), the previous state-of-the-art. Table shows our results. For the majority of categories, it seems to begin to be 50/50 between TriAN and MOOD, with TriAN showing more strength in commonsense categories. However, B. MOOD begins to get large jumps in accuracy in categories that it is beat in (such as "Who" and "Where"). For knowledge

System	Accuracy	
	Dev	Test
Human	97.4	98.0
Logistic Baseline	-	60.8
TriAN (Wang, 2018)	76.1	-
BERT$_{LARGE}$	82.3	-
B. MOOD (with ConceptNet)	83.1	-
B. MOOD (with WebChild)	82.7	-
B. MOOD (with ATOMIC)	82.5	-
B. MOOD (w/o final attention)	82.4	-
B. MOOD (with all KB)	**83.3**	**80.7**

Table 2: Results with B. MOOD on task dev and test set. "with all KB" describes results using all Concept-Net, WebChild, and ATOMIC embeddings. "Human" and "Regression Baseline" accuracy is from the shared task paper (Ostermann et al., 2018). TriAN (Wang, 2018) uses ConceptNet as features.

Category	System Accuracy		
	TriAN	BERT	B. MOOD
What	79.3	81.6	84.5
When	69.4	80.0	81.3
Where	75.1	77.3	78.3
Who	79.4	86.5	86.6
How	76.8	83.2	83.4
Overall	76.1	82.3	**83.3**

Table 3: Question type comparison between different models on the shared task: previous state-of-the-art TriAN (Wang, 2018), BERT$_{LARGE}$, and B. MOOD (with all 3 knowledge bases).

embeddings, we use a size of 10 for each knowledge graph, combining for a size 30 knowledge graph embedding. We randomly init each embedding, and if there is more than one embedding for token, we pick one at random (Wang, 2018). For BERT fine-tuning, we use a maximum sequence length of 450, a train batch size of 32, four epochs, $1e - 5$ learning rate, and a 20% warmup.

4.2 Results

We show our results and give analysis for MOOD. We show that each of the knowledge bases help the accuracy of our model, and our strongest model involves the union of all three knowledge bases. ConceptNet gives the largest increase, likely because there are the most matches between the prompts and ConceptNet, since ConceptNet covers everyday concepts that are relatively more common. WebChild gives a boost also, but not as large as ConceptNet. ATOMIC gives the small-

est boost, likely because 1) ATOMIC queries are the longest, and thus, least likely to match, and 2) there is not as much inferential commonsense present.

We also note that the base B. MOOD accuracy is higher than the base TriAN (Wang, 2018) accuracy, the previous state of the art. By appending similar knowledge embeddings, we find that we can bring the TriAN accuracy up to 77.8%, which is more comparable with MOOD. This shows that the additional knowledge bases (ATOMIC, WebChild) contribute to the overall accuracy even without the contextual embeddings. However, we find that the knowledge bases combined with TriAN still do not provide an improvement above that of MOOD, and thus, the knowledge bases alone are not enough to capture the necessary information. Instead, the knowledge graphs must be used through combination with contextual embeddings for the most effective model. This shows that BERT may lack the complete amount of information needed to understand this dataset. We also show that the attention is needed to understand the knowledge graphs alongside BERT, showing the importance of learning the different knowledge base embeddings within the text. This highlights the fact that using the knowledge base embeddings is helpful, and also comparisons between different sections of text is helpful for reading comprehension tasks.

5 Conclusion

We introduce a method of fine-tuning with graphical embeddings alongside contextual embeddings, MOOD. Our method uses three different knowledge bases, and introduces ways of improving both learning speed and knowledge embedding effectiveness. First, we preprocess the dataset, showing that both language model preprocessing and knowledge graph preprocessing is important to the final result. Then, we tune our language model on the shared task, stabilizing the hyperparameter search. We create knowledge graph embeddings and concatenate the embeddings via token realignment. Then, we introduce a final layer of attention that learns both contextual and explicit graph embeddings through contextualization. We show the effect of various knowledge bases, and show our accuracy across various question types. Our model gets fifth on the task leaderboard and outperforms BERT across all question types. We hope that this investigation motivates and furthers additional research in combining commonsense knowledge awareness with transformers.

Acknowledgments

The author thanks Maxwell Forbes, as well as the anonymous reviewers, for their helpful and insightful feedback. The author also thanks the shared task organizers for evaluation on the test set. JD is supported by NSF Multimodal.

References

Luis von Ahn, Mihir Kedia, and Manuel Blum. 2006. Verbosity: a game for collecting common-sense facts. In *CHI*.

Sören Auer, Christian Bizer, Georgi Kobilarov, Jens Lehmann, Richard Cyganiak, and Zachary G. Ives. 2007. Dbpedia: A nucleus for a web of open data. In *ISWC/ASWC*.

Jim Breen. 2004. Jmdict: A japanese-multilingual dictionary.

Nathanael Chambers and Daniel Jurafsky. 2008. Unsupervised learning of narrative event chains. In *ACL*.

Zihang Dai, Zhilin Yang, Yiming Yang, Jaime G. Carbonell, Quoc V. Le, and Ruslan Salakhutdinov. 2019. Transformer-xl: Attentive language models beyond a fixed-length context. *ArXiv*, abs/1901.02860.

Jacob Devlin, Ming-Wei Chang, Kenton Lee, and Kristina Toutanova. 2018. Bert: Pre-training of deep bidirectional transformers for language understanding. *ArXiv*, abs/1810.04805.

Catherine Havasi, R. Speer, Kenneth C. Arnold, Henry Lieberman, Jason B. Alonso, and Jesse Moeller. 2010. Open mind common sense: Crowd-sourcing for common sense. In *Collaboratively-Built Knowledge Sources and AI*.

Guokun Lai, Qizhe Xie, Hanxiao Liu, Yiming Yang, and Eduard H. Hovy. 2017. Race: Large-scale reading comprehension dataset from examinations. In *EMNLP*.

Douglas B. Lenat and Ramanathan V. Guha. 1989. Building large knowledge-based systems; representation and inference in the cyc project.

Hongyu Lin, Le Sun, and Xianpei Han. 2017. Reasoning with heterogeneous knowledge for commonsense machine comprehension. In *EMNLP*.

Yinhan Liu, Myle Ott, Naman Goyal, Jingfei Du, Mandar S. Joshi, Danqi Chen, Omer Levy, Miranda Paige Linscott Lewis, Luke S. Zettlemoyer, and Veselin Stoyanov. 2019. Roberta: A robustly optimized bert pretraining approach. *ArXiv*, abs/1907.11692.

Elizabeth M. Merkhofer, John C. Henderson, David Bloom, Laura Strickhart, and Guido Zarrella. 2018. Mitre at semeval-2018 task 11: Commonsense reasoning without commonsense knowledge. In *SemEval@NAACL-HLT*.

Christian M. Meyer and Iryna Gurevych. 2012. Wiktionary: A new rival for expert-built lexicons? exploring the possibilities of collaborative lexicography.

George A. Miller. 1992. Wordnet: A lexical database for english. *Commun. ACM*, 38:39–41.

Simon Ostermann, Ashutosh Modi, Michael Roth, Stefan Thater, and Manfred Pinkal. 2018. Mcscript: A novel dataset for assessing machine comprehension using script knowledge. *ArXiv*, abs/1803.05223.

Matthew E. Peters, Mark Neumann, Mohit Iyyer, Matt Gardner, Christopher Clark, Kenton Lee, and Luke S. Zettlemoyer. 2018. Deep contextualized word representations. *ArXiv*, abs/1802.05365.

Martin F. Porter. 1980. An algorithm for suffix stripping. *Program*, 40:211–218.

Maarten Sap, Ronan Le Bras, Emily Allaway, Chandra Bhagavatula, Nicholas Lourie, Hannah Rashkin, Brendan Roof, Noah A. Smith, and Yejin Choi. 2018. Atomic: An atlas of machine commonsense for if-then reasoning. *ArXiv*, abs/1811.00146.

Roy Schwartz, Jesse Dodge, Noah A. Smith, and Oren Etzioni. 2019. Green ai.

R. Speer and Catherine Havasi. 2013. Conceptnet 5: A large semantic network for relational knowledge. In *The People's Web Meets NLP*.

Emma Strubell, Ananya Ganesh, and Andrew McCallum. 2019. Energy and policy considerations for deep learning in nlp. *ArXiv*, abs/1906.02243.

Yu Sun, Shuohuan Wang, Yukun Li, Shikun Feng, Xuyi Chen, Han Zhang, Xin Tian, Danxiang Zhu, Hao Tian, and Hua Wu. 2019. Ernie: Enhanced representation through knowledge integration. *ArXiv*, abs/1904.09223.

Niket Tandon, Gerard de Melo, and Gerhard Weikum. 2017. WebChild 2.0 : Fine-grained commonsense knowledge distillation. In *Proceedings of ACL 2017, System Demonstrations*, pages 115–120, Vancouver, Canada. Association for Computational Linguistics.

Ashish Vaswani, Noam Shazeer, Niki Parmar, Jakob Uszkoreit, Lawrence Jones, Aidan N. Gomez, Lukasz Kaiser, and Illia Polosukhin. 2017. Attention is all you need. In *NIPS*.

Liang Wang. 2018. Yuanfudao at semeval-2018 task 11: Three-way attention and relational knowledge for commonsense machine comprehension. In *SemEval@NAACL-HLT*.

Yonghui Wu, Mike Schuster, Zhifeng Chen, Quoc V. Le, Mohammad Norouzi, Wolfgang Macherey, Maxim Krikun, Yuan Cao, Qin Gao, Klaus Macherey, Jeff Klingner, Apurva Shah, Melvin Johnson, Xiaobing Liu, Lukasz Kaiser, Stephan Gouws, Yoshikiyo Kato, Taku Kudo, Hideto Kazawa, Keith Stevens, George Kurian, Nishant Patil, Wei Wang, Cliff Young, Jason Smith, Jason Riesa, Alex Rudnick, Oriol Vinyals, Gregory S. Corrado, Macduff Hughes, and Jeffrey Dean. 2016. Google's neural machine translation system: Bridging the gap between human and machine translation. *ArXiv*, abs/1609.08144.

Bishan Yang and Tom M. Mitchell. 2017. Leveraging knowledge bases in lstms for improving machine reading. In *ACL*.

Zhilin Yang, Zihang Dai, Yiming Yang, Jaime G. Carbonell, Ruslan Salakhutdinov, and Quoc V. Le. 2019. Xlnet: Generalized autoregressive pretraining for language understanding. *ArXiv*, abs/1906.08237.

Rowan Zellers, Yonatan Bisk, Roy Schwartz, and Yejin Choi. 2018. Swag: A large-scale adversarial dataset for grounded commonsense inference. *ArXiv*, abs/1808.05326.

Jiacheng Zhang, Yang Liu, Huanbo Luan, Jingfang Xu, and Maosong Sun. 2017. Prior knowledge integration for neural machine translation using posterior regularization. *ArXiv*, abs/1811.01100.

Yukun Zhu, Jamie Ryan Kiros, Richard S. Zemel, Ruslan Salakhutdinov, Raquel Urtasun, Antonio Torralba, and Sanja Fidler. 2015. Aligning books and movies: Towards story-like visual explanations by watching movies and reading books. *2015 IEEE International Conference on Computer Vision (ICCV)*, pages 19–27.

A Appendices

A.1 Hyperparameters

Seen in Table 4 is a list of hyperparameters for our experiments. We use the same parameters for both uses of explicit knowledge embeddings.

Explicit Knowledge Embeddings	
Embedding size	10
Knowledge bases used	3
BERT Fine-Tuning	
Maximum sequence length	450
Train batch size	32
Learning rate	1e-5
Epochs	4
Warmup	20%
TriAN Parameters	
Optimizer	adamax
Learning rate	2e-3
Batch size	32
Hidden size	96
RNN type	lstm
Embedding dropout	0.4

Table 4: Hyperparameters used throughout experiments. TriAN parameters are used for TriAN comparison only.

Pingan Smart Health and SJTU at COIN - Shared Task: utilizing Pre-trained Language Models and Common-sense Knowledge in Machine Reading Tasks

Xiepeng Li[1*]   Zhexi Zhang[2*]   Wei Zhu[1*†]   Zheng Li[1]   Yuan Ni[1]
Peng Gao[1]   Junchi Yan[2]   Guotong Xie[1]
[1] Pingan Health Tech, Shanghai, China
[2] Shanghai Jiaotong University, Shanghai, China

Abstract

To solve the shared tasks of COIN: COmmonsense INference in Natural Language Processing) Workshop in EMNLP-IJCNLP 2019, we need explore the impact of knowledge representation in modeling commonsense knowledge to boost performance of machine reading comprehension beyond simple text matching. There are two approaches to represent knowledge in the low-dimensional space. The first is to leverage large-scale unsupervised text corpus to train fixed or contextual language representations. The second approach is to explicitly express knowledge into a knowledge graph (KG), and then fit a model to represent the facts in the KG. We have experimented both (a) improving the fine-tuning of pre-trained language models on a task with a small dataset size, by leveraging datasets of similar tasks; and (b) incorporating the distributional representations of a KG onto the representations of pre-trained language models, via simply concatenation or multi-head attention. We find out that: (a) for task 1, first fine-tuning on larger datasets like RACE (Lai et al., 2017) and SWAG (Zellers et al., 2018), and then fine-tuning on the target task improve the performance significantly; (b) for task 2, we find out the incorporating a KG of commonsense knowledge, WordNet (Miller, 1995) into the Bert model (Devlin et al., 2018) is helpful, however, it will hurts the performace of XL-NET (Yang et al., 2019), a more powerful pre-trained model. Our approaches achieve the state-of-the-art results on both shared task's official test data, outperforming all the other submissions.

1   Introduction

Machine reading comprehension (MRC) tasks have always been the most studied tasks in the field of natural language understanding. Common forms of reading comprehension tasks involve question answer (QA) , cloze-style and multiple-choice questions. Many models have achieved excellent results on MRC datasets such as (Rajpurkar et al., 2016; Nguyen et al., 2016; Lai et al., 2017; Zhang et al., 2018a). However, Kaushik and Lipton (2018) demonstrate that most questions in previous MRC tasks can be answered by simply matching the patterns in the textual level even with passage or question only, but existing models perform badly on questions that require incorporating knowledge in more sophisticated ways. In contrast, human beings can easily reason with knowledge from contexts or commonsense knowledge when doing MRC task. Thus, it is of significance for models to be able to reason with knowledge, especially commonsense knowledge.

Various deep learning models have been proposed and shown pretty good performance on MRC tasks (Parikh et al., 2019; Zhu et al., 2018; Sun et al., 2018; Xu et al., 2017). Majority of these approaches utilize sequence relevant neural networks such as GRU (Cho et al., 2014), LSTM (Hochreiter and Schmidhuber, 1997) and Attention mechanism (Vaswani et al., 2017) to model the implicit relation among passages, questions and answers.

As pre-trained language models have shown miraculous performance on several NLP tasks, a large number of methods utilize this pre-trained language model to extract textual level features in MRC tasks. (Zhang et al., 2019; Ran et al., 2019) compute the contextual representation of passages, questions and options separately with BERT and match the representation in downstream networks. They achieved the best results on RACE dataset at their submission time.

Shared task 1 in COIN workshop is a two-choice question task with short narrations about

---

* Equal contribution.
† Corresponding email: michaelwzhu91@gmail.com; zhuwei972@pingan.com.cn.

Proceedings of the First Workshop on Commonsense Inference in Natural Language Processing, pages 93–98
Hongkong, China, November 3, 2019. ©2019 Association for Computational Linguistics

everyday scenarios, which is an extended version of SemEval 2018 Task 11 (Ostermann et al., 2018). Shared task 2 uses the ReCoRD dataset (Zhang et al., 2018a), a machine reading comprehension dataset in news articles. It annotates named entities in the news articles and additionally provides some brief bullet points that summarize the news. It then asks for cloze-style answers, filling in a blank in a sentence related to the news article. Accomplishing these tasks requires both the capability of reading comprehension and commonsense knowledge inference.

Our system is based on XLNet (Yang et al., 2019), a generalized auto-regressive pretraining method which achieves state-of-the-art results on many NLP tasks. For task 1, We first pre-train the model on multiple-choice question dataset RACE (Lai et al., 2017) to gain certain reading comprehension abilities. Afterwards, we mine commonsense knowledge by fine-tuning grounded commonsense inference dataset SWAG (Zellers et al., 2018) on XLNet instead of introducing knowledge graph of general knowledge such as ConceptNet (Speer et al., 2017) or WordNet (Miller, 1995). For task 2, other than utilizing XLNet's representation power, we also experiment on enhancing the representation and regularizing predicted prior of named entities, by concatenating the pre-trained embedding of WordNet of contextual word embedding. We finally implement a series of post-processing strategies to improve the model prediction results. Our system achieves state-of-the-art performance on the both shared tasks' official test data, even though we only train on the train sets and only submit single models.

2 Model settings

In this section, we present the system designs we experimented for the two shared tasks.

2.1 Pretrained language model Fine-tuning

As shown in Devlin et al. (2018) and Yang et al. (2019), the usual way to employ pre-trained language models in representing multiple text input is concatenation of text inputs in certain orders. For this section, the denotations mainly follow Yang et al. (2019) since we mainly use XLNet as the text encoder. Since the notations for Bert will be quite similar, which will not be included in this work.

For task 1, the inputs are a context passage (denoted as P), two queries (denoted as Q_i, $i = 1, 2$), and two answer options for each query, $A_{i,j}$, for $j = 1, 2$. Following Yang et al. (2019)'s solution on the RACE dataset, we concatenate the inputs as follows:

$$Concat\,_{i=1}^{2}[P, [SEP], QA_i, [SEP], [CLS]], \tag{1}$$

where QA_i is the concatenation of the query-answer pairs:

$$QA_i = Concat\,_{j=1}^{2}[Q_i, A_{i,j}]. \tag{2}$$

As for Task 2, the inputs are a context passage (denoted as P), which in this case is a piece of a newspaper article, and a assertive sentence (denoted as S) part of which is masked out, thus they are concatenated as follows:

$$Concat\,[P, [SEP], S, [SEP], [CLS]]. \tag{3}$$

After the text inputs are concatenated accordingly, they will go through XLNet to get a contextual representation. The output layer for the two tasks are different. For task 1, a fully-connected layer is put on the $[CLS]$ token's representation two give out the likelihood of which answer option is the answer. For task 2, the answer is selected from the context passage, thus we have to predict the start position and end position. Thus two fully-connected layers are needed, where the first is to estimate the likelihood of being the start position for each token, and the second combines the encoded representation and the output of the first fully-connected layer and predicts the end position.

2.2 Multi-funetuning

Finetuning a pre-trained language model on a small target task dataset has shown significant performance gains, as is shown in Devlin et al. (2018) and Yang et al. (2019). However, directly finetuning is proven not to be the most effective way, since although pre-trained LMs are known to generalize well, overfitting problem is still inevitable. Thus, related corpus or similar datasets are often used, such as Wang et al. (2019) and Phang et al. (2018), to form a multi-stage fine-tuning procedure. For example, Wang et al. (2019) first finetune on the MultiNLI datset before training the CB, RTE, and BoolQ tasks. The intuition behind why this multi-stage fine-tuning strategy works is

Dataset	Options	Sentence A	Sentence B
RACE	4	passage	query+option
SWAG	4	query	option
Task 1	2	passage	query+option

Table 1: Structure of inputs for the two supplementary tasks and the target task dataset

Dataset	Train	Dev
RACE	87866	4887
SWAG	73546	20006
Task 1	14191	2020

Table 2: Basic statistics for the three datasets involved in solving task 1

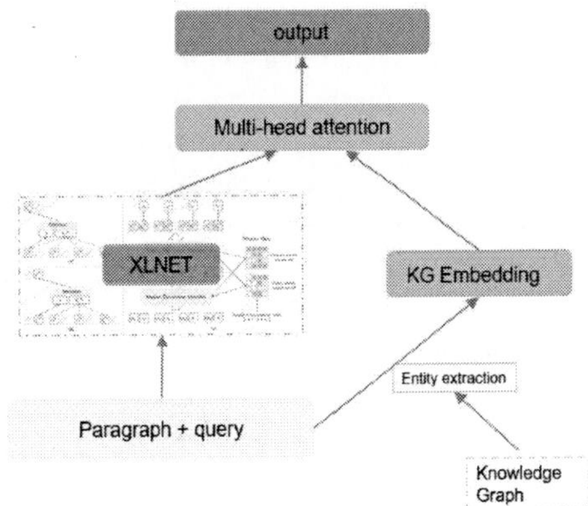

Figure 1: The architecture of our KG infusing model with XLNet as text encoder

that (a) to let the pre-trained LMs to adopt to the similar contextual environment, (b) and make the model more suitable for this specific task formation.

Due to the fact that task 1 dataset is small and during fine-tuning the original XLNet model overfits very quickly, we experimented on a multi-stage fine-tuning strategy. The first additional dataset we choose is RACE, which is relatively larger. Then we choose to fune-tune on SWAG, whose queries are similar to our target task and requires commonsense reasoning. Then we fine-tune till convergence on the task 1 train set.

Table 1 presents the structure of the inputs for the three datasets, where k is the number of options for each query. After each stage before the final fine-tuning, we disregard the final fully-connected output layer and use the updated XLNet layers to fine-tune on the next dataset.

2.3 Knowledge fusing

Besides the original basic fine-tuning architecture adopted by the XLNet, we also experiment on involving commonsense knowledge for context encoding, as is depicted in Figure 1.

The commonsense knowledge graph we use is the WordNet (Miller, 1995). The KG embedding is trained using DistMult (Yang et al., 2014a). First, we will match the phrases in the passage to entities in the WordNet, using Aho-Corasick algorithm (Arudchutha et al., 2014).[1] Then each token in the entity will be given the same embedding vector, which is the embedding of the entity in WordNet. Tokens not in any entity will be given a zero vector as embedding. The KG encoded text input will be incorporated with the encoded output of XLNet using a multi-head attention layer (Vaswani et al., 2017), where the XLNet encoded output acts as the query and the KG encoded output acts the key and value. Then the output layer is the same with answer span prediction layers described in the previous subsection.

2.4 Answer Verification

To improve the prediction results of a model, we implement a series of answer verification strategies, which are the following:

- as there are additional entity information provided with the dataset, at the span predict stage, we filter invalid predicted spans according to whether it match a named entity

- if we can not find any entities in all predictions, we randomly select one from the entities provided to us

- some entity is a part of the '-' concatenation span, then we match the answer by its left or right concatenated contexts

3 Experiment

3.1 Dataset

Statistics for the datasets involved in training for task 1, which are RACE, SWAG and the official task 1 dataset are shown in Table 2. The statistics represent the total number of queries in the corresponding dataset. The final submission result on

---

[1] If a phrase is matched to multiple entities in the KG, we will take the average of all entity embeddings as the entity embedding for the phrase.

the leader-board is calculated on official test data, which will not be published. Only training and development data for the task are available to us.

Task 2, which is the ReCoRD dataset (Zhang et al., 2018b) has 65, 000 queries on the train set and 10, 000 queries on the dev set. The answer for the ReCoRD dataset is not unique, since an entity is likely to be mentioned multiple times in a news article. Thus, we take each passage-query-answer-span as one sample during training, which can also be seen as a kind of data augmentation.

For both tasks, we only submit the models trained on the train sets of the target tasks.

3.2 Experimental setting

We use XLNet (large, cased) as the pre-trained language model. For task 1 dataset, we truncate the query-answer pair to a maximum length of 128, and set the maximum length of the passage-query-answer pair to 384. So the max length of the whole text inputs of one sample is 768. With a Tesla V100-PCIE-16GB GPU card, the batch size can only be set to be 2 on each card, thus we employ 8 GPUs for training. Firstly we fine-tune the original XLNet on RACE for 100,000 steps with the sequence length of 192, query-answer length of 96 and Adam optimizer leaning rate of 1e-6. Afterwards, we fine-tune the model on SWAG for 12,500 steps with the same parameters as RACE's. Eventually, the model is fine-tuned on the task 1 dataset till convergence, where the learning rate is set as 8e-6.

For task 2, the maximum length of the passage-querypair is set to be 384, in which the maximum length for the query is 64. During training the learning rate is 5e-6 and batch size is 4 on each GPU card.

When we try to infuse the KG into the XLNet, we use the OpenKE library (Han et al., 2018) to train the KG representions of WordNet. We choose DistMult (Yang et al., 2014b) as the embedding model, set the embedding size as 100, epoches as 10, batch size as 32 and the learning rate as 1e-4. The multi-head attention between the XLNet encoded output and the entity encoded output has the same number of attention head as the XLNet large model. During training, we will keep the KG embedding trainable. Besides multi-head attention, we also experiment using a whole transformer block, i.e., a multi-head attention layer followed by a position-wise feed-forward network,

Model	Dev	Test
Human	-	97.4%
Final submission	91.44%	90.6%
XLNet	91.09%	-
XLNet+RACE	92.46%	-
XLNet+SWAG	89.36%	-
XLNet+RACE+SWAG	**92.76%**	-

Table 3: Main results on the task 1.

and combining the entity encoding by simply concatenating it onto the XLNet encoded output. For comparison, we switch XLNet with Bert (large model), and repeat the above experiments.

3.3 Results

The main experimental accuracy results for task 1 are shown in Table 3, in which human performance is provided by task organizers. Our system consists of fine-tuning XLNet on RACE and SWAG. We also conduct an ablation experiment to investigate the effects of the two external dataset. As a result, Table 3 illustrates that pre-training on RACE plays a significant role in the system. Origin XLNet achieves an accuracy of 91.09%, indicating its powerful text representation ability, especially in the reading comprehension task. Pre-training on SWAG without RACE does not improve the accuracy perhaps because SWAG misleads the model to better adjust its task formation, thus making it worse on the machine reading comprehension. Meanwhile, combining SWAG together with RACE makes sense, indicating the model can improve its commonsense inference ability.

We achieved the best performance on the official dev dataset with the training steps described in section 3.2 while our submission result on the official leader-board was obtained with fewer training steps due to queue submission time impact on Codalab. Despite being not fully trained, our system still achieve the best result with the accuracy of 90.6%, outperforming other participating teams.

For task 2, the results are presented on Table 4, where the bolded models are our submissions on the test leaderboard. Due to limited resources and, the results are not run multiple times, thus the results may be affected by random effects. We find out the original XLNet performs the best, significantly outperforming the Bert models. While it seems adding a commonsense KG is beneficial for

Model	Dev EM	Dev F1	Test EM	Test F1
Human	-	-	91.31 %	91.69 %
Bert	69.83 %	71.05 %	-	-
Bert + KG (multi-head attn)	71.08 %	72.69 %	-	-
Bert + KG (transformer)	70.36 %	71.84 %	-	-
Bert + KG (concat)	70.74 %	72.09 %	-	-
XLNet	80.64 %	82.10 %	81.46 %	82.66 %
XLNet + KG (multi-head attn)	80.31 %	81.62 %	-	-
XLNet + KG (transformer)	80.16 %	81.55 %	-	-
XLNet + KG (concat)	80.25 %	81.67 %	-	-
XLNet + answer verification	**82.72 %**	**83.38 %**	**83.09 %**	**83.74 %**

Table 4: The main results on task 2.

Bert, it does not help improving XLNet models. For the models with KG, regardless of what the underlying pre-trained langugae model is, multi-head attention works best on infusing the knowledge, and simple concatenation works better than adding a whole transformer block.

For task 2, implementing the answer verification process after we obtain the predictions of XLNet model boost the performance significantly, both on the dev set and the test set. Since we did not see significant improvements by adding KG into the model, we did not submit results from KG infused models.

Conclusions

To conclude, we have shown that XLNet, a recently proposed pre-trained language model, is powerful in text representation for machine reading tasks. Simply fine-tuning XLNet on the shared tasks already outperforms the other models which use Bert as text encoder. However, we demonstrate on task 1 that multi-stage fine-tuning on similar tasks can help providing more stable convergence and improve the final results significantly. For task 2, we also show that the model predictions can be improved by adding human designed post-processing strategies. We also experiments on incorporating commonsense KG into the architecture of XLNet, however, due to our limited experiments, we haven't obtain significant improvements by adding KG into the model, especially models based on XLNet. However, it is a direction worth further research.

References

S. Arudchutha, T. Nishanthy, and R. G. Ragel. 2014. String matching with multicore cpus: Performing better with the aho-corasick algorithm. In *IEEE International Conference on Industrial Information Systems*.

Kyunghyun Cho, Bart Van Merriënboer, Caglar Gulcehre, Dzmitry Bahdanau, Fethi Bougares, Holger Schwenk, and Yoshua Bengio. 2014. Learning phrase representations using rnn encoder-decoder for statistical machine translation. *arXiv preprint arXiv:1406.1078*.

Jacob Devlin, Ming-Wei Chang, Kenton Lee, and Kristina Toutanova. 2018. Bert: Pre-training of deep bidirectional transformers for language understanding. *arXiv preprint arXiv:1810.04805*.

Xu Han, Shulin Cao, Xin Lv, Yankai Lin, Zhiyuan Liu, Maosong Sun, and Juanzi Li. 2018. Openke: An open toolkit for knowledge embedding. In *Proceedings of EMNLP*, pages 139–144.

Sepp Hochreiter and Jürgen Schmidhuber. 1997. Long short-term memory. *Neural computation*, 9(8):1735–1780.

Divyansh Kaushik and Zachary C Lipton. 2018. How much reading does reading comprehension require? a critical investigation of popular benchmarks. *arXiv preprint arXiv:1808.04926*.

Guokun Lai, Qizhe Xie, Hanxiao Liu, Yiming Yang, and Eduard Hovy. 2017. Race: Large-scale reading comprehension dataset from examinations. *arXiv preprint arXiv:1704.04683*.

George A Miller. 1995. Wordnet: a lexical database for english. *Communications of the ACM*, 38(11):39–41.

Tri Nguyen, Mir Rosenberg, Xia Song, Jianfeng Gao, Saurabh Tiwary, Rangan Majumder, and Li Deng. 2016. Ms marco: A human-generated machine reading comprehension dataset.

Simon Ostermann, Michael Roth, Ashutosh Modi, Stefan Thater, and Manfred Pinkal. 2018. Semeval-2018 task 11: Machine comprehension using commonsense knowledge. In *Proceedings of The 12th International Workshop on Semantic Evaluation*, pages 747–757.

Soham Parikh, Ananya B Sai, Preksha Nema, and Mitesh M Khapra. 2019. Eliminet: A model for eliminating options for reading comprehension with multiple choice questions. *arXiv preprint arXiv:1904.02651*.

Jason Phang, Thibault Fvry, and Samuel R. Bowman. 2018. Sentence encoders on stilts: Supplementary training on intermediate labeled-data tasks.

Pranav Rajpurkar, Jian Zhang, Konstantin Lopyrev, and Percy Liang. 2016. Squad: 100,000+ questions for machine comprehension of text. *arXiv preprint arXiv:1606.05250*.

Qiu Ran, Peng Li, Weiwei Hu, and Jie Zhou. 2019. Option comparison network for multiple-choice reading comprehension. *arXiv preprint arXiv:1903.03033*.

Robert Speer, Joshua Chin, and Catherine Havasi. 2017. Conceptnet 5.5: An open multilingual graph of general knowledge. In *Thirty-First AAAI Conference on Artificial Intelligence*.

Kai Sun, Dian Yu, Dong Yu, and Claire Cardie. 2018. Improving machine reading comprehension with general reading strategies. *arXiv preprint arXiv:1810.13441*.

Ashish Vaswani, Noam Shazeer, Niki Parmar, Jakob Uszkoreit, Llion Jones, Aidan N Gomez, Łukasz Kaiser, and Illia Polosukhin. 2017. Attention is all you need. In *Advances in neural information processing systems*, pages 5998–6008.

Alex Wang, Yada Pruksachatkun, Nikita Nangia, Amanpreet Singh, Julian Michael, Felix Hill, Omer Levy, and Samuel R. Bowman. 2019. Superglue: A stickier benchmark for general-purpose language understanding systems.

Yichong Xu, Jingjing Liu, Jianfeng Gao, Yelong Shen, and Xiaodong Liu. 2017. Dynamic fusion networks for machine reading comprehension. *arXiv preprint arXiv:1711.04964*.

Bishan Yang, Wen-tau Yih, Xiaodong He, Jianfeng Gao, and Li Deng. 2014a. Embedding Entities and Relations for Learning and Inference in Knowledge Bases. *arXiv e-prints*, page arXiv:1412.6575.

Bishan Yang, Wen-tau Yih, Xiaodong He, Jianfeng Gao, and Li Deng. 2014b. Embedding Entities and Relations for Learning and Inference in Knowledge Bases. *arXiv e-prints*, page arXiv:1412.6575.

Zhilin Yang, Zihang Dai, Yiming Yang, Jaime Carbonell, Ruslan Salakhutdinov, and Quoc V Le. 2019. Xlnet: Generalized autoregressive pretraining for language understanding. *arXiv preprint arXiv:1906.08237*.

Rowan Zellers, Yonatan Bisk, Roy Schwartz, and Yejin Choi. 2018. Swag: A large-scale adversarial dataset for grounded commonsense inference. *arXiv preprint arXiv:1808.05326*.

Sheng Zhang, Xiaodong Liu, Jingjing Liu, Jianfeng Gao, Kevin Duh, and Benjamin Van Durme. 2018a. Record: Bridging the gap between human and machine commonsense reading comprehension. *CoRR*, abs/1810.12885.

Sheng Zhang, Xiaodong Liu, Jingjing Liu, Jianfeng Gao, and Benjamin Van Durme. 2018b. Record: Bridging the gap between human and machine commonsense reading comprehension.

Shuailiang Zhang, Hai Zhao, Yuwei Wu, Zhuosheng Zhang, Xi Zhou, and Xiang Zhou. 2019. Dual co-matching network for multi-choice reading comprehension. *arXiv preprint arXiv:1901.09381*.

Haichao Zhu, Furu Wei, Bing Qin, and Ting Liu. 2018. Hierarchical attention flow for multiple-choice reading comprehension. In *Thirty-Second AAAI Conference on Artificial Intelligence*.

BLCU-NLP at COIN - Shared Task: Stagewise Fine-tuning BERT for Commonsense Inference in Everyday Narrations

Chunhua Liu [*] **Shike Wang** [*] **Bohan Li** [*] **Dong Yu** [†*✉]

[*] Beijing Language and Culture University
[†] Key Laboratory of Intelligent Information Processing,
Institute of Computing Technology, Chinese Academy of Sciences

{chunhualiu596, shikewang98, bohanli.lavida}@gmail.com
yudong_blcu@126.com

Abstract

This paper describes our system for COIN Shared Task 1: Commonsense Inference in Everyday Narrations. To inject more external knowledge to better reason over the narrative passage, question and answer, the system adopts a stagewise fine-tuning method based on pre-trained BERT model. More specifically, the first stage is to fine-tune on additional machine reading comprehension dataset to learn more commonsense knowledge. The second stage is to fine-tune on target-task (MCScript2.0) with MCScript (2018) dataset assisted. Experimental results show that our system achieves significant improvements over the baseline systems with 84.2% accuracy on the official test dataset.

1 Introduction

The COIN Shared Task1 aims to evaluate a system's commonsense inference ability in everyday narrations by selecting an appropriate answer from two candidates for each question, which also can be seen as a multiple-choice reading comprehension (MCRC) task. The most difficult part of this task lies in about 50% of the questions cannot be answered directly from the passage, because commonsense knowledge required to answer questions is not missing. Commonsense knowledge is essential but challenging to acquire and represent because of its invisible and implicit proprieties. Accordingly, the key solution to this problem is how to introduce world knowledge contained in additional databases or datasets into the system.

Neural networks have gained amazing results in various machine reading comprehension tasks. Typical strategy adapts neural encoder such as LSTM (Long Short-Term Memory) (Hochreiter and Schmidhuber, 1997) or CNN (Convolutional Neural Network)(LeCun and Bengio, 1998) to encode a passage, a question and a candidate answer separately and then employs attention mechanism to model interactions among them. This kind of method performs well on questions that can be answered from given passage texts but shows limited performance on questions demanding external knowledge to answer. Recently, the approach of the pre-training language model on large-scale free-texts to acquire external knowledge and then transferring learned background knowledge to a downstream task has displayed promising improvements in a variety of natural language processing tasks.

Compared with existing pre-trained language models, like ELMo (Peters et al., 2018) and GPT (Alec Radford, 2018), BERT stands out in language representation and understanding by introducing masked language model and next sentence prediction task. Hence, we choose BERT as the basic model to explore how much a pre-trained language model can help to solve the commonsense inference problem. In this process, two primary questions are guiding this work:

- How much gains can a pre-trained language model bring for the commonsense inference task?

- How to add more commonsense knowledge to a pre-trained language model to assist commonsense inference?

For the first question, we designed several groups of experiments to compare the performance of BERT$_{base}$ and BERT$_{large}$ on three types of questions provided in the target task, including text-based, script-based (also called commonsense-based), and text-or-script.

For another question, we present a two-staged fine-tuning approach to add more commonsense knowledge to the model. This first stage is to fine-tune on pre-trained encoder with additional

Proceedings of the First Workshop on Commonsense Inference in Natural Language Processing, pages 99–103
Hongkong, China, November 3, 2019. ©2019 Association for Computational Linguistics

corpus beyond English Wikipedia and BooksCorpus Some other genre corpus, like news-wire texts, English examine texts, and everyday narrations are considered in this phase. This way empowers the encoder to learn and store more knowledge about the world and thus improve its commonsense inference ability. The second stage is to fine-tune the updated encoder with a top classification layer on target-task with the support of additional commonsense datasets.

2 BERT for COIN-Everyday Narrations

2.1 How to Fine-tune BERT?

BERT is a bidirectional transformer encoder trained on the task of masked language model and next sentence prediction, equipping with powerful language encoding capacity. Devlin et al. (2018) provides two pre-trained model sizes: $BERT_{base}$ and $BERT_{large}$ with the different parameters, such as layers $\{12, 24\}$, self-attention heads $\{12, 16\}$, and hidden size $\{768, 1024\}$. BERT can encode any sequence less than 512 tokens, like a sentence or a paragraph. Generally, the final hidden outputs of the first token [CLS] is considered as the overall representation of the whole input sequence.

When applying BERT to MCRC task, the input token sequence is the concatenation of each candidate answer with the corresponding question and passage in the following format:
[CLS] Passage [SEP] Question Candidate [SEP]. So, the final hidden state of [CLS] represents the comprehensive understanding of the passage, question and candidate answer. Additionally, a classification layer is required to stack on the top of the BERT model to score for each candidate answer. The candidate who has the highest score would be regarded as the correct answer. When fine-tuning, the weight of both the BERT and classification layer are modified to adapt to the target task with the goal of minimizing the cross-entropy loss.

2.2 How powerful is BERT?

In this part, $BERT_{base}$ and $BERT_{large}$ model are fine-tuned as above described. Figure 1 show the gap between baseline model Attentive Reader (Hermann et al., 2015) re-implemented by Ostermann et al. (2019) and two pre-trained BERT models. The pre-trained models brings about 12.2% to 15.6% improvements, which obviously outperform the baseline system.

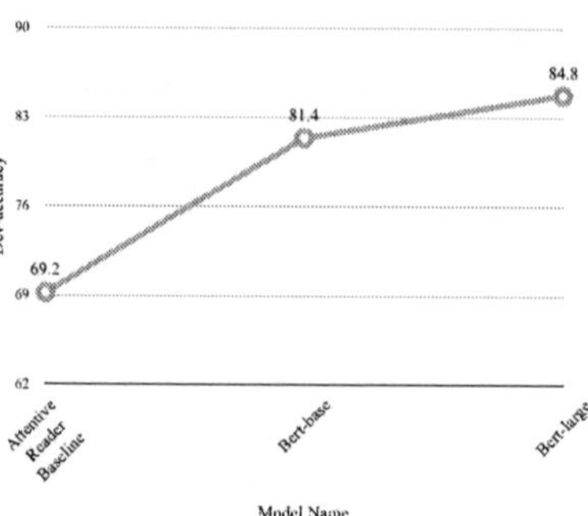

Figure 1: Comparing pre-trained models with baseline model.

Moreover, in order to compare the difference between $BERT_{base}$ and $BERT_{large}$, we give the statistics of their performance on three question labels. Figure 2 illustrates that 1) Both models are good at answering questions whose answer are given in the corresponding passages. 2) Even text-script questions can be answered based on either given passages or external commonsense, it's still hard for $BERT_{base}$ model to answer. 3) Compared with $BERT_{base}$, $BERT_{large}$ shows significant improvements in both script-based questions and text-script questions. These observations reveal that training more texts with a larger model is more likely to learn more commonsense knowledge. So, we use $BERT_{large}$ model in the following experiments.

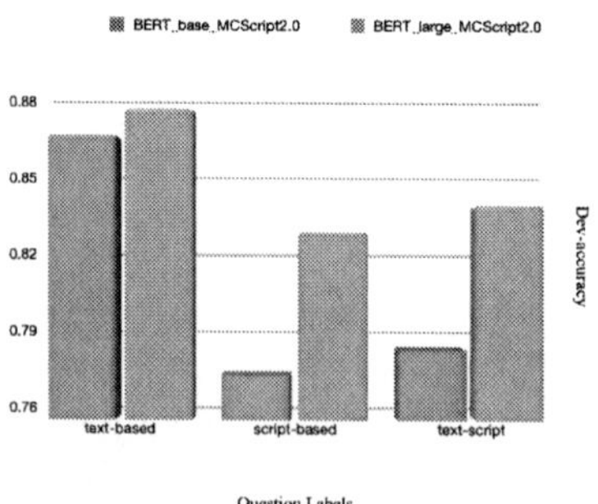

Figure 2: Comparing two BERT models on three question labels.

3 Stagewise Fine-tuning BERT

The overview of stage-wise fine-tuning BERT presented in this work is shown in Figure 3. It consists of two phases: encoder fine-tuning stage, classifier and encoder fine-tuning stage.

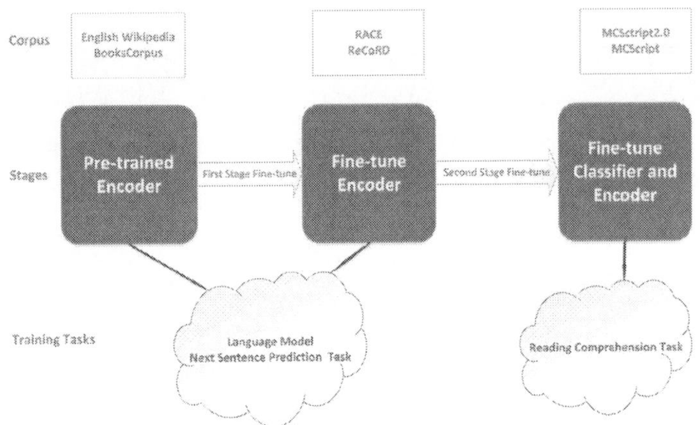

Figure 3: A view of two fine-tuning stages.

Dataset Name	Content	#Passages
RACE (Lai et al., 2017)	Mid/High Exam	25K
ReCoRD (Zhang et al., 2018)	News articles	80K
ROCStories (Mostafazadeh et al., 2016)	Narrations	3K (dev + test)
MCScript (Ostermann et al., 2018)	Narrations	2.1K
MCScript2.0 (Ostermann et al., 2019)	Narrations	3.5K
Inscript (Modi et al., 2017)	Narrations	1K
DES (Wanzare et al., 2019)	Narrations	0.5K

Table 1: Datasets used in this paper for fine-tuning.

3.1 Encoder Fine-tuning

In this work, we denote the pre-trained $BERT_{large}$ model including the embedding part as well as the 12 layers of transformer blocks as a whole and name them as the encoder.

The encoder is responsible for sequence representation by transforming raw input tokens into a fixed representation. Weights in the encoder decide how one token is represented and how one token in a sequence interacts with another. Therefore, allowing the encoder to witness more and train longer can enhance its representation ability and thus able to encode new input with a wide range of structures, writing styles and expressions.

Hence, in this phase, the key lies in how to find more applicable data to train the encoder further, also called fine-tune the encoder based on the pre-trained $BERT_{large}$. When choosing new data, we take two aspects, the task form pertaining to the MCRC and the content relating to everyday narrations into consideration. In addition, based on the number of datasets used for training, the encoder fine-tuning can be classified into two categories: single-dataset fine-tuning and multi-datasets fine-

tuning. The former means to fine-tune the encoder using only a single dataset. The latter fine-tunes the encoder by taking data from multiple datasets as input. Table 1 lists datasets selected in this paper.

For most datasets, only paragraphs or passages are used as training data, whose questions and answers are ignored. But to add more question-answering information, we add some questions and their answers to the passages, which is motivated by the task of the next sentence prediction. For dataset like RACE, whose questions and candidate answer is free-text, we randomly pick a question for the passage as well as its answer and then append it to the end of the passage. In this way, the question is treated as the next sentence for the final sentence of the passage, and similarly, the answer can be seen as the next sentence for the question. This technique makes it possible for the encoder to learn the potential questioning and its answer.

When fine-tuning, the model is still jointly trained on the task of masked language model and next sentence prediction. All weights are modified

Datasets for first stage	Datasets for second stage	Dev-acc(%)	Test-acc(%)
-		84.8	
MCScript2.0		84.8	
MCScript		83.6	
RACE	MCScript2.0	84.9	-
ReCoRD		85.9	
ROCStories		83.5	
Inscript		83.6	
DES		83.9	
RACE	MCScript2.0 + MCScript	85.1	-
RACE	MCScript2.0 + MCScript-w/o-who-how	85.7	-
RACE+ReCoRD	MCScript2.0	85.0	-
RACE+ReCoRD	MCScript2.0 + MCScript	86.0	-
RACE+ReCoRD	MCScript2.0 + MCScript-w/o-who-how	**86.6**	**84.2**
RACE+ReCoRD	MCScript2.0 + SWAG	85.9	-
All Datasets	MCScript2.0 + MCScript-w/o-who-how	84.7	-

Table 2: Main results.

when fine-tuned.

3.2 Classifier and Encoder Fine-tuning

The fist stage fine-tuning endows the encoder with more new knowledge, while the second stage fine-tuning focuses on adjusting weights in the encoder to adapt to the target task. This phase is carried on the fine-tuned encoder with the support of additional commonsense datasets, like MCScript (Ostermann et al., 2018), SWAG (Zellers et al., 2018). The most benefits come from the MCScript, which is the dataset used for evaluation of SemEval 2018 Task 11. When doing experiments, an interesting discovery is found that using the entire MCScript is not the best choice. Filtering some types of questions leads to better results on the development set of MCScript2.0. During fine-tuning, a classification layer is also added on the top of BERT and the training is guided by minimizing the cross-entropy loss.

4 Experiments and Results

4.1 Data

COIN Shared Task 1 uses MCScript2.0 corpus, which consists of three kinds of question labels, including text-based, script-based, and text-script. For text-based question, the answer can be deduced from the information provided in passages, while script-based question can only be answered with the support of external commonsense knowledge. The text-script question can be answered either depends on passages or external script knowledge.

4.2 Experiment Setup

We use the Pytorch version of pre-trained BERT implemented by huggingface[1]. Adam Optimizer (Kingma and Ba, 2014) is used to optimize the model, which is trained on TITAN RTX with 2 GPUs. Important hyper-parameters for training are listed in Table 3.

Description	first stage	second stage
t: tokens max length	350	300
e: fine-tune epoch	{3,4}	{3,4}
α: learning rate	3e-5	1e-5
b: batch size	32	64
g:gradient accumulation step	4	8

Table 3: Hyper-parameters settings used during training.

4.3 Results and Analysis

Table 2 demonstrates results of various trained models, consisting of three groups. This first group experiment is designed for first stage fintune, so only the target dataset, which refers to the MCScript2.0, is used in the second stage. The second group is conducted to help find the most suitable dataset to assist second-stage fine-tuning. The last group is a combination of the previous two groups.

---

[1] https://github.com/huggingface/pytorch-transformers

By observing the results in the first group, we can see that using the dataset from target task to first fine-tune the encoder didn't bring any improvements, indicating that using the same data to train model twice is unnecessary. Also, instead of raising the accuracy, training with some datasets even damage the model and diminish the accuracy. This can be attributed to many reasons, for example, the passage in ROCStories is too short compared with the target task, the data size of Inscript and DES is too small. However, with the prop of RACE and ReCoRD, the model has secured some advances. So, in the next phase fine-tuning, the two datasets are mixed to fine-tune the encoder in the first stage.

The second group of results points out that removing the question types with who and how in the MCScript can surprisingly increase the accuracy compared with using the whole set of MCScript. This is possibly caused by the different data distribution in the two datasets.

Our final submitted model is first fine-tuned on both RACE and ReCoRD and then fine-tuned with data in MCScript without the question type of who and how in MCScript2.0, which achieves the accuracy of 86.6% and 84.2% on the development set and test set separately and ranks fourth on the final test leaderboard.

5   Conclusion

This paper depicts our system that fine-tunes the pre-trained BERT model with two stages, which outperforms far further than the baseline model and achieves the accuracy of 84.2% in the official test dataset. Experimental results indicate that both stages fine-tuning bring benefits to the model. Besides, experiments reveal that $BERT_{large}$ excels at commonsense inference task.

Acknowledgement

This work is funded by the open project of Key Laboratory of Intelligent Information Processing, Institute of Computing Technology, Chinese Academy of Sciences (IIP2019-4).

References

Tim Salimans Ilya Sutskever Alec Radford, Karthik Narasimhan. 2018. Improving language understanding by generative pre-training.

Jacob Devlin, Ming-Wei Chang, Kenton Lee, and Kristina Toutanova. 2018. Bert: Pre-training of deep bidirectional transformers for language understanding. In *NAACL-HLT*.

Karl Moritz Hermann, Tomás Kociský, Edward Grefenstette, Lasse Espeholt, Will Kay, Mustafa Suleyman, and Phil Blunsom. 2015. Teaching machines to read and comprehend. In *NIPS*.

Sepp Hochreiter and Jürgen Schmidhuber. 1997. Long short-term memory. *Neural Computation*.

Guokun Lai, Qizhe Xie, Hanxiao Liu, Yiming Yang, and Eduard H. Hovy. 2017. Race: Large-scale reading comprehension dataset from examinations. In *EMNLP*.

Yann LeCun and Yoshua Bengio. 1998. Convolutional networks for images, speech, and time series.

Ashutosh Modi, Tatjana Anikina, Simon Ostermann, and Manfred Pinkal. 2017. Inscript: Narrative texts annotated with script information. *CoRR*, abs/1703.05260.

Nasrin Mostafazadeh, Nathanael Chambers, Xiaodong He, Devi Parikh, Dhruv Batra, Lucy Vanderwende, Pushmeet Kohli, and James F. Allen. 2016. A corpus and evaluation framework for deeper understanding of commonsense stories. *ArXiv*, abs/1604.01696.

Simon Ostermann, Ashutosh Modi, Michael Roth, Stefan Thater, and Manfred Pinkal. 2018. Mcscript: A novel dataset for assessing machine comprehension using script knowledge.

Simon Ostermann, Michael Roth, and Manfred Pinkal. 2019. MCScript2.0: A machine comprehension corpus focused on script events and participants. In *Proceedings of the Eighth Joint Conference on Lexical and Computational Semantics (*SEM 2019)*, pages 103–117, Minneapolis, Minnesota. Association for Computational Linguistics.

Matthew Peters, Mark Neumann, Mohit Iyyer, Matt Gardner, Christopher Clark, Kenton Lee, and Luke Zettlemoyer. 2018. Deep contextualized word representations. In *Proceedings of NAACL*.

Lilian D. A. Wanzare, Michael Roth, and Manfred Pinkal. 2019. Detecting everyday scenarios in narrative texts. *ArXiv*, abs/1906.04102.

Rowan Zellers, Yonatan Bisk, Roy Schwartz, and Yejin Choi. 2018. Swag: A large-scale adversarial dataset for grounded commonsense inference. In *EMNLP*.

Shenmin Zhang, Xiaodong Liu, Jingjing Liu, Jianfeng Gao, Kevin Duh, and Benjamin Van Durme. 2018. Record: Bridging the gap between human and machine commonsense reading comprehension. *ArXiv*, abs/1810.12885.

Commonsense inference in human-robot communication

Aliaksandr Huminski
Institute of High Performance Computing,
Singapore
huminskia@ihpc.a-star.edu.sg

Ng Yan Bin
A*STAR AI, Singapore
Singapore
ng_yan_bin@scei.a-star.edu.sg

Kenneth Kwok
Institute of High Performance Computing,
Singapore
kenkwok@ihpc.a-star.edu.sg

Francis Bond
Nanyang Technological University,
Singapore
fcbond@ntu.edu.sg

Abstract

Natural language communication between machines and humans are still constrained. The article addresses a gap in natural language understanding about actions, specifically that of understanding commands. We propose a new method for commonsense inference (grounding) of high-level natural language commands into specific action commands for further execution by a robotic system. The method allows to build a knowledge base that consists of a large set of commonsense inferences. The preliminary results have been presented.

1 Introduction

There is a significant progress in movement from early natural language understanding computer programs like SHRDLU (Winograd, 1972) with its deterministic actions in the virtual world to modern cognitive robots operating in the physical world and mapping language to actions. Artificial agents enter our lives and the end users of such systems are not technical experts. The only way for them to communicate with AI is to use natural language. For example, humans can give a natural language command expecting a follow-up action by the agent.

Nowadays in robotics, in order to execute a natural language command which is considered as a high-level instruction, an agent needs to transform it to a sequence of lower-level primitive actions (Figure 1.). For example, the industrial arm SCHUNK has three primitives: *open-gripper*, *close-gripper*, *move-to* and for this agent any high-level command should be transformed into a sequence of these 3 actions to be performed (Kress-Gazit et al., 2008). For smarter agents with more primitives, complicated commands like *fill up the cup with water* can be executed by transformation into a long sequence of the lower-level actions: *pick up the cup, move to your left, put the*

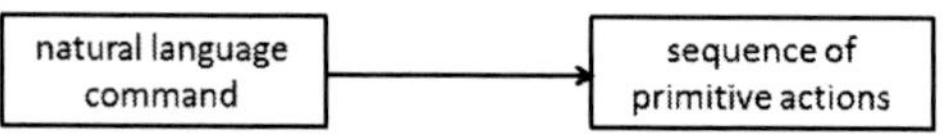

Figure 1: Transformation of high-level command for an agent.

cup under the faucet, turn on the faucet, turn off the faucet, etc. In other words, natural language command decomposition is a necessary step for an agent to be capable of executing.

To make such transformations possible, previous works (Misra et al., 2015; She and Chai, 2016) explicitly model verbs with predicates describing the resulting states of actions. Their empirical evaluations have demonstrated how incorporating result states into verb representations can link language with underlying planning modules for robotic systems (Gao et al., 2016). Recent investigations use reinforcement learning to transform language commands into primitive actions (Misra et al., 2017) or representation of actions (Arumugam et al., 2017).

The current studies in human-robot communication (She and Chai, 2017; Chai et al., 2018) show that natural language understanding of commands is difficult for machines because commands in human-human communications are usually expressed through a desired change of state.

2 Problem Statement

As Rappaport Hovav and Levin (2010) pointed out, any action can be expressed in two different ways. Firstly, there are manner verbs that describe how actions are carried out – i.e. manners of doing: *hit, stab, scrub, sweep, wipe, yell*, etc. Secondly, there are verbs that describe results of an action or a change of state: *break, clean, crush, destroy, shatter*, etc.

Further we will use a term "action verb" as a

Proceedings of the First Workshop on Commonsense Inference in Natural Language Processing, pages 104–112
Hongkong, China, November 3, 2019. ©2019 Association for Computational Linguistics

synonym for a manner verb and a term "result verb" as a synonym for a verb that describes a result of an action or a change of state.

For commands in human-human communication, people mostly use result verbs. We say *open the door*, not *push the door*; *clean the table*, not *wipe the table*.

It should be underlined that result verbs don't express any concrete action. For instance, the command *open the door* represents a particular kind of change of state in an entity but it is silent about **how** this change comes about. The verb *clean* doesn't indicate whether it was done by sweeping, wiping, washing or sucking; the same way the verb *kill* does not indicate how a killing was done[1].

On the contrary, the action verbs in the commands *pull the door, push the door, kick the door,* etc. represent different kinds of action necessary to implement the change of state *open the door*.

The obvious question arises: if a command is expressed through a desired change of state, how humans know what actions to do? The point is that humans derive the information about the concrete actions related to the desired change from shared background knowledge about the world. There is no need to explicitly represent it in human communication. It is commonsense knowledge that enables us to understand each other (Clark, 1996; Tomasello, 2008) and to know how to open the door or how to clean the table (see Figure 2.).

AI systems, even new generations of cognitive agents, have significantly less knowledge about the world and are not able to ground result-verb commands into action-verb commands. A command with a result verb does not give AI any information on *what actions* should be performed to achieve the disable change of state. As a result of that, commands to robots are directly linked to primitive actions implemented by a robot without the intermediate step of identifying them with action verbs (see Figure 1.).

The straightforward approach "command → primitive actions" fails to achieve two significant

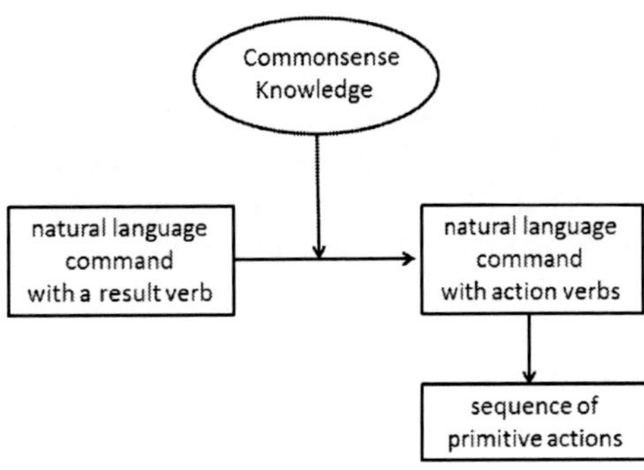

Figure 2: Transformation of high-level command for a human.

points.

First, a result verb being applied to the same object can be executed by different action-verb commands. For instance, the command with the result verb *fill up (the cup with water)* can be executed by the action verb *pour (water into the cup)* or by the action verb *scoop (water from the bucket)*.

Second, a result verb being applied to different objects assumes different action verbs. For instance, the following commands with the same result verb *open* require different action verbs to be executed: *open the door; open the book; open the refrigerator; open the can; open the envelope,* etc. Even for the similar commands *open the door* and *open the refrigerator* there is a difference that must be noted: the last command cannot be implemented by pushing.

The general problem of overcoming the gap in human-robot natural language understanding being applied to the high-level natural language commands can be formulated the following way. How can AI systems transform high-level natural language commands with result verbs into commands with action verbs[2]?

3 Related Work

Although commonsense inference between action verbs and result verbs has been described in linguistic studies (Rappaport Hovav and Levin, 2010), there is still a lack of detailed account of potential causality that could be denoted by an action verb (Gao et al., 2016).

From the AI domain, there were investigations

---

[1]The separation of verbs on action verbs and result verbs got further elaboration in cognitive science where an event representation is considered to be based on 2-vector structure model: a force vector representing the cause of a change and a result vector representing a change in object properties (Gardenfors, 2017; Gardenfors and Warglien, 2012; Warglien et al., 2012). It is argued that this framework gives a cognitive explanation for manner verbs as force vectors and for result verbs as result vectors.

[2]In the article we do not consider the follow-up step in the transformation of action verbs into action primitives for further execution by AI agent. This kind of transformation depends on the type of the agent.

devoted to learning the physics of the world from videos (Fire and Zhu, 2016) and simulations (Wu et al., 2017). However, except for a few works that explored the physical properties of verbs (Forbes and Choi, 2017; Zellers and Choi, 2017), how verbs and their corresponding actions affect the state of the physical world is still largely under-explored.

Well-known knowledge bases like Freebase, YAGO or DBPedia, even being automatically populated by modern NLP methods, do not contain commonsense inferences we are going to create.

Crowd-sourcing resources such as ConceptNet have an incomplete coverage, which is its main drawback. A human knowledge engineer may not list all possible events related to a particular action verb or a result verb. For example, the inference *scrub → clean* might be listed while others such as *mop → clean*, *suck → clean*, or *sweep → clean* might be missed.

Existing linguistic resources such as Propbank, FrameNet or VerbNet provide important information about verb classification, its arguments and semantic roles, but they do not distinguish action verbs and result verbs. For instance, in the largest domain-independent computational verb lexicon VerbNet (Kipper Schuler, 2005), that provides semantic role representation for 6394 verbs (version 3.2b), the action verb *hit* and the result verb *break* have the same structure: [Agent, Instrument, Patient, Result]. Even if the semantic representation for a verb may indicate that a change of state is involved, it does not provide the specifics associated with the verb's meaning (e.g., to what attribute of its patient the changes might occur) (Gao et al., 2016).

WordNet, manually created by professional linguists, to the best of our knowledge, is the only linguistic resource that partly provides information about causal links between action verbs and result verbs. As we will indicate below, these links overlap with the hypernym-hyponym relations in WordNet.

Finally, the broad-coverage resource VerbOcean (Chklovski and Patel, 2004) set a semantic relation "enablement" between verbs using the following 4 patterns: "Xed * by Ying the"; "Xed * by Ying or"; "to X * by Ying the" and "to X * by Ying or", where "X" and "Y" are verbs; (*) matches any single word. The patterns are similar to the one we are going to use. The only signifi-

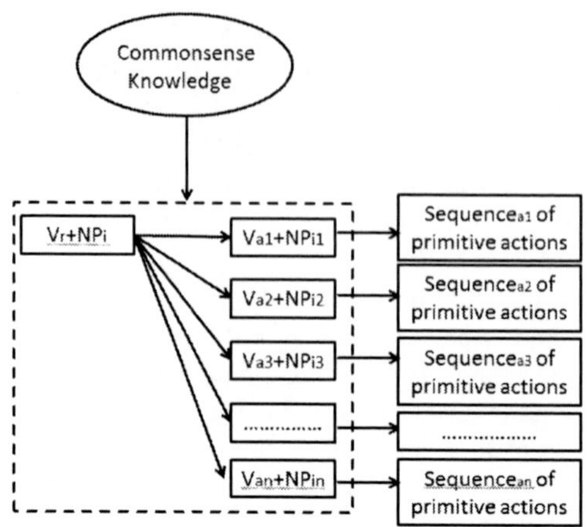

Figure 3: Transformation of high-level command.

cant difference is that all of them do not include a noun after a verb "X". As it was mentioned in the section 3 (2nd point), a result verb being applied to different objects assumes different action verbs.

4 Proposed Approach

We consider the transformation formulated in section 3 as a process of grounding where a high-level command representing a desired change of state is grounded to an action(s) command.

The following two assumptions will be made to formalize the process of grounding.

1) The commands in human-robot interactions can occur in various forms and patterns. Some of them can be rather complicated. Our work addresses the simplest case where a command is represented by the structure V+NP, where V is a verb, NP is a noun phrase.

2) The grounding of a result-verb command into an action-verb command is represented as: $V_r+NP_1+by+V_a+NP_2$, where V_r is a result verb; V_a is an action verb[3].

Since a result verb being applied to the same object can be executed by different action-verb commands, the schema on the Figure 2. will be unfolded as one-to-multi relations between a result-verb command and an action-verb command (see Figure 3.).

The key point here is how to extract one-to-multi relations. In reality, these relations are commonsense inferences that allow humans easily to

---

[3]NP_1 can be the same or different from NP_2. Compare: *open the door by pulling the door* and *open the door by pushing the button*

transform result-verb commands into action-verb commands. These commonsense inferences are so obvious and so well-known to everybody that are very rarely expressed anywhere in a written form. It makes it hard to find and extract from any source of information. As a consequence of that, we cannot apply deep learning techniques for extraction of above-mentioned one-to-multi relations. Deep learning has proved incredibly powerful and effective for many practical tasks from perceptual classification to self-driving cars. But we have to acknowledge the data-hungry nature of systems based on deep learning. The side-effect of that is a long tail of low-frequency data that cannot be treated the same way. Our research deals with such data.

The method suggested for one-to-multi relations extraction is based on 3 non-related approaches and includes three steps accordingly.

1. Getting 2 sets of verbs: a set of result verbs $\{V_r\}$ and a set of action verbs $\{V_a\}$;

2. Getting a set of the most frequent pairs $\{V_r+NP\}$;

3. Getting a set of commonsense inferences $\{V_r+NP_1+by+V_a+NP_2\}$.

In the first step, result verbs (V_r) and action verbs (V_a) are separated. The separation is based on analysis of Wordnet; this is a domain-independent step that aims to cover generally result and action verbs representing the physical world. In the second step, the set of the most frequent pairs $\{V_r+NP\}$ are extracted using the N-gram approach to form result-verb commands: *clean the floor, cool the beer*, etc. In the third step, we use a search engine to check all around the web if there is a commonsense inference between an action-verb command and a result-verb command (*open the door by pressing the button*). If a commonsense inference exists in the web it is considered as being validated and added to the set.

4.1 Step #1: Getting Two Sets of Verbs

The output of the step #1 is two sets of verbs: a set of action verbs $\{V_a\}$ and a set of result verbs $\{V_r\}$. The separation is based on the analysis of the entire set of verbs through Princeton WordNet (WN) (Fellbaum, 1998) which is widely used in a variety of tasks related to extraction of semantic relations. The verb part of WN contains 11529 unique verbs (version WN 3.0)[4]. They are organized in verb synsets ordered mainly by troponym-hypernym hierarchical relations (Fellbaum and Miller, 1990). According to the definitions, a hypernym is a verb with a more generalized meaning, while a troponym replaces the hypernym by indicating a manner of doing something. The closer a verb is to the bottom of a verb tree, the more specific the manners that are expressed by troponyms: *communicate-talk-whisper*[5].

Meanwhile, action verbs are hidden in the WN verb structure since troponyms are not always action verbs. In some troponym-hypernym relations the verbs are in fact action verbs like in {kill}-{drown}. However, there are no explicit ways to extract them yet.

The idea is that action verbs can be extracted from WN if at least one of four conditions, applied to a verb is valid[6] :

1. A verb in WN is an action verb if its gloss contains the following template: "V + by [...]ing", where V=hypernym. Example: {sweep} (*clean by sweeping*);

2. A verb in WN is an action verb if its gloss contains the following template: "V + with + [concrete object]", where V=hypernym. Example: {brush} (*clean with a brush*). Restriction on the concrete object is made to avoid cases like *with success (pleasure, preparation,* etc).

3. A verb in WN is an action verb if it represents movement in any direction: *lift, turn, descend,* etc.

4. A verb in WN is an action verb if its hypernym is an action verb. In other words, once a verb is an action verb, all branches located below consist of action verbs as well, regardless of their glosses.

The procedure of using conditions 1-4 goes from all top verbs to the bottom verbs. For ex-

---

[4] https://wordnet.princeton.edu/documentation/wnstats 7wn. The following paper (McCrae et al., 2019) outlines a roadmap for adding new entries to WordNet, so the number of verbs is not fixed, but increasing over time.

[5] Note that these are defined on verb-senses, not verbs. For example, the verb *see* "perceive: I see the picture" will behave differently from the verb *see* "understand: I see the problem".

[6] These 4 conditions elaborate the approach developed in (Huminski and Zhang, 2018a,b)

ample, we start from the top synset {change, alter, modify} (gloss: *cause to change; make different; cause a transformation*). It doesn't satisfy the 1st or the 2nd condition, so we go down on 1 level and examine one of its troponyms: {clean, make clean} (*make clean by removing dirt, filth, or unwanted substances from*). It is still not an action verb synset: in the pattern from the 1st condition – "V + by [...]ing" – the verb *make clean* is not a hypernym. On the next level there are synsets with glosses that satisfy either the 1st or the 2nd condition:

- {sweep} (*clean by sweeping*);

- {brush} (*clean with a brush*);

- {steam, steam clean} (*clean by means of steaming*).

So, the verbs *sweep, brush, steam, steam clean* are action verbs. Applying the 3rd condition on them, one can state that all synsets located below these 3 synsets (if any) are action verb synsets. The framework is the basis of the procedure for action extraction.

We implemented the procedure following the conditions 1.-4. and got the following results:

1. 191 verb synsets have been extracted by matching the template "V + by [...]ing";

2. 329 verb synsets have been extracted by matching the template "V + with + (a/an)? + ..." ;

3. 1408 verb synsets have been extracted from the motion lexicographer file;

4. a total of 3063 verb synsets have been extracted as a total number of action verbs including all the verb synsets that are located under the hypernyms as action verbs; 3063 extracted verb synsets contain 3294 unique action verbs.

All other verbs are potentially result verbs. Also some restrictions need to be applied to consider only the result and action verbs that are represented in the physical world and necessary for robot actions.

We will evaluate the results intrinsically (a linguist will judge the validity), and extrinsically, i.e. for English verbs also found in Levin's *English Word Classes and Alternations* (1992) we will compare our results to her classes. For example, class 10.3 "clear" verbs (*clean, clear, drain, empty*) are result verbs while 10.4.1 "wipe" verbs (*bail, buff, dab, distill, dust, erase, expunge, flush, leach, lick ..*) are action verbs.

4.2 Step #2: Getting Set of Pairs {V_r+NP}

The output of the step #2 is a set of the most frequent (commonly used) pairs {V_r+NP}. The purpose of this step is based on the observation that a result verb being applied to different objects assumes different action-verb commands.

To generate the set {V_r+NP} we use N-grams (which are a contiguous sequence of n items from a given text) extracted from the largest publicly-available, genre-balanced corpus of English: the Corpus of Contemporary American English[7] with about 430 million words in size. With this N-grams data (2, 3, 4, 5-word sequences, with their frequency), the subset of N-grams are extracted where the 1st word is a result verb in any grammatical form. A threshold was set for the frequency. For example, for the result verb *open* we extracted all 3-grams that look like the following (with frequency at the beginning):

3459 opened the door
2611 open the door
....
201 open the window
169 opened the window
......
130 opened the box
89 open the box
etc.

If the data from N-grams is insufficient we use larger, noisier corpora such as the common crawl[8].

4.3 Step #3: Getting a Set of Commonsense Inferences

The output of the final step #3 is a set of commonsense inferences between an action-verb command and a result-verb command validated by a search engine from the web. The search engine is used to check (validate) if a commonsense inference exists in the web. Each commonsense inference for the checking has a structure V_r+NP_1+by+V_a+NP_2 (*open the door by pressing the button*).

The procedure is the following:

---

[7]https://www.ngrams.info/
[8]https://commoncrawl.org/

1. make a cartesian multiplication of pairs $\{V_r+NP\}$ and action verbs $\{V_a\}$: $\{(V_r+NP), V_a\}$;

2. create a sequence for each element from 1.: $V_r+NP+by+V_a$ (*fill the cup by pouring*);

3. run the sequence from 2. on the search engine looking for the sequence $V_r+NP_1+by+V_a+NP_2$(concrete object) in the web. Estimate the frequency (or getting no result).

4. If we do not find sufficient action-verb templates V_a+NP_2(concrete object), we will use the learned combinations to learn new templates, extending the approach (Snow et al., 2006) to learning wordnet relations.

All validated commonsense inferences will be added to the set with frequencies and stored.

5 Implementation and Preliminary Results

The flowchart (Fig. 4) shows the general approach of causal relations extraction from text. Three modules on the bottom in grey color represent three steps from section 5. The details of the approach are given below.

Raw data. WordNet is used as raw data.

Algorithm of separation. For getting preliminary results, commonly used result verbs and action verbs were taken from the linguistic literature. We extracted 12 result verbs and 50 action verbs.

Result verbs: *break, clean, clear, close, raise, cut, fill, heat, kill, lift, open, remove.*

Action verbs: *blow, brush, chip, chop, clip, comb, compress, drown, flap, grab, grasp, grind, grip, hack, hammer, hit, kick, knead, lever, mow, pound, pour, press, pull, push, rinse, rub, saw, scoop, scrape, scratch, scribble, scrub, shake, shave, shoot, shovel, slap, slash, smear, soap, splash, sponge, squeeze, stab, steam, sweep, touch, wash, wipe.*

N-gram approach. For each of 12 result verbs, we extracted five 3-grams V_r+NP. Each 3-gram contains the most frequent noun phrase with the corresponding verb. Totally 60 3-grams were extracted (see Table 1 for details).

Web-search. Cartesian multiplication of 60 3-grams and 50 action verbs produces 3000 combinations "V_r+NP by V_a". We use search engine Bing for running the template "V_r+NP by V_a...".

Accordingly, 3000 searches were made. The results were taken and analyzed from the first 10 web pages that appeared. We were looking for the results corresponding the template "V_r+NP by V_a+NP/Pronoun".

Results. As a result we got 497 causal relations. Sample of 20 extracted causal relations is given in Table 2.

Examples of causal relations for the 3-gram "open the window" is given in Table 3.

6 Evaluation

The evaluation was based on a sample of 100 causal relations randomly taken from extracted 497 ones.

Due to the restrictions applied on event and causal relation between events we can not evaluate the recall of the extraction.

The precision (validity) of extracted causal relations were evaluated by five human judges. They were given instructions to rate the causal relations by marking each relation with a number from 1 (very bad) to 5 (very good). Examples of invalid (*break the ice by seeing it*) and valid (*opened the box by pulling on the handle*) causal extractions were provided.

6.1 Simple Average

After 5 judges put their marks, the simple average was calculated by dividing the sum of all marks by 500. We got 3.1.

6.2 Extraction of valid causal relations

We calculated the average between judges for each causal relation and extracted 62 causal relations (among 100 randomly taken) with average score more or equal 3.

6.3 Analysis of invalid causal relations

38 causal relations with the average score lower than 3 were preliminarily analyzed for detecting the reasons. We found the following:

a) bad parsing or bad POS tagging (*kill the bacteria by pouring a half cup; fill the hole by pushing thousands; open the window by grabbing the opening*);

b) unusual causal relations that require a context: *heat the oil by pressing the palms; cut the engine by pulling both paddles.*

c) meaningless causal relations: *break the ice by seeing it; killing each other by slashing the rate;*

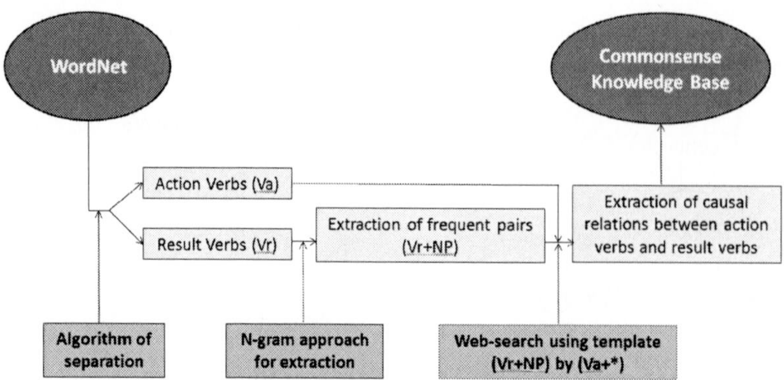

Figure 4: Flowchart of causal relations extraction from text

	five the most frequent 3-grams for each of twelve result verbs				
1	breaking new ground	break the ice	broke a window	broke the surface	break the mold
2	clean drinking water	clean the house	clean the air	clean kitchen towel	cleaning the kitchen
3	clear the air	clear the table	clear the area	clear plastic bag	clear the decks
4	closed the door	closed the book	close the window	close the lid	close the gate
5	raised his hand	raised his glass	raise the money	raise the price	raised his arms
6	cut the grass	cut the engine	cut his hair	cut a hole	cut the cake
7	filled the room	fills the screen	fill the space	fill the hole	fill the tank
8	heat the oil	heat olive oil	heat the oven	heat the butter	heat the water
9	killing each other	killed a man	killed his wife	killed the engine	kill the bacteria
10	lifted the lid	lifted his head	lifted a hand	lifted his glass	lift the weight
11	opened the door	open the window	open the gate	opened the box	opened the car
12	remove from heat	remove from oven	removed from office	remove from pan	remove from skillet

Table 1: Most frequent 3-grams for extracted result verbs

	samples of extracted causal relations
1	clean the house by wiping surfaces
2	closed the door by pushing it
3	opened the door by shaking it
4	heat the oil by pressing the palms
5	opened the box by pulling on the handle
6	close the gate by slashing it
7	fill the tank by pouring containers
8	cleaning the kitchen by washing the dishes
9	clean the house by wiping down the kitchen cabinets
10	remove from pan by grasping foil
11	cut the engine by pulling the kill control
12	close the window by pulling up the switch
13	fill the hole by pouring gravel
14	opened the car by pressing the little button
15	break the ice by pounding it
16	close the window by pushing the switch
17	close the window by pulling down the shutter
18	close the window by pulling the switch
19	kill the bacteria by pouring some bleach
20	broke a window by shooting a rock

Table 2: Samples of extracted causal relations

open the window by grabbing the window crank
open the window by pressing SHIFT + F10
open the window by pulling downwards
open the window by pulling it
open the window by pulling on that side
open the window by pulling the knob
open the window by pulling the lock
open the window by pulling the window inwards
open the window by pushing back the fastener
open the window by pushing down the multiplex network master switch assembly
open the window by pushing it
open the window by pushing on the button
open the window by scratching at the window
open the window by shaking the device
open the window by shooting the button
open the window by touching the glass pane

Table 3: Examples of causal relations for the 3-gram "open the window"

7 Conclusion and Further Work

Commonsense inferences allow us to equip and empower cognitive robots with an ability to understand high-level natural language commands (or instructions). We present a method for acquiring the knowledge needed to transform high-level result-verb commands into action-verb commands for further implementation into primitive actions.

In the future, to improve the results and increase the quality of retrieved actions we are planning to:

- improve the instruction for judges to decrease the deviation in evaluation;

- use better NLP tools for POS tagging and parsing;

- develop more elaborated procedure for commonsense inferences, for example, to exclude search results with negation ("don't open the window by throwing the stone") that produce wrong commonsense inferences;

- use metrics for calculation of consistency (reliability) of the results (for example, Krippendorff's alpha coefficient);

- enlarge the set of verbs used for commonsense inferences using resource such as WordNets.

- build multilingual commonsense inferences (starting with Chinese and Indonesian) based on (Bond and Foster, 2013; Bond et al., 2014), (Wang and Bond, 2013).

References

Dilip Arumugam, Siddharth Karamcheti, Nakul Gopalan, Lawson L.S. Wong, and Stefanie Tellex. 2017. Accurately and efficiently interpreting human-robot instructions of varying granularities. In *Proceedings of the Conference on Robotics: Science and Systems*.

Francis Bond and Ryan Foster. 2013. Linking and extending an open multilingual wordnet. In *51st Annual Meeting of the Association for Computational Linguistics: ACL-2013*, pages 1352–1362.

Francis Bond, Lian Tze Lim, Enya Kong Tang, and Hammam Riza. 2014. The combined wordnet bahasa. In *NUSA: Linguistic studies of languages in and around Indonesia 57*, pages 83–100.

Joyce Y. Chai, Qiaozi Gao, Lanbo She, Shaohua Yang, Sari Saba-Sadiya, and Guangyue Xu. 2018. Language to action: Towards interactive task learning with physical agents. In *Proceedings of the Twenty-Seventh International Joint Conference on Artificial Intelligence (IJCAI-18)*.

Timothy Chklovski and Patrick Patel. 2004. Verbocean: Mining the web for fine-grained semantic verb relations. In *Proceedings of the Conference on Empirical Methods in Natural Language Processing (EMNLP)*, Barcelona, Spain.

Herbert H. Clark. 1996. *Using language*. Cambridge University Press, Cambridge, UK.

Christiane Fellbaum. 1998. *WordNet: An Electronic Lexical Database*. MIT Press, Cambridge, MA, USA.

Christiane Fellbaum and George A. Miller. 1990. Folk psychology or semantic entailment? a reply to rips and conrad. *The Psychological Review*, 97:565–570.

Amy Fire and Song-Chun Zhu. 2016. Learning perceptual causality from video. *ACM Transactions on Intelligent Systems and Technology (TIST)*, 7(2):23.

Maxwell Forbes and Yejin Choi. 2017. Verb physics: Relative physical knowledge of actions and objects. In *Proceedings of the 55th Annual Meeting of the Association for Computational Linguistics: ACL-2017 (Volume 1: Long Papers)*, pages 266–276.

Qiaozi Gao, Malcolm Doering, Shaohua Yang, and Joyce Y. Chai. 2016. Physical causality of action verbs in grounded language understanding. In *Proceedings of the 54th Annual Meeting of the Association for Computational Linguistics: ACL-2016*, pages 1814–1824, Berlin, Germany.

Peter Gardenfors. 2017. *The Geometry of Meaning: Semantics Based on Conceptual Spaces*. MIT Press, Cambridge, MA, USA.

Peter Gardenfors and Massimo Warglien. 2012. Using conceptual spaces to model actions and events. *Journal of Semantics*, 29(4):487–519.

Aliaksandr Huminski and Hao Zhang. 2018a. Action hierarchy extraction and its application. In *Proceedings of the Eleventh International Conference on Language Resources and Evaluation (LREC-2018). Workshop "Annotation, Recognition & Evaluation of Actions (AREA)"*, Miyazaki, Japan.

Aliaksandr Huminski and Hao Zhang. 2018b. Wordnet troponymy and extraction of "manner-result" relations. In *Proceedings of the 9th Global WordNet Conference (GWC 2018)*, Singapore.

Karin Kipper Schuler. 2005. *VerbNet: A broad-coverage, comprehensive verb lexicon*. Ph.D. thesis. Computer and Information Science Dept. University of Pennsylvania. Philadelphia. PA.

Hadas Kress-Gazit, Georgios E. Fainekos, and George J. Pappas. 2008. Translating structured english to robot controllers. *Advanced Robotics*, 22(12):1343–1359.

Beth Levin. 1992. *English Verb Classes And Alternations*. University of Chicago Press, Chicago, IL.

John P. McCrae, Alexandre Rademaker, Francis Bond, Ewa Rudnicka, and Christiane Fellbaum. 2019. English wordnet 2019 – an open-source wordnet for english. In *Proceedings of the 10th Global WordNet Conference GWC-2019*, Wroclaw, Poland.

Dipendra Kumar Misra, Tao Kejia, Liang Percy, and Saxena Ashutosh. 2015. Environment-driven lexicon induction for high-level instructions. In *Proceedings of the 53rd Annual Meeting of the Association for Computational Linguistics and the 7th International Joint Conference on Natural Language*

Processing: ACL-2015 (Volume 1: Long Papers), pages 992–1002, Beijing, China.

Dipendra Kumar Misra, John Langford, and Yoav Artzi. 2017. Mapping instructions and visual observations to actions with reinforcement learning. In *Proceedings of the Conference on Empirical Methods in Natural Language Processing (EMNLP)*.

Malka Rappaport Hovav and Beth Levin. 2010. Reflections on manner/result complementarity. In *Syntax, Lexical Semantics, and Event Structure*, pages 21–38, Oxford University Press, Oxford, UK.

Lanbo She and Joyce Y. Chai. 2016. Incremental acquisition of verb hypothesis space towards physical world interaction. In *Proceedings of the 54th Annual Meeting of the Association for Computational Linguistics: ACL-2016 (Volume 1: Long Papers)*, pages 108–117, Berlin, Germany.

Lanbo She and Joyce Y. Chai. 2017. Interactive learning of grounded verb semantics towards human-robot communication. In *Proceedings of the 55th Annual Meeting of the Association for Computational Linguistics: ACL-2017 (Volume 1: Long Papers)*, pages 1634–1644.

Rion Snow, Daniel Jurafsky, and Andrew Y Ng. 2006. Semantic taxonomy induction from heterogenous evidence. In *Proceedings of the 21st International Conference on Computational Linguistics and the 44th Annual meeting of the Association for Computational Linguistics: ACL-2006*, pages 801–808.

Michael Tomasello. 2008. *The Origins of Human Communication*. MIT Press, Cambridge, MA, USA.

Shan Wang and Francis Bond. 2013. Building the chinese open wordnet (cow): Starting from core synsets. In *Proceedings of the 11th Workshop on Asian Language Resources: ALR-2013*, pages 10–18.

Massimo Warglien, Peter Gardenfors, and Matthijs Westera. 2012. Event structure, conceptual spaces and the semantics of verbs. *Theoretical Linguistics*, 38(3-4):159–193.

Terry Winograd. 1972. *Understanding natural language*. Academic Press, Oxford, England.

Jiajun Wu, Erika Lu, Pushmeet Kohli, William T. Freeman, and Josh Tenenbaum. 2017. Learning to see physics via visual deanimation. In *Proceedings of the 31th Annual Conference on Neural Information Processing Systems (NIPS)*.

Rowan Zellers and Yejin Choi. 2017. Zero-shot activity recognition with verb attribute induction. In *Proceedings of the Conference on Empirical Methods in Natural Language Processing (EMNLP)*.

Diversity-aware Event Prediction
based on a Conditional Variational Autoencoder with Reconstruction

Hirokazu Kiyomaru   **Kazumasa Omura**

Yugo Murawaki   **Daisuke Kawahara**   **Sadao Kurohashi**

Graduate School of Informatics, Kyoto University

Yoshida-honmachi, Sakyo-ku, Kyoto, 606-8501, Japan

`{kiyomaru, omura, murawaki, dk, kuro}@nlp.ist.i.kyoto-u.ac.jp`

Abstract

Typical event sequences are an important class of commonsense knowledge. Formalizing the task as the generation of a next event conditioned on a current event, previous work in event prediction employs sequence-to-sequence (seq2seq) models. However, what can happen after a given event is usually diverse, a fact that can hardly be captured by deterministic models. In this paper, we propose to incorporate a conditional variational autoencoder (CVAE) into seq2seq for its ability to represent diverse next events as a probabilistic distribution. We further extend the CVAE-based seq2seq with a reconstruction mechanism to prevent the model from concentrating on highly typical events. To facilitate fair and systematic evaluation of the diversity-aware models, we also extend existing evaluation datasets by tying each current event to multiple next events. Experiments show that the CVAE-based models drastically outperform deterministic models in terms of precision and that the reconstruction mechanism improves the recall of CVAE-based models without sacrificing precision.[1]

1 Introduction

Typical event sequences are an important class of commonsense knowledge that enables deep text understanding (Schank and Abelson, 1975; LoBue and Yates, 2011). Following previous work (Nguyen et al., 2017), we work on the task of generating a next event conditioned on a current event, which we call event prediction. For example, we want a computer to recognize that the event "board bus" is typically followed by another event "pay bus fare" and to generate the latter word sequence given the former.

---

[1]The source code and the new test sets are publicly available at `https://github.com/hkiyomaru/diversity-aware-event-prediction`.

Early studies memorized event sequences extracted from a corpus and inevitably suffered from low generalization capability and a scalability problem. A promising approach to modeling wide-coverage knowledge is to generalize events by representing them in a continuous space (Granroth-Wilding and Clark, 2016; Nguyen et al., 2017; Hu et al., 2017). Nguyen et al. (2017) generate a next event using the sequence-to-sequence (seq2seq) framework, which was first proposed for machine translation (Bahdanau et al., 2014) and subsequently applied to various NLP tasks including text summarization (Rush et al., 2015; Chopra et al., 2016) and dialog generation (Sordoni et al., 2015; Serban et al., 2016).

One limitation of the simple seq2seq models, which are deterministic in nature, is their inability to take into account an important characteristic of events: What can happen after a current event is usually diverse. For the example of "board bus" mentioned above, "get off bus" as well as "pay bus fare" is a valid next event. The inherent diversity makes it difficult to train deterministic models, and during testing, they can hardly generate multiple next events that are both valid and diverse.

To address this problem, we first propose to incorporate a conditional variational autoencoder (CVAE) into seq2seq models (Kingma et al., 2014; Sohn et al., 2015). As a probabilistic model, the CVAE draws a latent variable, representing the next event, from a probabilistic distribution, and this distribution encodes the diversity of next events.

Through experiments, we found that, as indicated by high precision, the CVAE made learning from diverse training data more effective. However, the outputs of the CVAE-based seq2seq model concentrated on a small number of highly typical events (i.e., low recall), possibly due to the mode-seeking property of variational infer-

Proceedings of the First Workshop on Commonsense Inference in Natural Language Processing, pages 113–122

Hongkong, China, November 3, 2019. ©2019 Association for Computational Linguistics

ence (Bishop, 2006, pp. 466–470). This tendency is also reminiscent of seq2seq models' preference to generic outputs (Sordoni et al., 2015; Serban et al., 2016).

We alleviate this problem by extending the CVAE-based seq2seq model with a reconstruction mechanism (Tu et al., 2017). During training, the reconstruction mechanism forces the model to reconstruct the input from the hidden states of the decoder. This has an effect of restraining the model from outputting highly typical next events because they make the reconstruction more difficult.

We evaluate the proposed models using two event pair datasets provided by Nguyen et al. (2017). One problem with these datasets is that each current event in the test sets is tied to only one next event. For a fair evaluation of diversity-aware models, we extend the test sets so that each given event has multiple next events.

Experiments show that the CVAE-based seq2seq models consistently outperformed the simple seq2seq models in terms of precision (i.e., validity) without hurting recall (i.e., diversity) while forcing the simple seq2seq models to generate diverse outputs yielded low precision. The reconstruction mechanism consistently improved recall of the CVAE-based models while keeping or even increasing precision. We also confirmed that the original test sets failed to detect the clear differences between the models.

2   Related Work

2.1   Event Prediction

There is a growing body of work on learning typical event sequences (Chambers and Jurafsky, 2008; Jans et al., 2012; Pichotta and Mooney, 2014; Granroth-Wilding and Clark, 2016; Pichotta and Mooney, 2016; Hu et al., 2017; Nguyen et al., 2017). While early studies explicitly store event sequences in a symbolic manner, a recent approach to this task is to train neural network models that implicitly represent event sequence knowledge as continuous model parameters. In both cases, models are usually evaluated by how well they restore a missing portion of an event sequence. We collectively refer to this task as event prediction.

Event prediction can be categorized into two tasks: classification and generation. In the classification task, a model is to choose one from a pre-defined set of candidates for a missing event. A popular strategy is to rank candidates by similarity with the remaining part of the event sequence. Similarity measures include pointwise mutual information (Chambers and Jurafsky, 2008), conditional bigram probability (Jans et al., 2012), and cosine similarities based on latent semantic indexing and word embeddings (Granroth-Wilding and Clark, 2016). For its reliance on pre-defined candidates, however, the classification approach is constrained by its limited flexibility.

In the generation task, a model is to directly generate a missing event, usually in the form of a word sequence (Pichotta and Mooney, 2016; Hu et al., 2017; Nguyen et al., 2017), although one previous study adopted a predicate-argument structure-based event representation (Weber et al., 2018). Nguyen et al. (2017) worked on the task of generating a next event given a single event, which we follow in this paper. They adopted the seq2seq framework (Sutskever et al., 2014) and investigated how recurrent neural network (RNN) variants, the number of RNN layers, and the presence or absence of an attention mechanism (Bahdanau et al., 2014) affected the performance. Hu et al. (2017) gave a sequence of events to the model to generate the next one. Accordingly, they worked on hierarchically encoding the given event sequence using word-level and event-level RNNs.

All of these models are deterministic in nature and do not take into account the fact that there could be more than one valid next event. For example, both "get off bus" and "pay bus fare" seem to be appropriate next events of "board bus". The inherent diversity makes it difficult to train deterministic models. During testing, they can hardly generate multiple next events that are both valid and diverse.

2.2   Conditional Variational Autoencoders

Variational autoencoders (VAEs) are a neural network-based framework to learn probabilistic generation (Kingma and Welling, 2013; Rezende et al., 2014). The basic idea of VAEs is to reconstruct an input y via a latent representation z in a way similar to autoencoders (AEs). While AEs learn the process as deterministic transformation, VAEs adopt probabilistic generation: a VAE encodes y into the probability distribution of z, instead of a point in a low-dimensional vector space. It then reconstructs the input y from z drawn from the posterior distribution. z is assumed to have a prior distribution, for which a multivariate Gaussian distribution is often used. As straightforward extensions of VAEs, conditional VAEs (CVAEs) let probabilistic distributions be conditioned on a common observed variable x (Kingma et al., 2014; Sohn et al., 2015). In our case, x is a current event while y is a next event to predict.

Bowman et al. (2016) applied VAEs to text generation. They constructed VAEs using RNNs as its components and found that VAEs with an RNN-based decoder failed to encode meaningful information to z. To alleviate this problem, they proposed simple but effective heuristics: KL cost annealing and word dropout. We also employ these techniques.

If a VAE-based text generation model is conditioned on text, it can be seen as a CVAE-based seq2seq model (Zhao et al., 2017; Serban et al., 2017; Zhang et al., 2016). Since a CVAE learns probabilistic generation, it is suitable for tasks where the output is not uniquely determined according to the input. One of the representative applications of CVAE-based text generation is dialogue response generation, or the task of generating possible replies to a human utterance (Zhao et al., 2017; Serban et al., 2017). Applying CVAEs to next event prediction is a natural choice because the task is also characterized by output diversity.

2.3 Diversity-Promoting Objective Functions

In dialogue response generation, seq2seq is known to suffer from the generic response problem: The model often ends up blindly generating uninformative responses such as "I don't know". A popular approach to this problem is to rerank the candidate outputs, which are usually produced by beam search, according to the mutual information with the conversational context (Li et al., 2016).

We notice that the reconstruction mechanism (Tu et al., 2017) serves the same purpose in a more straightforward manner, albeit stemming from a different motivation. The reconstruction mechanism forces the model to reconstruct the input from the hidden states of the decoder. Although it was originally proposed for machine translation to prevent over-translation and under-translation, it could counteract the event prediction model's tendency to concentrate on highly typical outputs.

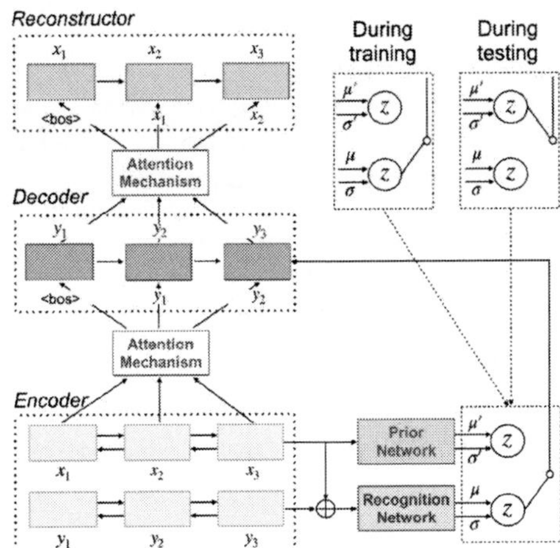

Figure 1: The neural network architecture of our event prediction model. $\oplus$ denotes vector concatenation.

3 Problem Setting

Given a current event x, we are to generate a variety of events, each of which, y, often happens after x. x and y are represented by word sequences like "board bus" and "get off bus". Our goal is to learn from training data an event prediction model $p_\theta(y|x)$, where θ is the set of model parameters.

4 Conditional VAE with Reconstruction

Figure 1 illustrates an overview of our model. To capture the diversity of next events, we use a conditional variational autoencoder (CVAE) based seq2seq model. The CVAE naturally represents diverse next events as a probability distribution. Additionally, we extend the CVAE with a reconstruction mechanism (Tu et al., 2017) to alleviate the model's tendency to concentrate on a small number of highly typical events.

4.1 Objective Function

We introduce a probabilistic latent variable z and assume that y depends on both x and z. The conditional log likelihood of y given x is written as:

$$\log p(y|x) = \log \int_z p_\theta(y, z|x)dz \tag{1}$$

$$= \log \int_z p_\theta(y|z, x)p_\theta(z|x)dz. \tag{2}$$

We refer to $p_\theta(z|x)$ and $p_\theta(y|z, x)$ as the *prior network* and the *decoder*, respectively. Eq. 2 involves an intractable marginalization over the latent variable z. The CVAE circumvents this problem by maximizing the *evidence lower bound* (ELBO) of Eq. 2. To approximate the true posterior distribution $p_\theta(z|y, x)$, we introduce a *recognition network* $q_\phi(z|y, x)$, where ϕ is the set of model parameters. The ELBO is then written as:

$$\mathcal{L}_{\text{CVAE}}(\theta, \phi; y, x) = -KL(q_\phi(z|y, x) \parallel p_\theta(z|x))$$
$$+ \mathbb{E}_{q_\phi(z|y,x)}[\log p_\theta(y|z, x)] \quad (3)$$
$$\leq \log p(y|x). \quad (4)$$

We extend the CVAE with a reconstruction mechanism $p_\psi(x|y)$, where ψ is the set of model parameters. During training, it forces the model to reconstruct x from y drawn from the posterior distribution. Adding the corresponding term, we obtain the following objective function:

$$\mathcal{L}(\theta, \phi, \psi; y, x) = \mathcal{L}_{\text{CVAE}}(\theta, \phi; y, x)$$
$$+ \lambda \mathbb{E}_{q_\phi(z|y,x)}[\log p_\psi(x|y)p_\theta(y|z, x)], \quad (5)$$

where λ is the weight for the reconstruction term. Because outputting highly typical next events makes the reconstruction more difficult, the reconstruction mechanism counteracts the model's tendency to do so.

4.2 Neural Network Architecture

We first assign distributed representations to words in x and y using the same encoder. The encoder is a bi-directional LSTM (Hochreiter and Schmidhuber, 1997) with two layers. We concatenate the representations of the first and last words to obtain h^x and h^y, the representations of x and y, respectively.

We assume that z is distributed according to a multivariate Gaussian distribution with a diagonal covariance matrix. During training, the recognition network provides the posterior distribution $q_\phi(z|y, x) \sim \mathcal{N}(\boldsymbol{\mu}, \boldsymbol{\sigma}^2 \boldsymbol{I})$:

$$\begin{bmatrix} \boldsymbol{\mu} \\ \log(\boldsymbol{\sigma}^2) \end{bmatrix} = \boldsymbol{W}_1 \begin{bmatrix} h^y \\ h^x \end{bmatrix} + \boldsymbol{b}_1. \quad (6)$$

During testing, the prior network gives the prior distribution $p_\theta(z|x) \sim \mathcal{N}(\boldsymbol{\mu}', \boldsymbol{\sigma}'^2 \boldsymbol{I})$:

$$\begin{bmatrix} \boldsymbol{\mu}' \\ \log(\boldsymbol{\sigma}'^2) \end{bmatrix} = \boldsymbol{W}_2 h^x + \boldsymbol{b}_2. \quad (7)$$

We employ the reparametrization trick (Kingma and Welling, 2013) to sample z from the posterior distribution so that the error signal can propagate to the earlier part of the networks.

We use a single-layer LSTM as the decoder. When the decoder predicts y_i, the i-th word of y, it receives its previous hidden state, the word embedding of y_{i-1}, the latent variable z, and the context representation calculated by an attention mechanism (Bahdanau et al., 2014).

We use a single-layer LSTM as the reconstructor. When the reconstructor predicts x_j, the j-th word of x, the inputs are its previous hidden state, the word embedding of x_{j-1}, and the context representation calculated by an attention mechanism. The parameters of the reconstructor's attention mechanism are different from those used in the decoder.

As indicated by Eqs. 3 and 5, we sum up three terms to get the loss: the cross entropy loss of the decoder, the cross entropy loss of the reconstructor, and the KL divergence between the posterior and prior. Since these loss terms are differentiable with respect to the model parameters θ, ϕ and ψ, we can optimize them in an end-to-end fashion.

4.3 Optimization Techniques

Encoding meaningful information in z using CVAEs with an RNN decoder is known to be hard (Bowman et al., 2016). We employ two common techniques to alleviate the issue: (1) KL cost annealing (gradually increasing the weight of the KL term) and (2) word dropout (replacing target words with unknown words with a certain probability). For KL cost annealing, we increase the weight of the KL term using the sigmoid function. For word dropout, we start with no dropout, and gradually increase the dropout rate by 0.05 every epoch until it reaches a predefined value.

5 Datasets

We used the following two datasets provided by Nguyen et al. (2017).

Wikihow: Wikihow[2] organizes on a large scale descriptions of how to accomplish tasks. Each task is described by sub-tasks with detailed descriptions. Nguyen et al. (2017) created an event pair dataset by extracting adjacent sub-task descriptions.

Descript: The original DESCRIPT corpus is a collection of event sequence descriptions created through crowdsourcing (Wanzare et al., 2016). Nguyen et al. (2017) built a new corpus of event

---

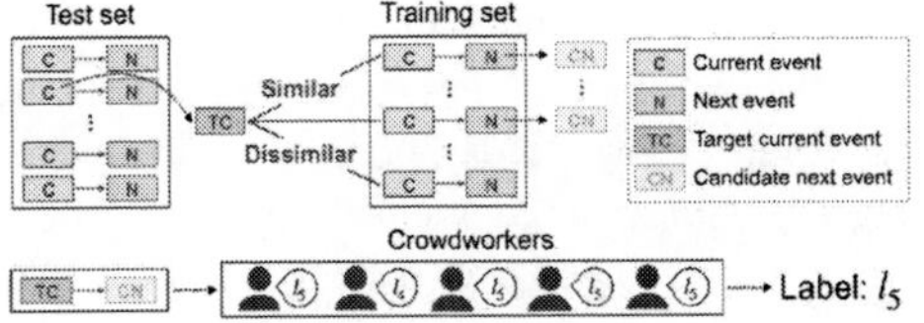

Figure 2: The workflow of test data construction.

pairs by extracting the contiguous two event descriptions in the DESCRIPT corpus. Descript is of higher quality but smaller than Wikihow.

5.1 Construction of New Test Sets

One problem with these datasets is that each current event in their test sets is tied to only one next event. As discussed by Nguyen et al. (2017), test sets for event prediction should have reflected the fact that there could be more than one valid next event.

Inspired by Zhao et al. (2017), we addressed this problem by extending the test sets through an information retrieval technique and crowdsourcing. Figure 2 illustrates the overall workflow. For each of the two test sets, we first randomly chose 200 target event pairs. Our goal was to add multiple next events to each of the current events. For each event pair, we focused on the current event and retrieved 20 similar current events in the training set. As a similarity measure, we used cosine similarity based on the averaged word2vec[3] embeddings of constituent words. We then used the corresponding 20 next events of the retrieved event pairs as candidates for the next events of the target current event.

We asked crowdworkers to check if a given event pair was appropriate. Note that our crowdsourcing covered not only the automatically retrieved event pairs but also the original event pairs. To remove a potential bias caused by wording, we presented a current event and a candidate next event as **A** and **B**, respectively. Each event pair was given one of the following five labels:

l_1: Strange expression.

l_2: No relation.

l_3: A and B are related, but one does not happen after the other.

l_4: A happens after B.

l_5: B happens after A.

[3]https://code.google.com/archive/p/word2vec/

	l_1	l_2	l_3	l_4	l_5
Wikihow (orig.)	7.3%	20.2%	30.6%	6.5%	35.5%
Wikihow (cand.)	6.9%	37.4%	25.4%	10.0%	20.3%
Descript (orig.)	0.0%	4.5%	8.0%	3.5%	84.1%
Descript (cand.)	1.7%	19.7%	12.0%	13.3%	53.2%

Table 1: The result of crowdsourcing. Each number indicates the ratio of events with the corresponding label. The labels were selected by taking the majority. In no majority cases, we gave priority to the labels with smaller subscripts.

	Train	Dev	Test	New Test
Wikihow	1,287,360	26,820	26,820	858 (174)
Descript	23,320	2,915	2,915	2,203 (199)

Table 2: Statistics of the datasets. The training, development and test sets are the original ones provided by Nguyen et al. (2017). For each dataset, we built new test sets with multiple next events. The numbers of unique current events are in parentheses.

Event pairs with label l_5 were desirable. We distributed each event pair to five workers and aggregated the five judgments by taking the majority. We used the Amazon Mechanical Turk platform and employed crowdworkers living in the US or Canada whose average work approval rates were higher than 95%. The total cost was $240.

Table 1 shows the ratio of event pairs with each label. We selected event pairs with label l_5 to build new test sets. The sizes of the resultant datasets are listed in Table 2. One current event in Wikihow and Descript had 4.9 and 11.0 next events on average, respectively. Note that the number of unique current events in our test sets was not equal to 200 because some current events happened to have no next event with label l_5.

5.2 The Quality of Original Datasets

As shown in Table 1, only 84.1% of the original event pairs of Descript were given label l_5. Even worse, the majority of the original event pairs of Wikihow were given labels other than l_5. We had two possible explanations for this. First, because Wikihow was an open-domain dataset, it contained descriptions with which crowdworkers were not necessarily familiar (e.g., creating a website). Second, the event pairs were sometimes hard to interpret because they were extracted from adjacent descriptions out of context. The results suggest that further studies in this area should use Wikihow with caution.

6 Experiments

6.1 Model Setup

We initialized word embeddings by pre-trained word2vec embeddings. Specifically, we used the embeddings with 300 dimensions trained on the Google News corpus. The encoder, decoder, and reconstructor had hidden vectors with size 256. The prior network and the recognition network consisted of a linear map to 256-dimensional space. The latent variable z had a size of 256. We used the Adam optimizer (Kingma and Ba, 2015) for updating model parameters. The learning rate was selected from $\{0.0001, 0.001, 0.01\}$. For CVAEs, we selected the word dropout ratio from $\{0.0, 0.1, 0.3\}$. To investigate the effect of the weight parameter for the reconstruction loss, we trained and compared models with different $\lambda \in \{0.1, 0.5, 1.0\}$. Hyper-parameter tuning was done based on the *original* development sets.

6.2 Baselines

We compared eight seq2seq models: deterministic models (**S2S**) (Nguyen et al., 2017) and CVAE-based models (**CVAE**) with and without the attention mechanism (**att**) and the reconstruction mechanism (**rec**). The hyper-parameters were the same as those reported in Section 6.1. The models without the attention mechanism calculated the context representation by concatenating the forward and backward last hidden states of the encoder.

To stochastically generate next events using deterministic models, we sampled words at each decoding step from the vocabulary distribution.[4] For CVAE-based models, we sampled the latent variable z and then decoded y greedily.

6.3 Quantitative Evaluation

Following Zhao et al. (2017), we evaluated precision and recall. For a given current event x, there were M_x reference next events r_j, $j \in [1, M_x]$. A model generated N hypothesis events h_i, $i \in [1, N]$. The precision and recall were as follows:

$$\text{precision}(x) = \frac{\sum_{i=1}^{N} \max_{j \in [1, M_x]} \text{BLEU}(r_j, h_i)}{N}$$

$$\text{recall}(x) = \frac{\sum_{j=1}^{M_x} \max_{i \in [1, N]} \text{BLEU}(r_j, h_i)}{M_x}$$

---

[4]We did not employ a beam search algorithm because it was not easy to compare the results with those of the probabilistic models. Beam search yields a specified number of *distinct* events while the probabilistic models can generate duplicate events.

where BLEU is the sentence-level variant of a well-known metric that measures the geometric mean of modified n-gram precision with the penalty of brevity (Papineni et al., 2002). The final score was averaged over the entire test set. We refer to the precision and recall as **P@N** and **R@N**, respectively. **F@N** is the harmonic mean of P@N and R@N. We report the scores with $N = 5$ and 10, in accordance with the average number of next events in our new test sets.

For comparison, we also followed the experimental procedure of Nguyen et al. (2017), where event prediction models deterministically output a single next event using greedy decoding. For CVAEs, we did this by setting z at the mean of the predicted Gaussian prior. The outputs were evaluated by BLEU. We refer to the criterion as **greedy-BLEU**. We used the original test sets for this experiment.

Table 3 lists the evaluation results. In terms of precision (i.e., validity), the CVAE-based models consistently outperformed the deterministic models with large margins. The deterministic models achieved better recall (i.e., diversity) than the CVAE-based models, but this came with a cost of drastically low precision. The results may be somewhat surprising because our focus is on generating diverse next events. However, generating valid next events is a precondition of success, and we found that the CVAE-based models were able to satisfy the two requirements while the deterministic models were not.

For both deterministic and probabilistic models, the attention mechanism exhibited tendencies to improve precision and recall on Wikihow but to lower the scores on Descript. Our results were consistent with those of Nguyen et al. (2017). We conjecture that Descript was so small that the attention mechanism led to overfitting.

For CVAEs, the reconstruction mechanism mostly improved recall without hurting precision, regardless of the presence or absence of the attention mechanism. Note that the best F-scores were consistently achieved by CVAEs with reconstruction. Such consistent improvements were not observed for the deterministic models. The reconstruction mechanism had evidently no effect on mitigating the difficulty of deterministic models in learning from diverse data.

In terms of greedy-BLEU, our deterministic models were competitive with the previously re-

	P@5	R@5	F@5	P@10	R@10	F@10	greedy-BLEU
S2S (Nguyen et al., 2017)	-	-	-	-	-	-	2.69 ± 0.00
S2S+att (Nguyen et al., 2017)	-	-	-	-	-	-	2.81 ± 0.00
S2S	2.75 ± 0.19	$\mathbf{3.10 \pm 0.16}$	2.91 ± 0.17	2.69 ± 0.12	4.22 ± 0.16	3.28 ± 0.14	2.62 ± 0.23
S2S+att	2.66 ± 0.05	$\mathbf{3.10 \pm 0.11}$	2.86 ± 0.08	2.74 ± 0.08	4.15 ± 0.11	3.30 ± 0.06	2.64 ± 0.07
S2S+rec ($\lambda = 0.1$)	2.68 ± 0.22	3.05 ± 0.15	2.85 ± 0.19	2.61 ± 0.15	4.08 ± 0.31	3.18 ± 0.20	2.63 ± 0.08
S2S+rec ($\lambda = 0.5$)	2.44 ± 0.16	2.86 ± 0.19	2.63 ± 0.17	2.56 ± 0.06	4.12 ± 0.14	3.16 ± 0.09	2.43 ± 0.13
S2S+rec ($\lambda = 1.0$)	2.44 ± 0.18	2.97 ± 0.26	2.68 ± 0.21	2.61 ± 0.17	3.99 ± 0.19	3.15 ± 0.18	2.32 ± 0.06
S2S+att+rec ($\lambda = 0.1$)	2.63 ± 0.09	3.05 ± 0.05	2.82 ± 0.06	2.72 ± 0.24	$\mathbf{4.32 \pm 0.09}$	3.33 ± 0.19	2.64 ± 0.09
S2S+att+rec ($\lambda = 0.5$)	2.63 ± 0.02	3.04 ± 0.10	2.82 ± 0.05	2.60 ± 0.07	4.08 ± 0.15	3.17 ± 0.09	2.48 ± 0.06
S2S+att+rec ($\lambda = 1.0$)	2.50 ± 0.14	2.97 ± 0.07	2.71 ± 0.10	2.59 ± 0.07	4.08 ± 0.13	3.17 ± 0.09	2.35 ± 0.07
CVAE	4.94 ± 0.11	2.07 ± 0.08	2.92 ± 0.10	4.92 ± 0.08	2.09 ± 0.07	2.93 ± 0.08	2.62 ± 0.03
CVAE+att	5.35 ± 0.25	2.33 ± 0.11	3.25 ± 0.15	5.35 ± 0.21	2.33 ± 0.09	3.25 ± 0.13	2.60 ± 0.07
CVAE+rec ($\lambda = 0.1$)	5.52 ± 0.42	2.50 ± 0.21	3.44 ± 0.25	5.50 ± 0.43	2.50 ± 0.22	3.44 ± 0.27	$\mathbf{2.79 \pm 0.11}$
CVAE+rec ($\lambda = 0.5$)	5.71 ± 0.08	2.44 ± 0.13	3.42 ± 0.14	5.70 ± 0.12	2.48 ± 0.10	3.46 ± 0.11	2.52 ± 0.15
CVAE+rec ($\lambda = 1.0$)	5.11 ± 0.41	2.24 ± 0.19	3.11 ± 0.26	5.13 ± 0.41	2.28 ± 0.17	3.16 ± 0.24	2.48 ± 0.01
CVAE+att+rec ($\lambda = 0.1$)	$\mathbf{5.86 \pm 0.53}$	2.40 ± 0.10	3.40 ± 0.02	$\mathbf{5.87 \pm 0.53}$	2.42 ± 0.11	3.42 ± 0.02	2.63 ± 0.07
CVAE+att+rec ($\lambda = 0.5$)	5.48 ± 0.13	2.61 ± 0.27	3.54 ± 0.27	5.41 ± 0.06	2.60 ± 0.26	3.50 ± 0.25	2.52 ± 0.14
CVAE+att+rec ($\lambda = 1.0$)	5.32 ± 0.28	2.86 ± 0.28	$\mathbf{3.71 \pm 0.28}$	5.23 ± 0.19	3.01 ± 0.24	$\mathbf{3.82 \pm 0.23}$	2.48 ± 0.04

(a) Results on Wikihow.

	P@5	R@5	F@5	P@10	R@10	F@10	greedy-BLEU
S2S (Nguyen et al., 2017)	-	-	-	-	-	-	5.42 ± 0.00
S2S+att (Nguyen et al., 2017)	-	-	-	-	-	-	5.29 ± 0.00
S2S	7.21 ± 0.68	5.34 ± 0.32	6.13 ± 0.46	7.59 ± 0.59	7.81 ± 0.36	7.70 ± 0.48	5.09 ± 0.31
S2S+att	7.59 ± 0.46	5.78 ± 0.49	6.56 ± 0.49	7.84 ± 0.33	7.99 ± 0.35	7.91 ± 0.33	4.87 ± 0.19
S2S+rec ($\lambda = 0.1$)	9.04 ± 0.42	$\mathbf{6.12 \pm 0.26}$	7.30 ± 0.32	8.91 ± 0.31	$\mathbf{8.58 \pm 0.25}$	8.74 ± 0.28	5.49 ± 0.22
S2S+rec ($\lambda = 0.5$)	8.00 ± 0.38	5.71 ± 0.30	6.66 ± 0.31	8.07 ± 0.29	8.09 ± 0.34	8.08 ± 0.30	5.14 ± 0.22
S2S+rec ($\lambda = 1.0$)	6.92 ± 0.11	5.19 ± 0.04	5.93 ± 0.06	6.91 ± 0.16	7.08 ± 0.07	6.99 ± 0.06	4.92 ± 0.12
S2S+att+rec ($\lambda = 0.1$)	8.27 ± 0.18	5.78 ± 0.21	6.80 ± 0.20	8.51 ± 0.16	8.39 ± 0.31	8.45 ± 0.24	5.15 ± 0.32
S2S+att+rec ($\lambda = 0.5$)	8.40 ± 0.77	6.04 ± 0.52	7.02 ± 0.62	8.05 ± 0.28	7.95 ± 0.18	8.00 ± 0.22	$\mathbf{5.73 \pm 0.29}$
S2S+att+rec ($\lambda = 1.0$)	7.58 ± 0.49	5.58 ± 0.23	6.43 ± 0.31	7.35 ± 0.20	7.51 ± 0.27	7.43 ± 0.23	5.34 ± 0.16
CVAE	17.27 ± 0.94	4.77 ± 0.12	7.47 ± 0.22	17.35 ± 0.95	5.01 ± 0.12	7.77 ± 0.21	5.03 ± 0.18
CVAE+att	16.13 ± 1.91	4.51 ± 0.20	7.04 ± 0.42	15.99 ± 2.21	4.75 ± 0.33	7.32 ± 0.61	4.65 ± 0.33
CVAE+rec ($\lambda = 0.1$)	18.19 ± 0.69	5.40 ± 0.24	8.33 ± 0.36	18.44 ± 0.33	5.89 ± 0.17	8.92 ± 0.22	5.50 ± 0.24
CVAE+rec ($\lambda = 0.5$)	17.33 ± 0.61	5.10 ± 0.42	7.87 ± 0.48	17.35 ± 0.57	5.67 ± 0.40	8.55 ± 0.47	5.34 ± 0.09
CVAE+rec ($\lambda = 1.0$)	17.20 ± 2.05	5.03 ± 0.26	7.78 ± 0.52	17.10 ± 2.41	5.42 ± 0.33	8.23 ± 0.63	5.24 ± 0.11
CVAE+att+rec ($\lambda = 0.1$)	16.96 ± 1.09	5.19 ± 0.12	7.95 ± 0.10	17.44 ± 1.00	5.78 ± 0.12	8.67 ± 0.10	5.18 ± 0.26
CVAE+att+rec ($\lambda = 0.5$)	$\mathbf{18.57 \pm 1.41}$	5.45 ± 0.36	$\mathbf{8.42 \pm 0.55}$	$\mathbf{18.52 \pm 1.59}$	5.91 ± 0.34	$\mathbf{8.96 \pm 0.53}$	5.58 ± 0.37
CVAE+att+rec ($\lambda = 1.0$)	16.47 ± 1.30	5.35 ± 0.24	8.07 ± 0.38	16.27 ± 1.38	5.89 ± 0.36	8.65 ± 0.53	5.33 ± 0.32

(b) Results on Descript.

Table 3: Event prediction performance evaluated by automatic evaluation metrics. Each model is trained three times with different random seeds. The scores are the average and standard deviation. The bold scores indicate the highest ones over models.

ported models of Nguyen et al. (2017), though our models were optimized based on the loss while the previous models were tuned according to greedy-BLEU. Curiously enough, greedy-BLEU indicated no big difference between the deterministic and probabilistic models, while our new test sets yielded large gaps between them in terms of precision and recall. As we will see in the next section, these differences were not spurious and did demonstrate the limitation of a single pair-based evaluation.

6.4 Qualitative Analysis

Table 4 shows next events generated by the deterministic and probabilistic models, with Table 4a being an example from Wikihow. The deterministic model generated events without any duplication, leading to a high recall. However, most of the generated events, such as "choose high speed goals", look irrelevant to the current event. This suggests that, as indicated by low precision, the deterministic model fails to generate valid next events when being forced to diversify the outputs.

The CVAE without the reconstruction mechanism appears to have generated next events that were generally valid and, at a first glance, diverse. However, a closer look reveals that they expressed a small number of highly typical events and that their semantic diversity was not large. For example, "consider the risks of psychotherapy" was semantically identical with "consider the risk factors" in this context. Compared with the vanilla CVAE, the CVAEs with reconstruction successfully generated semantically diverse next events. We would like to emphasize that the diversity was improved without sacrificing precision.

Table 4b shows an example from Descript. As

Current event: talk to mental health professional
Reference next events: [1] find support group, [2] reestablish your sense of safety, [3] spend time facing why you distrust people, [4] talk to your doctor about medication, [5] try cognitive behavioral therapy cbt, and [6] visit more than one counselor

S2S	CVAE	CVAE+att+rec ($\lambda = 0.1$)	CVAE+att+rec ($\lambda = 1.0$)
1. adjust your support system (1)	1. seek therapy (11)	1. consider the possibility of medical treatment (14)	1. get referral to therapist (8)
2. choose high speed goals (1)	2. consider psychotherapy (5)	2. ask your doctor about medications (4)	2. ask your doctor about medication (8)
3. join support group (1)	3. consider your therapist (2)	3. ask your family (2)	3. get support (4)
4. understand your parent lifestyle (1)	4. consider the risks of psychotherapy (2)	4. be aware of your depressive symptoms (2)	4. get an overview of the various topics (2)
5. listen to someone knowledgeable (1)	5. consider the risk factors (2)	5. be aware of your own mental health (2)	5. be aware of the benefits of testosterone (1)

(a) Frequently generated events by models trained on Wikihow.

Current event: board bus
Reference next events: [1] buy a ticket, [2] find a seat if available or stand if necessary, [3] give bus driver token or money, [4] pay driver or give prepaid card or ticket, [5] pay fare or give ticket if needed, [6] pay for the bus [7] pay the driver, [8] place your luggage overhead or beneath seat, [9] reach the destination, [10] sit down, [11] sit down and ride, [12] sit in your seat, [13] sit on the bus, and [14] take a seat in the bus

S2S	CVAE	CVAE+rec ($\lambda = 0.1$)	CVAE+rec ($\lambda = 1.0$)
1. pay for ticket (1)	1. get off bus (9)	1. find seat (10)	1. pay fare (29)
2. delivery driver (1)	2. pay bus fare (7)	2. pay fare (5)	2. pay the fare (1)
3. get on train (1)	3. get on bus (6)	3. get off bus (4)	3. -
4. sit down (1)	4. pay fare (4)	4. put bag in overhead compartment (2)	4. -
5. check mirrors (1)	5. pay for ticket (2)	5. wait for bus to stop (2)	5. -

(b) Frequently generated events by models trained on Descript.

Table 4: Next events generated by the deterministic and probabilistic models. We sampled 30 next events for each current event. Note that the samples can be duplicate. The numbers in parentheses indicate the frequencies.

with Wikihow, the deterministic model generated next events that were diverse but mostly invalid. The vanilla CVAE also lacked semantic diversity as with the case of Wikihow. The CVAE with reconstruction ($\lambda = 0.1$) alleviated the problem and was able to produce next events that were both valid and diverse. However, care must be taken in tuning λ, as the model with $\lambda = 1.0$ ended up concentrating on a small number of next events, which was indicated by low recall. With a too large λ, the model was strongly biased toward next events that had one-to-one correspondences with current events. Note that we could tune λ if we had new development sets with multiple next events, in addition to new test sets.

Finally, we have to acknowledge that there is still room for improvement in the new test sets. Although we successfully collected valid and diverse next events, the data construction procedure provided no guarantee of typicality. For the reference next events of "board bus" (Table 4b), "pay for the bus" and its variants dominate, but we are unsure if they are truly more typical than "place your luggage overhead or beneath seat". One way to take typicality into account is to ask a large number of crowdworkers to type next events given the current event, rather than to check the validity of a given event pair. Although we did not do this for the high cost and difficulty in quality control, it is worth exploring in the future.

7 Conclusion

We tackled the task of generating next events given a current event. Aiming to capture the diversity of next events, we proposed to use a CVAE-based seq2seq model with a reconstruction mechanism. To fairly evaluate diversity-aware models, we built new test sets with multiple next events. The CVAE-based models drastically outperformed deterministic models in terms of precision and that the reconstruction mechanism improved the recall of CVAE-based models without sacrificing precision. Although we focused on event pairs in the present work, the use of longer sequence of events would be a promising direction for future work.

Acknowledgments

We are grateful to the anonymous reviewers for their constructive feedback. This work was supported by Yahoo Japan Corporation.

References

Dzmitry Bahdanau, Kyunghyun Cho, and Yoshua Bengio. 2014. Neural machine translation by jointly learning to align and translate. *arXiv preprint arXiv:1409.0473*.

Christopher M. Bishop. 2006. *Pattern Recognition and Machine Learning*. Springer.

Samuel R. Bowman, Luke Vilnis, Oriol Vinyals, Andrew Dai, Rafal Jozefowicz, and Samy Bengio. 2016. Generating sentences from a continuous space. In *Proceedings of The 20th SIGNLL Conference on Computational Natural Language Learning*, pages 10–21. Association for Computational Linguistics.

Nathanael Chambers and Dan Jurafsky. 2008. Unsupervised learning of narrative event chains. In *Proceedings of ACL-08: HLT*, pages 789–797. Association for Computational Linguistics.

Sumit Chopra, Michael Auli, and Alexander M. Rush. 2016. Abstractive sentence summarization with attentive recurrent neural networks. In *Proceedings of the 2016 Conference of the North American Chapter of the Association for Computational Linguistics: Human Language Technologies*, pages 93–98, San Diego, California. Association for Computational Linguistics.

Mark Granroth-Wilding and Stephen Clark. 2016. What happens next? event prediction using a compositional neural network model. In *Proceedings of the Thirtieth AAAI Conference on Artificial Intelligence*, AAAI'16, pages 2727–2733. AAAI Press.

Sepp Hochreiter and Jürgen Schmidhuber. 1997. Long short-term memory. *Neural computation*, 9(8):1735–1780.

Linmei Hu, Juanzi Li, Liqiang Nie, Xiao-Li Li, and Chao Shao. 2017. What happens next? Future subevent prediction using contextual hierarchical lstm. In *AAAI Conference on Artificial Intelligence*.

Bram Jans, Steven Bethard, Ivan Vulić, and Marie-Francine Moens. 2012. Skip n-grams and ranking functions for predicting script events. In *Proceedings of the 13th Conference of the European Chapter of the Association for Computational Linguistics*, pages 336–344, Avignon, France. Association for Computational Linguistics.

Diederik P. Kingma and Jimmy Ba. 2015. Adam: A method for stochastic optimization. In *Proceedings of the Third International Conference on Learning Representations (ICLR)*.

Diederik P Kingma and Max Welling. 2013. Auto-encoding variational bayes. *arXiv preprint arXiv:1312.6114*.

Durk P Kingma, Shakir Mohamed, Danilo Jimenez Rezende, and Max Welling. 2014. Semi-supervised learning with deep generative models. In Z. Ghahramani, M. Welling, C. Cortes, N. D. Lawrence, and K. Q. Weinberger, editors, *Advances in Neural Information Processing Systems 27*, pages 3581–3589. Curran Associates, Inc.

Jiwei Li, Michel Galley, Chris Brockett, Jianfeng Gao, and Bill Dolan. 2016. A diversity-promoting objective function for neural conversation models. In *Proceedings of the 2016 Conference of the North American Chapter of the Association for Computational Linguistics: Human Language Technologies*, pages 110–119. Association for Computational Linguistics.

Peter LoBue and Alexander Yates. 2011. Types of common-sense knowledge needed for recognizing textual entailment. In *Proceedings of the 49th Annual Meeting of the Association for Computational Linguistics: Human Language Technologies*, pages 329–334. Association for Computational Linguistics.

Dai Quoc Nguyen, Dat Quoc Nguyen, Cuong Xuan Chu, Stefan Thater, and Manfred Pinkal. 2017. Sequence to sequence learning for event prediction. In *Proceedings of the Eighth International Joint Conference on Natural Language Processing (Volume 2: Short Papers)*, pages 37–42, Taipei, Taiwan. Asian Federation of Natural Language Processing.

Kishore Papineni, Salim Roukos, Todd Ward, and Wei-Jing Zhu. 2002. Bleu: a method for automatic evaluation of machine translation. In *Proceedings of the 40th annual meeting on association for computational linguistics*, pages 311–318. Association for Computational Linguistics.

Karl Pichotta and Raymond Mooney. 2014. Statistical script learning with multi-argument events. In *Proceedings of the 14th Conference of the European Chapter of the Association for Computational Linguistics*, pages 220–229, Gothenburg, Sweden. Association for Computational Linguistics.

Karl Pichotta and Raymond J. Mooney. 2016. Using sentence-level lstm language models for script inference. In *Proceedings of the 54th Annual Meeting of the Association for Computational Linguistics (Volume 1: Long Papers)*, pages 279–289. Association for Computational Linguistics.

Danilo Jimenez Rezende, Shakir Mohamed, and Daan Wierstra. 2014. Stochastic backpropagation and approximate inference in deep generative models. In *Proceedings of the 31st International Conference on Machine Learning*, volume 32 of *Proceedings of Machine Learning Research*, pages 1278–1286, Beijing, China. PMLR.

Alexander M. Rush, Sumit Chopra, and Jason Weston. 2015. A neural attention model for abstractive sentence summarization. In *Proceedings of the 2015 Conference on Empirical Methods in Natural Language Processing*, pages 379–389, Lisbon, Portugal. Association for Computational Linguistics.

Roger C. Schank and Robert P. Abelson. 1975. Scripts, plans, and knowledge. In *Proceedings of the 4th International Joint Conference on Artificial Intelligence - Volume 1*, IJCAI'75, pages 151–157, San Francisco, CA, USA. Morgan Kaufmann Publishers Inc.

Iulian V. Serban, Alessandro Sordoni, Yoshua Bengio, Aaron Courville, and Joelle Pineau. 2016. Building end-to-end dialogue systems using generative hierarchical neural network models. In *Proceedings of the Thirtieth AAAI Conference on Artificial Intelligence*, AAAI'16, pages 3776–3783. AAAI Press.

Iulian Vlad Serban, Alessandro Sordoni, Ryan Lowe, Laurent Charlin, Joelle Pineau, Aaron Courville, and Yoshua Bengio. 2017. A hierarchical latent variable encoder-decoder model for generating dialogues. In *Proceedings of the Thirty-First AAAI Conference on Artificial Intelligence*, AAAI'17, pages 3295–3301. AAAI Press.

Kihyuk Sohn, Honglak Lee, and Xinchen Yan. 2015. Learning structured output representation using deep conditional generative models. In C. Cortes, N. D. Lawrence, D. D. Lee, M. Sugiyama, and R. Garnett, editors, *Advances in Neural Information Processing Systems 28*, pages 3483–3491. Curran Associates, Inc.

Alessandro Sordoni, Michel Galley, Michael Auli, Chris Brockett, Yangfeng Ji, Margaret Mitchell, Jian-Yun Nie, Jianfeng Gao, and Bill Dolan. 2015. A neural network approach to context-sensitive generation of conversational responses. In *Proceedings of the 2015 Conference of the North American Chapter of the Association for Computational Linguistics: Human Language Technologies*, pages 196–205, Denver, Colorado. Association for Computational Linguistics.

Ilya Sutskever, Oriol Vinyals, and Quoc V Le. 2014. Sequence to sequence learning with neural networks. In Z. Ghahramani, M. Welling, C. Cortes, N. D. Lawrence, and K. Q. Weinberger, editors, *Advances in Neural Information Processing Systems 27*, pages 3104–3112. Curran Associates, Inc.

Zhaopeng Tu, Yang Liu, Lifeng Shang, Xiaohua Liu, and Hang Li. 2017. Neural machine translation with reconstruction. In *Proceedings of the Thirty-First AAAI Conference on Artificial Intelligence, February 4-9, 2017, San Francisco, California, USA.*, pages 3097–3103.

Lilian DA Wanzare, Alessandra Zarcone, Stefan Thater, and Manfred Pinkal. 2016. Descript: A crowdsourced corpus for the acquisition of high-quality script knowledge. In *The International Conference on Language Resources and Evaluation*.

Noah Weber, Leena Shekhar, Niranjan Balasubramanian, and Nathanael Chambers. 2018. Hierarchical quantized representations for script generation. In *Proceedings of the 2018 Conference on Empirical Methods in Natural Language Processing*,

pages 3783–3792, Brussels, Belgium. Association for Computational Linguistics.

Biao Zhang, Deyi Xiong, jinsong su, Hong Duan, and Min Zhang. 2016. Variational neural machine translation. In *Proceedings of the 2016 Conference on Empirical Methods in Natural Language Processing*, pages 521–530, Austin, Texas. Association for Computational Linguistics.

Tiancheng Zhao, Ran Zhao, and Maxine Eskenazi. 2017. Learning discourse-level diversity for neural dialog models using conditional variational autoencoders. In *Proceedings of the 55th Annual Meeting of the Association for Computational Linguistics (Volume 1: Long Papers)*, pages 654–664. Association for Computational Linguistics.

Can a Gorilla Ride a Camel?
Learning Semantic Plausibility from Text

Ian Porada[1], Kaheer Suleman[2], and Jackie Chi Kit Cheung[1,3]

[1]Mila, McGill University
{ian.porada@mail, jcheung@cs}.mcgill.ca
[2]Microsoft Research Montreal
kasulema@microsoft.com
[3]Canada CIFAR AI Chair

Abstract

Modeling semantic plausibility requires commonsense knowledge about the world and has been used as a testbed for exploring various knowledge representations. Previous work has focused specifically on modeling physical plausibility and shown that distributional methods fail when tested in a supervised setting. At the same time, distributional models, namely large pretrained language models, have led to improved results for many natural language understanding tasks. In this work, we show that these pretrained language models are in fact effective at modeling physical plausibility in the supervised setting. We therefore present the more difficult problem of learning to model physical plausibility directly from text. We create a training set by extracting attested events from a large corpus, and we provide a baseline for training on these attested events in a self-supervised manner and testing on a physical plausibility task. We believe results could be further improved by injecting explicit commonsense knowledge into a distributional model.

1 Introduction

A person riding a camel is a common event, and one would expect the subject-verb-object (s-v-o) triple *person-ride-camel* to be attested in a large corpus. In contrast, *gorilla-ride-camel* is uncommon, likely unattested, and yet still semantically plausible. Modeling semantic plausibility then requires distinguishing these plausible events from the semantically nonsensical, e.g. *lake-ride-camel*.

Semantic plausibility is a necessary part of many natural language understanding (NLU) tasks including narrative interpolation (Bowman et al., 2016), story understanding (Mostafazadeh et al., 2016), paragraph reconstruction (Li and Jurafsky, 2017), and hard coreference resolution (Peng

Event	Plausible?
bird-construct-nest	✓
bottle-contain-elephant	✗
gorilla-ride-camel	✓
lake-fuse-tie	✗

Table 1: Example events from Wang et al. (2018)'s physical plausibility dataset.

et al., 2015). Furthermore, the problem of modeling semantic plausibility has itself been used as a testbed for exploring various knowledge representations.

In this work, we focus specifically on modeling physical plausibility as presented by Wang et al. (2018). This is the problem of determining if a given event, represented as an s-v-o triple, is physically plausible (Table 1). We show that in the original supervised setting a distributional model, namely a novel application of BERT (Devlin et al., 2019), significantly outperforms the best existing method which has access to manually labeled physical features (Wang et al., 2018).

Still, the generalization ability of supervised models is limited by the coverage of the training set. We therefore present the more difficult problem of learning physical plausibility directly from text. We create a training set by parsing and extracting attested s-v-o triples from English Wikipedia, and we provide a baseline for training on this dataset and evaluating on Wang et al. (2018)'s physical plausibility task. We also experiment training on a large set of s-v-o triples extracted from the web as part of the NELL project (Carlson et al., 2010), and find that Wikipedia triples result in better performance.

Proceedings of the First Workshop on Commonsense Inference in Natural Language Processing, pages 123–129
Hongkong, China, November 3, 2019. ©2019 Association for Computational Linguistics

2   Related Work

Wang et al. (2018) present the semantic plausibility dataset that we use for evaluation in this work, and they show that distributional methods fail on this dataset. This conclusion aligns with other work showing that GloVe (Pennington et al., 2014) and word2vec (Mikolov et al., 2013) embeddings do not encode some salient features of objects (Li and Gauthier, 2017). More recent work has similarly concluded that large pretrained language models only learn attested physical knowledge (Forbes et al., 2019).

Other datasets which include plausibility ratings are smaller in size and missing atypical but plausible events (Keller and Lapata, 2003), or concern the more complicated problem of multi-event inference in natural language (Zhang et al., 2017; Sap et al., 2019).

Complementary to our work are methods of extracting physical features from a text corpus (Wang et al., 2017; Forbes and Choi, 2017; Bagherinezhad et al., 2016).

2.1   Distributional Models

Motivated by the distributional hypothesis that words in similar contexts have similar meanings (Harris, 1954), distributional methods learn the representation of a word based on the distribution of its context. The occurrence counts of bigrams in a corpus are correlated with human plausibility ratings (Lapata et al., 1999, 2001), so one might expect that with a large enough corpus, a distributional model would learn to distinguish plausible but atypical events from implausible ones. As a counterexample, Ó Séaghdha (2010) has shown that the subject-verb bigram *carrot-laugh* occurs 855 times in a web corpus, while *manservant-laugh* occurs zero.[1] Not everything that is physically plausible occurs, and not everything that occurs is attested due to reporting bias[2] (Gordon and Van Durme, 2013); therefore, modeling semantic plausibility requires systematic inference beyond a distributional cue.

We focus on the masked language model BERT as a distributional model. BERT has led to improved results across a variety of NLU bench-

marks (Rajpurkar et al., 2018; Wang et al., 2019), including tasks that require explicit commonsense reasoning such as the Winograd Schema Challenge (Sakaguchi et al., 2019).

2.2   Selectional Preference

Closely related to semantic plausibility is selectional preference (Resnik, 1996) which concerns the semantic preference of a predicate for its arguments. Here, *preference* refers to the typicality of arguments: while it is plausible that a gorilla rides a camel, it is not preferred. Current approaches to selectional preference are distributional (Erk et al., 2010; Van de Cruys, 2014) and have shown limited performance in capturing semantic plausibility (Wang et al., 2018).

Ó Séaghdha and Korhonen (2012) have investigated combining a lexical hierarchy with a distributional approach, and there have been related attempts at grounding selectional preference in visual perception (Bergsma and Goebel, 2011; Shutova et al., 2015).

Models of selectional preference are either evaluated on a pseudo-disambiguation task, where attested predicate-argument tuples must be disambiguated from pseudo-negative random tuples, or evaluated on their correlation with human plausibility judgments. Selectional preference is one factor in plausibility and thus the two should correlate.

3   Task

Following existing work, we focus on the task of single-event, physical plausibility. This is the problem of determining if a given event, represented as an s-v-o triple, is physically plausible.

We use Wang et al. (2018)'s physical plausibility dataset for evaluation. This dataset consists of 3,062 s-v-o triples, built from a vocabulary of 150 verbs and 450 nouns, and containing a diverse combination of both typical and atypical events balanced between the plausible and implausible categories. The set of events and ground truth labels were manually curated.

3.1   Supervised

In the supervised setting, a model is trained and tested on labelled events from the same distribution. Therefore, both the training and test set capture typical and atypical plausibility. We follow the same evaluation procedure as previous work

---

[1] This point was made based on search engine results. Some, but not all, of the *carrot-laugh* bigrams are false positives.

[2] Reporting bias describes the discrepancy between what is frequent in text and what is likely in the world. This is in part because people do not describe the obvious.

	male-have-income
Wikipedia	*village-have-population*
	event-take-place
	login-post-comment
NELL	*use-constitute-acceptance*
	modules-have-options

Table 2: Most frequent s-v-o triples for each corpus.

and perform cross validation on the 3,062 labeled triples (Wang et al., 2018).

3.2 Learning from Text

We also present the problem of learning to model physical plausibility directly from text. In this new setting, a model is trained on events extracted from a large corpus and evaluated on a physical plausibility task. Therefore, only the test set covers both typical and atypical plausibility.

We create two training sets based on separate corpora: first, we parse English Wikipedia using the StanfordNLP neural pipeline (Qi et al., 2018) and extract attested s-v-o triples. Wikipedia has led to relatively good results for selectional preference (Zhang et al., 2019), and in total we extract 6 million unique triples with a cumulative 10 million occurrences. Second, we use the NELL (Carlson et al., 2010) dataset of 604 million s-v-o triples extracted from the dependency parsed ClueWeb09 dataset. For NELL, we filter out triples with non-alphabetic characters or less than 5 occurrences, resulting in a total 2.5 million unique triples with a cumulative 112 million occurrences.

For evaluation, we split Wang et al. (2018)'s 3,062 triples into equal sized validation and test sets. Each set thus consists of 1,531 triples.

4 Methods

4.1 NN

As a baseline, we consider the performance of a neural method for selectional preference (Van de Cruys, 2014). This method is a two-layer artificial neural network (NN) over static embeddings.

Supervised. We reproduce the results of Wang et al. (2018) using GloVe embeddings and the same hyperparameter settings.

Self-Supervised. We use this same method for *learning from text* (Subsection 3.2). To do so, we turn the training data into a self-supervised train-

ing set: attested events are considered to be plausible, and pseudo-implausible events are created by sampling each word in an s-v-o triple independently by occurrence frequency. We do hyperparameter search on the validation set over learning rates in $\{1e-3, 1e-4, 1e-5, 2e-5\}$, batch sizes in $\{16, 32, 64, 128\}$, and epochs in $\{0.5, 1, 2\}$.

4.2 BERT

We use BERT for modeling semantic plausibility by simply treating this as a sequence classification task. We tokenize the input s-v-o triple and introduce new entity marker tokens to separate each word.[3] We then add a single layer NN to classify the input based on the final layer representation of the `[CLS]` token. We use BERT-large and fine-tune the entire model in training.[4]

Supervised. We do no hyperparameter search and simply use the default hyperparameter configuration which has been shown to work well for other commonsense reasoning tasks (Ruan et al., 2019). BERT-large sometimes fails to train on small datasets (Devlin et al., 2019; Niven and Kao, 2019); therefore, we restart training with a new random seed when the training loss fails to decrease more than 10%.

Self-Supervised. We perform *learning from text* (Subsection 3.2) by creating a self-supervised training set in exactly the same way as for the NN method. The hyperparameter configuration is determined by grid search on the validation set over learning rates in $\{1e-5, 2e-5, 3e-5\}$, batch sizes in $\{8, 16\}$, and epochs in $\{0.5, 1, 2\}$.

5 Results

5.1 Supervised

For the supervised setting, we follow the same evaluation procedure as Wang et al. (2018): we perform 10-fold cross validation on the dataset of 3,062 s-v-o triples, and report the mean accuracy of running this procedure 20 times all with the same model initialization (Table 3).

BERT outperforms existing methods by a large margin, including those with access to manually labeled physical features. We conclude from

---

[3]Our input to BERT is of the form: `[CLS] [SUBJ] <subject> [/SUBJ] [VERB] <verb> [/VERB] [OBJ] <object> [/OBJ] [SEP]`.

[4]We use Hugging Face's PyTorch implementation of BERT, `https://github.com/huggingface/pytorch-transformers`.

Model	Accuracy
Random	0.50
NN (Van de Cruys, 2014)	0.68
NN+WK (Wang et al., 2018)	0.76
Fine-tuned BERT	**0.89**

Table 3: Mean accuracy of classifying plausible events for models trained in a supervised setting. NN+WK combines the NN approach with manually labeled world knowledge (WK) features describing both the subject and object.

Event	Plausible?	
	BERT	GT
dentist-capsize-canoe	✓	✓
stove-heat-air	✗	✓
sun-cool-water	✓	✗
chair-crush-water	✗	✗

Table 4: Interpreting log-likelihood as confidence, example events for which BERT was highly confident and either correct or incorrect with respect to the ground truth (GT) label.

these results that distributional data does provide a strong cue for semantic plausibility in the supervised setting of Wang et al. (2018).

Examples of positive and negative results for BERT are presented in Table 4. There is no immediately obvious pattern in the cases where BERT misclassifies an event. We therefore consider events for which BERT gave a consistent estimate across all 20 runs of cross-validation. Of these, we present the event for which BERT was most confident.

We note that due to the limited vocabulary size of the dataset, the training set always covers the test set vocabulary when performing 10-fold cross validation. That is to say that every word in the test set has been seen in a different triple in the training set. For example, every verb occurs within 20 triples; therefore, on average a verb in the test set has been seen 18 times in the training set.

Supervised performance is dependent on the coverage of the training set vocabulary (Moosavi and Strube, 2017), and it is intractable to have 18 plausibility labels for all verbs across English. Furthermore, supervised models are susceptible to annotation artifacts (Gururangan et al., 2018; Poliak et al., 2018) and do not necessarily even learn

Model	Wikipedia		NELL	
	Valid	Test	Valid	Test
Random	0.50	0.50	0.50	0.50
NN	0.53	0.52	0.50	0.51
BERT	**0.65**	**0.63**	**0.57**	**0.56**

Table 5: Accuracy of classifying plausible events for models trained on a corpus in a self-supervised manner.

the desired relation, or in fact any relation, between words (Levy et al., 2015).

This is our motivation for reframing semantic plausibility as a task to be learned directly from text, a new setting in which the training set vocabulary is independent of the test set.

5.2 Learning from Text

For *learning from text* (Subsection 3.2), we report both the validation and test accuracies of classifying physically plausible events (Table 5).

BERT fine-tuned on Wikipedia performs the best, although only partially captures semantic plausibility with a test set accuracy of 63%. Performance may benefit from injecting explicit commonsense knowledge into the model, an approach which has previously been used in the supervised setting (Wang et al., 2018).

Interestingly, BERT is biased towards labelling events as plausible. For the best performing model, for example, 78% of errors are false positives.

Models trained on Wikipedia events consistently outperform those trained on NELL which is consistent with our subjective assessment of the cleanliness of these datasets. The baseline NN method in particular seems to learn very little from training on the NELL dataset.

6 Conclusion

We show that large, pretrained language models are effective at modeling semantic plausibility in the supervised setting. Supervised models are limited by the coverage of the training set, however; thus, we reframe modeling semantic plausibility as a self-supervised task and present a baseline based on a novel application of BERT.

We believe that self-supervised results could be further improved by incorporating explicit commonsense knowledge, as well as further incidental signals (Roth, 2017) from text.

Acknowledgments

We would like to thank Adam Trischler, Ali Emami, and Abhilasha Ravichander for useful discussions and comments. This work is supported by funding from Microsoft Research and resources from Compute Canada. The last author is supported by the Canada CIFAR AI Chair program.

References

Hessam Bagherinezhad, Hannaneh Hajishirzi, Yejin Choi, and Ali Farhadi. 2016. Are elephants bigger than butterflies? reasoning about sizes of objects. In *AAAI*.

Shane Bergsma and Randy Goebel. 2011. Using visual information to predict lexical preference. In *Proceedings of the International Conference Recent Advances in Natural Language Processing 2011*, pages 399–405, Hissar, Bulgaria. Association for Computational Linguistics.

Samuel R. Bowman, Luke Vilnis, Oriol Vinyals, Andrew Dai, Rafal Jozefowicz, and Samy Bengio. 2016. Generating sentences from a continuous space. In *Proceedings of The 20th SIGNLL Conference on Computational Natural Language Learning*, pages 10–21, Berlin, Germany. Association for Computational Linguistics.

Andrew Carlson, Justin Betteridge, Bryan Kisiel, Burr Settles, Estevam R. Hruschka, Jr., and Tom M. Mitchell. 2010. Toward an architecture for never-ending language learning. In *Proceedings of the Twenty-Fourth AAAI Conference on Artificial Intelligence*, AAAI'10, pages 1306–1313. AAAI Press.

Tim Van de Cruys. 2014. A neural network approach to selectional preference acquisition. In *Proceedings of the 2014 Conference on Empirical Methods in Natural Language Processing (EMNLP)*, pages 26–35, Doha, Qatar. Association for Computational Linguistics.

Jacob Devlin, Ming-Wei Chang, Kenton Lee, and Kristina Toutanova. 2019. BERT: Pre-training of deep bidirectional transformers for language understanding. In *Proceedings of the 2019 Conference of the North American Chapter of the Association for Computational Linguistics: Human Language Technologies, Volume 1 (Long and Short Papers)*, pages 4171–4186, Minneapolis, Minnesota. Association for Computational Linguistics.

Katrin Erk, Sebastian Padó, and Ulrike Padó. 2010. A flexible, corpus-driven model of regular and inverse selectional preferences. *Computational Linguistics*, 36(4):723–763.

Maxwell Forbes and Yejin Choi. 2017. Verb physics: Relative physical knowledge of actions and objects. In *Proceedings of the 55th Annual Meeting of the Association for Computational Linguistics (Volume 1: Long Papers)*, pages 266–276, Vancouver, Canada. Association for Computational Linguistics.

Maxwell Forbes, Ari Holtzman, and Yejin Choi. 2019. Do neural language representations learn physical commonsense? *arXiv preprint arXiv:1908.02899*.

Jonathan Gordon and Benjamin Van Durme. 2013. Reporting bias and knowledge acquisition. In *Proceedings of the 2013 Workshop on Automated Knowledge Base Construction*, AKBC '13, pages 25–30, New York, NY, USA. ACM.

Suchin Gururangan, Swabha Swayamdipta, Omer Levy, Roy Schwartz, Samuel Bowman, and Noah A. Smith. 2018. Annotation artifacts in natural language inference data. In *Proceedings of the 2018 Conference of the North American Chapter of the Association for Computational Linguistics: Human Language Technologies, Volume 2 (Short Papers)*, pages 107–112, New Orleans, Louisiana. Association for Computational Linguistics.

Zellig S. Harris. 1954. Distributional structure. *WORD*, 10(2-3):146–162.

Frank Keller and Mirella Lapata. 2003. Using the web to obtain frequencies for unseen bigrams. *Computational Linguistics*, 29(3):459–484.

Maria Lapata, Frank Keller, and Scott McDonald. 2001. Evaluating smoothing algorithms against plausibility judgements. In *Proceedings of the 39th Annual Meeting on Association for Computational Linguistics*, ACL '01, pages 354–361, Stroudsburg, PA, USA. Association for Computational Linguistics.

Maria Lapata, Scott McDonald, and Frank Keller. 1999. Determinants of adjective-noun plausibility. In *Proceedings of the Ninth Conference on European Chapter of the Association for Computational Linguistics*, EACL '99, pages 30–36, Stroudsburg, PA, USA. Association for Computational Linguistics.

Omer Levy, Steffen Remus, Christian Biemann, and Ido Dagan. 2015. Do supervised distributional methods really learn lexical inference relations? In *HLT-NAACL*.

Jiwei Li and Dan Jurafsky. 2017. Neural net models of open-domain discourse coherence. In *Proceedings of the 2017 Conference on Empirical Methods in Natural Language Processing*, pages 198–209, Copenhagen, Denmark. Association for Computational Linguistics.

Lucy Li and Jon Gauthier. 2017. Are distributional representations ready for the real world? evaluating word vectors for grounded perceptual meaning. In *Proceedings of the First Workshop on Language Grounding for Robotics*, pages 76–85, Vancouver, Canada. Association for Computational Linguistics.

Tomas Mikolov, Ilya Sutskever, Kai Chen, Greg S Corrado, and Jeff Dean. 2013. Distributed representations of words and phrases and their compositionality. In *Advances in neural information processing systems*, pages 3111–3119.

Nafise Sadat Moosavi and Michael Strube. 2017. Lexical features in coreference resolution: To be used with caution. In *Proceedings of the 55th Annual Meeting of the Association for Computational Linguistics (Volume 2: Short Papers)*, pages 14–19, Vancouver, Canada. Association for Computational Linguistics.

Nasrin Mostafazadeh, Nathanael Chambers, Xiaodong He, Devi Parikh, Dhruv Batra, Lucy Vanderwende, Pushmeet Kohli, and James Allen. 2016. A corpus and cloze evaluation for deeper understanding of commonsense stories. In *Proceedings of the 2016 Conference of the North American Chapter of the Association for Computational Linguistics: Human Language Technologies*, pages 839–849, San Diego, California. Association for Computational Linguistics.

Timothy Niven and Hung-Yu Kao. 2019. Probing neural network comprehension of natural language arguments. In *Proceedings of the 57th Annual Meeting of the Association for Computational Linguistics*, pages 4658–4664, Florence, Italy. Association for Computational Linguistics.

Diarmuid Ó Séaghdha. 2010. Latent variable models of selectional preference. In *Proceedings of the 48th Annual Meeting of the Association for Computational Linguistics*, ACL '10, pages 435–444, Stroudsburg, PA, USA. Association for Computational Linguistics.

Diarmuid Ó Séaghdha and Anna Korhonen. 2012. Modelling selectional preferences in a lexical hierarchy. In **SEM 2012: The First Joint Conference on Lexical and Computational Semantics – Volume 1: Proceedings of the main conference and the shared task, and Volume 2: Proceedings of the Sixth International Workshop on Semantic Evaluation (SemEval 2012)*, pages 170–179, Montréal, Canada. Association for Computational Linguistics.

Haoruo Peng, Daniel Khashabi, and Dan Roth. 2015. Solving hard coreference problems. In *Proceedings of the 2015 Conference of the North American Chapter of the Association for Computational Linguistics: Human Language Technologies*, pages 809–819, Denver, Colorado. Association for Computational Linguistics.

Jeffrey Pennington, Richard Socher, and Christopher Manning. 2014. Glove: Global vectors for word representation. In *Proceedings of the 2014 Conference on Empirical Methods in Natural Language Processing (EMNLP)*, pages 1532–1543, Doha, Qatar. Association for Computational Linguistics.

Adam Poliak, Jason Naradowsky, Aparajita Haldar, Rachel Rudinger, and Benjamin Van Durme. 2018. Hypothesis only baselines in natural language inference. In *Proceedings of the Seventh Joint Conference on Lexical and Computational Semantics*, pages 180–191, New Orleans, Louisiana. Association for Computational Linguistics.

Peng Qi, Timothy Dozat, Yuhao Zhang, and Christopher D. Manning. 2018. Universal dependency parsing from scratch. In *Proceedings of the CoNLL 2018 Shared Task: Multilingual Parsing from Raw Text to Universal Dependencies*, pages 160–170, Brussels, Belgium. Association for Computational Linguistics.

Pranav Rajpurkar, Robin Jia, and Percy Liang. 2018. Know what you don't know: Unanswerable questions for squad. *arXiv preprint arXiv:1806.03822*.

Philip Resnik. 1996. Selectional constraints: An information-theoretic model and its computational realization. *Cognition*, 61(1-2):127–159.

Dan Roth. 2017. Incidental supervision: Moving beyond supervised learning. In *AAAI*.

Yu-Ping Ruan, Xiaodan Zhu, Zhen-Hua Ling, Zhan Shi, Quan Liu, and Si Wei. 2019. Exploring unsupervised pretraining and sentence structure modelling for winograd schema challenge. *CoRR*, abs/1904.09705.

Keisuke Sakaguchi, Ronan Le Bras, Chandra Bhagavatula, and Yejin Choi. 2019. Winogrande: An adversarial winograd schema challenge at scale. *ArXiv*, abs/1907.10641.

Maarten Sap, Ronan Le Bras, Emily Allaway, Chandra Bhagavatula, Nicholas Lourie, Hannah Rashkin, Brendan Roof, Noah A Smith, and Yejin Choi. 2019. Atomic: an atlas of machine commonsense for if-then reasoning. In *Proceedings of the AAAI Conference on Artificial Intelligence*, volume 33, pages 3027–3035.

Ekaterina Shutova, Niket Tandon, and Gerard de Melo. 2015. Perceptually grounded selectional preferences. In *Proceedings of the 53rd Annual Meeting of the Association for Computational Linguistics and the 7th International Joint Conference on Natural Language Processing (Volume 1: Long Papers)*, pages 950–960, Beijing, China. Association for Computational Linguistics.

Alex Wang, Amanpreet Singh, Julian Michael, Felix Hill, Omer Levy, and Samuel R. Bowman. 2019. GLUE: A multi-task benchmark and analysis platform for natural language understanding. In *International Conference on Learning Representations*.

Su Wang, Greg Durrett, and Katrin Erk. 2018. Modeling semantic plausibility by injecting world knowledge. In *Proceedings of the 2018 Conference of the North American Chapter of the Association for*

Computational Linguistics: Human Language Technologies, Volume 2 (Short Papers), pages 303–308, New Orleans, Louisiana. Association for Computational Linguistics.

Su Wang, Stephen Roller, and Katrin Erk. 2017. Distributional modeling on a diet: One-shot word learning from text only. In *Proceedings of the Eighth International Joint Conference on Natural Language Processing (Volume 1: Long Papers)*, pages 204–213, Taipei, Taiwan. Asian Federation of Natural Language Processing.

Hongming Zhang, Hantian Ding, and Yangqiu Song. 2019. SP-10K: A large-scale evaluation set for selectional preference acquisition. In *Proceedings of the 57th Annual Meeting of the Association for Computational Linguistics*, pages 722–731, Florence, Italy. Association for Computational Linguistics.

Sheng Zhang, Rachel Rudinger, Kevin Duh, and Benjamin Van Durme. 2017. Ordinal common-sense inference. *Transactions of the Association for Computational Linguistics*, 5:379–395.

How Pre-trained Word Representations Capture Commonsense Physical Comparisons

Pranav Goel
Computer Science
University of Maryland
pgoel1@cs.umd.edu

Shi Feng
Computer Science
University of Maryland
shifeng@umiacs.umd.edu

Jordan Boyd-Graber
Computer Science, iSchool,
UMIACS, and LSC
University of Maryland
jbg@umiacs.umd.edu

Abstract

Understanding common sense is important for effective natural language reasoning. One type of common sense is how two objects compare on physical properties such as size and weight: e.g., 'is a house bigger than a person?'. We probe whether pre-trained representations capture comparisons and find they, in fact, have higher accuracy than previous approaches. They also generalize to comparisons involving objects not seen during training. We investigate *how* such comparisons are made: models learn a consistent ordering over all the objects in the comparisons. Probing models have significantly higher accuracy than those baseline models which use dataset artifacts: e.g., memorizing some words are larger than any other word.

1 Introduction

Pre-trained word representations or embeddings (Mikolov et al., 2013) such as GloVe (Pennington et al., 2014) underpin modern NLP. To understand what information is encoded, supervised models *probe* (Adi et al., 2016; Linzen et al., 2016; Conneau et al., 2018) a particular property, for example, part-of-speech (Belinkov et al., 2017), morphology (Peters et al., 2018a), etc. in these representations. With the advent of contextualized word embeddings such as ELMo (Peters et al., 2018a) and BERT (Devlin et al., 2018), efforts to understand the information encoded in representations learned by neural model have increased (Peters et al., 2018b; Tenney et al., 2019; Liu et al., 2019). Apart from linguistic properties, what do these representations learn about the world? Commonsense reasoning over language that incorporates world knowledge such as 'an elephant is heavier than a person' can help agents make better decisions and understand 'complex' phenomena like humor and irony. However, extracting common sense from text corpora is challenging since we rarely state obvious things directly (Van Durme, 2010; Gordon and Van Durme, 2013; Misra et al., 2016; Zhang et al., 2017).

This paper asks if pre-trained representations encode a specific type of common sense: physical comparisons between objects.[1] The supervised classification task takes a pair of words being compared on a physical attribute such as size or speed, with the system's objective to decide which is 'bigger' or 'faster' (§ 2.1). We use a linear or a one-layer fully-connected neural network probing model with only a combination (concatenation or subtraction) of the frozen pre-trained embeddings for the words to be compared as input (§ 2.2). This probing model achieves better accuracy than previous approaches (§ 2.3) which use extra information other than the words (such as the verbs connecting the words) on the Verb Physics dataset (Forbes and Choi, 2017) (§ 3): it encodes physical commonsense comparisons.[2] It generalizes to objects not present in the training set (§ 3.1) with higher accuracy than baselines exploiting dataset artifacts (§ 4). We use a 'simple' probing model since more complex models make it difficult to disentangle the major contributing factor to results - model or embeddings (as in other probing studies like Liu et al. (2019)). Our other major contribution is analyzing how models compare objects. The output logits for labels (indicating model confidence) order objects consistently across orderings or rankings built around different objects (§ 4.1.1). Models also learn an ordering over all the objects and use this learned ordering for comparisons (§ 4.1.2).

---

[1] Note: Concurrent work by Forbes et al. (2019) also finds neural representations are proficient at capturing physical properties of objects (focus of this work) but not at tackling the relationship with actions applicable to objects.

[2] This work aims to probe representations for physical commonsense comparisons; better accuracy is a byproduct.

Proceedings of the First Workshop on Commonsense Inference in Natural Language Processing, pages 130–135
Hongkong, China, November 3, 2019. ©2019 Association for Computational Linguistics

2 Experimental Setup

2.1 Probing Task & Data

We use Verb Physics (Forbes and Choi, 2017) and follow their setup. Given a pair of words or objects, a system predicts if $word_1$ $</>/\approx$ $word_2$ when compared on an attribute, for example, $bed >^{weight} hand$ or $mouth \approx^{size} fist$. Verb Physics consists of five different datasets comparing objects on *size, weight, strength, rigidness,* and *speed.*[3] The train:dev:test split is 5:45:50 resulting in about 100 and 1000 comparisons in the training and dev sets respectively, with similar statistics for all attributes. This is the split used in the previous works and hence we use the same split in order to benchmark results. To test generalization to words not seen during training, we also use a different evaluation set released by Bagherinezhad et al. (2016) with 486 size-based comparisons of objects (§ 3.1).[4]

2.2 Our Probing Model

The probing model is a simple setup to assess if pre-trained representations capture physical object comparisons. We concatenate or subtract the word embeddings for the two words and pass it to a fully-connected neural network with zero (in which case, linear) or one hidden layer. Our primary experiments use GloVe (Pennington et al., 2014), ELMo (Peters et al., 2018a), and BERT (Devlin et al., 2018) embeddings. Training details (including the specific pre-trained models and training parameters) are presented in Appendix A. Following Yang et al. (2018), we pass the reversed combination of the two embeddings through the network, and align and combine the outputs for both input pairs ($word_1 - word_2$ and $word_2 - word_1$) for the final output. If $word_1 < word_2$ then $word_1 > word_2$ as well. Unlike Yang et al. (2018), we pass the reversed pair at training. This 'reversal' trick is visualized in Figure 2, and the empirical results showing its effect in increasing accuracy are discussed in Appendix B.

2.3 Baselines

Majority Class: This baseline predicts the label for a comparison on the dev set based on the highest-frequency label for both the words as per training set. If the two labels agree, e.g., $word_1$

---

[3]https://github.com/uwnlp/verbphysics
[4]http://grail.cs.washington.edu/projects/size/

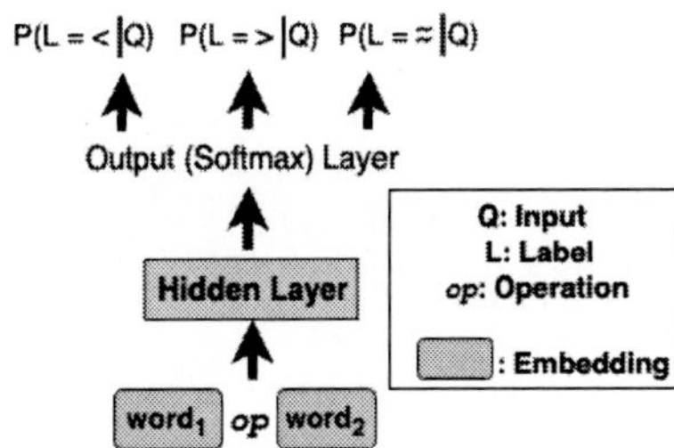

Figure 1: The Probing Model: We combine the pre-trained word embeddings of the two words being compared (via concatenation or subtraction) and pass it though zero (linear) or one hidden layer.

is 'bigger' and $word_2$ is 'smaller' in most training comparisons, this baseline predicts $word_1 > word_2$. If the two majority labels disagree (both words tend to be 'bigger' most of the times), this baseline uses the ratio of frequency of the majority label with the total number of comparisons involving the word to decide.

We also compare with the previous state-of-the-art approaches on the Verb Physics dataset:

Verb-centric Frame Semantics: (Forbes and Choi, 2017, **F&C**) use probabilistic graphical modeling for joint inference over objects as well as actions/verbs that can imply physical relationship their arguments (for example, 'x entered y' implies y is bigger than x).

Property Comparisons from Embeddings: (Yang et al., 2018, **PCE**) use a one-layer neural network over concatenated word embeddings and compare the projection with the embeddings of 'poles': words exemplifying a physical relation ('big', 'small' for size; 'fast', 'slow' for speed, etc.). Classification is the closest 'pole'. This use of poles is the main difference with our approach.

Apart from these baseline models, we devise additional baselines to test for possible artifacts in the dataset, such as using only one of the words as input to the model, in Section 4.

3 Results and Discussion

The probing model (Figure 1) with pre-trained representations has better accuracy than previous approaches which use extra information in addition to the words being compared (Table 1). This indicates that representations themselves capture physical commonsense comparisons.

GloVe is almost as accurate as ELMo and more accurate than BERT contrary to results seen on many NLP tasks (Peters et al., 2018a; Devlin et al.,

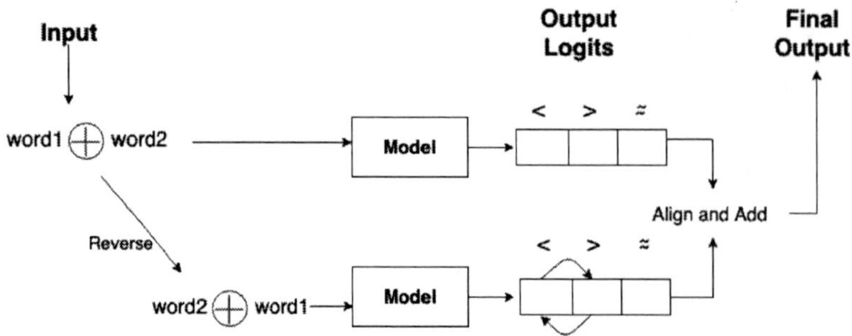

Figure 2: The Reversal Trick: As done by Yang et al. (2018) at test time, the reversed embedding is also passed through the network and the output logits for both pairs ($word_1$ concatenated with $word_2$ and $word_2$ concatenated with $word_1$) are aligned and combined for the final output. We try doing this at training time as well which leads to an improvement in accuracy.

2018). This task has no context to exploit and Tenney et al. (2019) also observe that contextualized embeddings win over non-contextual models on syntactic tasks but less for semantic tasks.

We also used **BERT-large** but saw similar accuracies as BERT-base. Concatenating word embeddings usually achieved slightly better accuracy (Appendix B) but subtracting gave more stable results across different random initializations. The reversed input pair embeddings (§ 2.2) at training and testing improves accuracy (Appendix B).

3.1 Generalization to New Objects

In Verb Physics, ~99% of the words or objects involved in comparisons in the dev set are seen at training. If word embeddings capture common sense well, they should compare two words not seen during training. To test this, we use the Verb Physics training set for the 'size' attribute and evaluate on a different test set (Bagherinezhad et al., 2016): **EB evaluation set** (§ 2.1) where *only ~33% of the words are seen during training.*

Since this evaluation set contains only $<$ and $>$ comparisons, we use comparisons in Verb Physics training set with just these two labels. Unlike Bagherinezhad et al. (2016) who use visual and textual cues, our model use only pre-trained text representations. Yet the probing model achieves at least 4% higher accuracy (Table 2).

4 Analysis

Levy et al. (2015) find that in models for hypernymy detection: the accuracy gap between the full model using both the words as input and using just one of the words is less than 10%. Their training set contains prototypical hypernyms: single word in a pair that models can latch onto to detect hypernymy. The unsupervised method of using the cosine similarity of the two words is also a strong baseline in that work. We experiment with these same baselines for our task.

On the Verb Physics dataset: Only $word_2$ seems to be a strong baseline (much like the ma-

	Majority Class Baseline	F&C	PCE	Probing Model (GloVe)	Probing Model (ELMo)	Probing Model (BERT-base)
Size	0.66	0.75	0.80	**0.82**	**0.82**	0.80
Weight	0.67	0.74	0.81	**0.82**	**0.82**	0.80
Strength	0.66	0.71	0.77	0.78	**0.79**	0.75
Rigidness	0.60	0.68	0.71	0.71	**0.72**	0.71
Speed	0.59	0.66	0.72	0.72	**0.76**	0.71
Overall	0.64	0.71	0.76	0.77	**0.78**	0.75

Table 1: Accuracy of the probing model compared with the baselines including previous approaches on the attributes in the Verb Physics dataset. The simple probing model achieves better accuracy indicating that the frozen pre-trained representations capture commonsense physical comparisons.

Model	Accuracy
The Visual+Textual Model by Bagherinezhad et al. (2016)	0.835
Probing Model (GloVe)	0.879
Probing Model (ELMo)	**0.905**
Probing Model (BERT)	0.893

Table 2: The probing model trained on the Verb Physics size dataset and evaluated on (Bagherinezhad et al., 2016). Only ~33% of the objects in this test set are present in training set: our model generalizes to new objects and gives better accuracy using the frozen pre-trained representations of the words alone.

jority class baseline for this dataset), but the drop in accuracy is higher than 10% for GloVe and ELMo (Table 3): Our model is *not* simply relying on lexical memorization. Randomly selecting a label gives ~33% accuracy while using the majority label for all comparisons gives ~50% accuracy. The unsupervised model gives low accuracy which suggests supervision is helpful.

On the EB Evaluation Set (Bagherinezhad et al., 2016): Using just one word when training and evaluating sees a drop of about 12 to 15% in accuracy (Table 4). This baseline is fairly strong in comparison to a random baseline (50% accuracy), but the difference in accuracy again indicates the model doing more than just lexical memorization.

4.1 Do Models Learn a Consistent Ordering?

Pre-trained representations encode commonsense physical comparisons, and do not rely on mere lexical memorization. One explanation is models could learn to rank or order the objects.

Using the given Verb Physics training set	$word_1$ - $word_2$	ONLY $word_2$ Baseline	Unsupervised Baseline
GloVe	0.78	0.66	0.49
ELMo	0.78	0.67	0.52
BERT	0.75	0.66	0.52

Table 3: Accuracy of probing models (averaged across the five attributes) on the Verb Physics dev sets. Unsupervised baseline takes cosine similarity of the embeddings and uses a threshold tuned on the dev set to classify. Using just one word when training and evaluating helps investigate possible lexical memorization.

On the Complete EB Evaluation Set; ~33% 'overlap'	$word_1$ - $word_2$	$word_1$	$word_2$
GloVe	0.88	0.74	0.73
ELMo	0.89	0.74	0.72
BERT	0.87	0.65	0.68

Table 4: Evaluation on Bagherinezhad et al. (2016). Accuracy drops by 15 to 20% when compared with the only one word baselines.

Examples of Orders Formed Around a Word
head < knee < meal < ***chair*** < back < place < street < world < *gate* < air < floor < *room*
eye < *chair* < child < king < daughter < wife < boy < messenger < father < coach < horse < door < house < ***gate*** < train < *room* < sun

Table 5: Two examples for orderings formed around the words ***chair*** and ***gate*** for the size attribute using GloVe. Comparisons between words occurring in both these orderings (italicized) are consistent.

4.1.1 Local Ordering formed via Logit Difference

A particular word gets compared with many other words in data. We can order those words to form a 'local' ordering, e.g., ordering around ***chair*** (Table 5). Orderings are *consistent* if the same pair of words in different local orderings hold the same relationship, e.g., chair < room in both orderings in Table 5. It is conceivable humans are more confident about a comparison when the difference in objects in terms of the property is large (a house is bigger than a chair). Larger difference in output logits (for label 0 (<) and 1 (>)) can indicate more model confidence and hence, objects being farther apart in an ordering. We form local orderings around a word using logit difference between the labels when compared with the other word.

All the local orderings formed around all words on Verb Physics are completely consistent for GloVe and BERT. For ELMo, more than 90% comparisons were usually consistent across any two orderings. Models seem to learn to arrange all the words in some sort of consistent ordering.

	Linear	Neural Net with 1 or 2 hidden layers
GloVe	0.76	0.77
ELMo	0.77	0.78
BERT	0.74	0.75

Table 6: The best accuracies obtained by a Linear Model compared with the best accuracies obtained by a shallow Neural Network. For all three representations, the linear model gives similar accuracy and hence we often use it for our analysis. Since good accuracy is achieved by a simple linear model from the frozen word representations alone, we can reasonably conclude that pre-trained embeddings encode information required to compare words for physical common sense.

4.1.2 Global Ordering over all Words Using Learned Weights

We use a *linear* model (0 hidden layers in Figure 1) to order all the objects in one of the Verb Physics dev sets. Per Table 6, linear modela are almost at par (accuracy within 1%) with shallow fully connected neural networks on the Verb Physics dev set. A score for a word is its embedding multiplied with the weight learned for mapping the input to the label 1 which would be higher if $word_1 > word_2$. We use this score to rank the objects. Appendix C shows an example of a learned ordering over all the words in the dev set using GloVe. Using this ordering to classify the comparisons of pair of words achieves accuracy at par with the original models on a subset of the dev set containing only 0/1 labels. **This suggests the models assign an absolute value to every word to rank all the objects and then *use this global ranking* to compare any two objects.** Using the weight corresponding to the label 0 achieves similar results. An ordering can be used directly for $>$ or $<$ comparisons but is not that indicative for $\approx$ comparisons. This might explain the relative struggles GloVe, ELMo, and BERT face classifying comparisons labeled 2 (Table 7).

5 Conclusion

A linear or a small fully connected neural network probing model can compare two words on commonsense physical attributes using frozen pre-trained representations (GloVe, ELMo, and BERT) of the words alone with higher accuracy than previous approaches which use extra information in addition to the objects being compared.

	0 ($<$)	1 ($>$)	2 ($\approx$)
GloVe	0.79	0.77	0.33
ELMo	0.81	0.80	0.18
BERT	0.77	0.78	0.12

Table 7: Label-Wise Accuracy: The GloVe, ELMo, and BERT representations (fed to a linear model) struggle to capture the relationship $word_1 \approx word_2$ (label 2). This is likely due to the class imbalance in the dataset, with the rough distribution of the labels across all attributes in the Verb Physics training set being 41% for the label 0, 49% for the label 1, and just 10% for the label 2. The representations seem to learn an ordering over all the words and use it to compare objects (§4.1.2). This is also one possible explanation for comparatively poor accuracy on the label 2 since judging $\approx$ relationship between words is hard while the $<$ or $>$ relation can be inferred directly from an ordering. Accuracies here are averaged across the results for all the five attributes.

They also generalize to objects not seen during training and get significantly higher accuracy than using just one word: embeddings encode physical common sense. Models learn an ordering over of all the words involved in the comparisons and embeddings could be using this ordering to compare any two objects. The difference in the output logit values corresponding to the labels serves as a surprisingly good proxy to form completely consistent orderings around different words. One direction of future work would be to move beyond comparisons or relative information towards directly probing for size estimates for various physical properties for objects (without the setting being relative), using the recently released large-scale resource containing 'distributions over physical quantities associated with objects, adjectives, and verbs' (Elazar et al., 2019).

References

Yossi Adi, Einat Kermany, Yonatan Belinkov, Ofer Lavi, and Yoav Goldberg. 2016. Fine-grained analysis of sentence embeddings using auxiliary prediction tasks. *arXiv preprint arXiv:1608.04207.*

Hessam Bagherinezhad, Hannaneh Hajishirzi, Yejin Choi, and Ali Farhadi. 2016. Are elephants bigger than butterflies? reasoning about sizes of objects. In *Thirtieth AAAI Conference on Artificial Intelligence.*

Yonatan Belinkov, Nadir Durrani, Fahim Dalvi, Hassan Sajjad, and James Glass. 2017. What do neural machine translation models learn about morphology?

In *Proceedings of the 55th Annual Meeting of the Association for Computational Linguistics (Volume 1: Long Papers)*, pages 861–872.

Alexis Conneau, Germán Kruszewski, Guillaume Lample, Loïc Barrault, and Marco Baroni. 2018. What you can cram into a single $&!#* vector: Probing sentence embeddings for linguistic properties. In *Proceedings of the 56th Annual Meeting of the Association for Computational Linguistics (Volume 1: Long Papers)*, pages 2126–2136.

Jacob Devlin, Ming-Wei Chang, Kenton Lee, and Kristina Toutanova. 2018. Bert: Pre-training of deep bidirectional transformers for language understanding. *arXiv preprint arXiv:1810.04805*.

Yanai Elazar, Abhijit Mahabal, Deepak Ramachandran, Tania Bedrax-Weiss, and Dan Roth. 2019. How large are lions? inducing distributions over quantitative attributes. *arXiv preprint arXiv:1906.01327*.

Maxwell Forbes and Yejin Choi. 2017. Verb physics: Relative physical knowledge of actions and objects. In *Proceedings of the 55th Annual Meeting of the Association for Computational Linguistics (Volume 1: Long Papers)*, pages 266–276.

Maxwell Forbes, Ari Holtzman, and Yejin Choi. 2019. Do neural language representations learn physical commonsense? *arXiv preprint arXiv:1908.02899*.

Jonathan Gordon and Benjamin Van Durme. 2013. Reporting bias and knowledge acquisition. In *Proceedings of the 2013 workshop on Automated knowledge base construction*, pages 25–30. ACM.

Omer Levy, Steffen Remus, Chris Biemann, and Ido Dagan. 2015. Do supervised distributional methods really learn lexical inference relations? In *Proceedings of the 2015 Conference of the North American Chapter of the Association for Computational Linguistics: Human Language Technologies*, pages 970–976.

Tal Linzen, Emmanuel Dupoux, and Yoav Goldberg. 2016. Assessing the ability of lstms to learn syntax-sensitive dependencies. *Transactions of the Association for Computational Linguistics*, 4:521–535.

Nelson F. Liu, Matt Gardner, Yonatan Belinkov, Matthew E. Peters, and Noah A. Smith. 2019. Linguistic knowledge and transferability of contextual representations. In *Proceedings of the Conference of the North American Chapter of the Association for Computational Linguistics: Human Language Technologies*.

Tomas Mikolov, Ilya Sutskever, Kai Chen, Greg S Corrado, and Jeff Dean. 2013. Distributed representations of words and phrases and their compositionality. In *Advances in Neural Information Processing Systems*, pages 3111–3119.

Ishan Misra, C Lawrence Zitnick, Margaret Mitchell, and Ross Girshick. 2016. Seeing through the human reporting bias: Visual classifiers from noisy human-centric labels. In *Proceedings of the IEEE Conference on Computer Vision and Pattern Recognition*, pages 2930–2939.

Jeffrey Pennington, Richard Socher, and Christopher Manning. 2014. Glove: Global vectors for word representation. In *Proceedings of the 2014 conference on empirical methods in natural language processing (EMNLP)*, pages 1532–1543.

Matthew Peters, Mark Neumann, Mohit Iyyer, Matt Gardner, Christopher Clark, Kenton Lee, and Luke Zettlemoyer. 2018a. Deep contextualized word representations. In *Proceedings of the 2018 Conference of the North American Chapter of the Association for Computational Linguistics: Human Language Technologies, Volume 1 (Long Papers)*, pages 2227–2237.

Matthew Peters, Mark Neumann, Luke Zettlemoyer, and Wen-tau Yih. 2018b. Dissecting contextual word embeddings: Architecture and representation. In *Proceedings of the 2018 Conference on Empirical Methods in Natural Language Processing*, pages 1499–1509.

Ian Tenney, Patrick Xia, Berlin Chen, Alex Wang, Adam Poliak, R Thomas McCoy, Najoung Kim, Benjamin Van Durme, Sam Bowman, Dipanjan Das, and Ellie Pavlick. 2019. What do you learn from context? probing for sentence structure in contextualized word representations. In *International Conference on Learning Representations*.

Benjamin Van Durme. 2010. Extracting implicit knowledge from text.

Yiben Yang, Larry Birnbaum, Ji-Ping Wang, and Doug Downey. 2018. Extracting commonsense properties from embeddings with limited human guidance. In *Proceedings of the 56th Annual Meeting of the Association for Computational Linguistics (Volume 2: Short Papers)*, pages 644–649.

Sheng Zhang, Rachel Rudinger, Kevin Duh, and Benjamin Van Durme. 2017. Ordinal common-sense inference. *Transactions of the Association for Computational Linguistics*, 5:379–395.

Author Index